W9-CUB-400

Sharing the Work

Sharing the Work

What My Family and Career Taught Me about Breaking Through (and Holding the Door Open for Others)

Myra Strober

Foreword by John Donahoe

The MIT Press
Cambridge, Massachusetts
London, England

This book was set in Sabon by Toppan Best-set Premedia Limited. Printed and bound in the United States of America.

Library of Congress Cataloging-in-Publication Data

Names: Strober, Myra H., author.
Title: Sharing the work : what my family and career taught me about breaking through (and holding the door open for others) / Myra Strober; foreword by John Donahoe.
Description: Cambridge, MA : MIT Press, [2015] | Includes index.
Identifiers: LCCN 2015039699 | ISBN 9780262034388 (hardcover : alk. paper)
Subjects: LCSH: Strober, Myra H. | Women economists—United States—Biography. | Women college teachers—United States—Biography. | Women in the professions—United States. | Sex discrimination—United States. | Work and family—United States. | Feminism—United States.
Classification: LCC HB119.S76 A3 2015 | DDC 330.092—dc23 LC record available at http://lccn.loc.gov/2015039699

10   9   8   7   6   5   4   3   2   1

Dedication: The gender revolution of the past fifty years—women's increased participation in the world of work, combined with men's growing responsibilities for family life—has been one of the most profound transformations of recent decades. As an activist, I helped bring about some of that change. As a researcher, I studied it.

Many of you have also been on the ground floor of this transformation, and you will recognize your own exhilaration and pain in my story. But others of you may have little awareness of the struggles that brought us to where we are today. Whatever your history, this book is dedicated to you, with the hope that my journey inspires you to imagine and initiate the next round of change—to succeed not only in your own career and family, but also to take strong action to break down gender and other discriminatory barriers in your workplace and in society as a whole.

Contents

Foreword by John Donahoe   ix

Part I: 1970–1971

1   Sisterhood Is Powerful, 1970–1971   3

Part II: 1950–1970

2   Banished to the Balcony, 1950–1953   25
3   A Boost Up, 1954–1958   37
4   Into the Sanctum, 1958–1964   55
5   Add Children and Stir, 1964–1970   79

Part III: 1971–2012

6   Where the Rubber Hits the Road, 1971–1972   107
7   Ninety Men and Me, 1972–1974   123
8   Forging New Doors, 1974–1981   137
9   Reinvention, 1982–1989   163
10 Flow, 1989–2000   179
11 Transformation, 2000–2012   201
12 Lessons Learned about Sharing the Work   213

Acknowledgments   221
Index   223

Foreword

John Donahoe

The best memoirs teach us about ourselves. In sharing her personal story, Myra Strober has accomplished just that. In recounting her extraordinary life and trailblazing career as an activist, academic, wife, mother, and friend, she engages us with refreshing honesty, intellect, insight, and candor. For those of us who have lived through similar personal and professional experiences, as well as for those just starting out on this journey, Myra's memoir is a must-read.

Our progress on gender equality in Myra's lifetime is striking. And the work that remains to be done is equally sobering. Her powerful storytelling takes us back to moments and situations no longer imaginable. Yet she also pulls from those experiences and brings us dramatically into the present, reminding us of the challenges women still face each and every day to achieve true gender equality. The gender revolution is far from over.

Reading this compelling and timely memoir, I felt an uncanny familiarity. For more than 30 years, I have strived in my professional and personal life to promote, support, encourage, embrace, and model gender equality. A true partnership and shared vision with my wife, Eileen, has been foundational. That partnership enabled us to juggle demanding dual careers, raise four wonderful children, and navigate life's everyday ups and downs. It hasn't been easy, but together we've succeeded in ways we often thought impossible.

Myra's experience as a woman breaking into the male-dominated world of academia reminds me of Eileen's early challenges in the male-dominated legal profession. And Myra was a wise and invaluable coach for me as a young leader during the 1990s as we sought to bring more gender equality into Bain Consulting. Her insight and example continued to influence me during my tenure as CEO of eBay. It is clear that Myra's personal story reflects the confidence and courage of so many talented women who have persevered to create change and claim the careers they deserved.

In the end, we each deserve the opportunity to create the life we want. And that means the journey for gender equality continues. Many of the lessons Myra draws from her life are extremely relevant to us all today. Success requires hard work, but context matters. Public policies matter, workplace policies matter, attitudes and expectations matter. And no one can do it alone—each of us needs to rely on family, friends, and professional allies.

Myra's insights mirror my own experience and the advice I've shared with others. Success happens, and positive change occurs, when we act with courage and conviction, build strong community, and keep fighting the good fight.

Myra's memoir can inspire us all.

John Donahoe is Chair of the Board of Paypal and former CEO of eBay

I

1970–1971

1

Sisterhood Is Powerful, 1970–1971

"It's because you live in Palo Alto," the chairman of Berkeley's economics department tells me.

"I can't have a regular job here because I live in Palo Alto?"

He nods.

Chairman Break is tall, with football-player shoulders, and although I'm tall too, his massive frame towers over me. He's the bigshot in of one of the most prestigious economics departments in the country. I'm the assistant professor wannabe. If this meeting doesn't go well, he could decide not to hire me for next year. Under my jacket, rivulets of perspiration are making their way down my dress-for-success blouse.

"You have to live in Berkeley to be on your tenure track?"

Again he nods.

I'm baffled. I never knew that. My husband, Sam, is a medical resident at Stanford and works incredibly long hours. Often he goes back to his lab late at night to check on his experiments. We have to live in Palo Alto.

"OK," I say softly, getting up to leave. "Thanks very much."

When I get to my office, my hands are shaking. I can hardly insert my key into the lock. I feel drained, disoriented. Did I take something out of the freezer for tonight's dinner? Lamb chops? Hamburger? I dial home, but Margie, my babysitter, doesn't pick up. She's probably taken the kids out somewhere.

I leave my office and walk across Sproul Plaza, surprisingly quiet after all the years of student demonstrations. It's 1970, and the Vietnam War is beginning to wind down. I slide into my full-size blue Chevy with a trunk large enough to hold both a stroller and a carriage, and review my meeting with Break. I spend a lot of time in Big Blue these days. It's about an hour between Palo Alto and Berkeley in the morning and longer in the late afternoon, and I do the commute three days a week.

Gradually, crawling in stop-and-go traffic toward the Bay Bridge, the absurdity of Break's answer registers. My first response is to cry. I grope around in my purse, pull out some tissue, and dab at my eyes. But now the road is blurry. I switch my thoughts to my children.

"Mommy, Mommy!" Jason, my three-year-old, will scream with delight when he hears my key in the door. And Liz, eleven months, will follow his lead; she'll speed across the living room on all fours, tug on my leg, and make joyful noises.

Suddenly, the traffic starts to move. I can never tell why the snarls dissolve, but I'm always grateful. As I drive at normal speed, my thoughts turn back to Break, but this time, instead of tears, I'm aware of growing anger—at myself.

What's wrong with you? I scream inside my head. *You let him intimidate you. You let him make you mute. You're a smart woman, and you let him make you look stupid. Faculty don't have to live in Berkeley to be on the tenure track. He fed you pure bull, and you bought it. You want to know why you can't have a tenure-track job at Berkeley? Look at what's real. There are no women except Margaret in the whole economics department faculty, and though she's been there for more than twenty years, she's still a lecturer. Wake up!*

The difference between a lecturer and an assistant professor is monumental. Assistant professors have a regular job with an opportunity for promotion and lifetime tenure. Lecturers, on the other hand, are on a road to nowhere. They're appointed from year to year, generally only a few months before their teaching is to begin, and have no chance of advancing. I've worked too hard for too many years to be content with second-class citizenship. I intend to get the real deal at Berkeley.

When I finally get onto the Bay Bridge, my anger changes. Now I'm furious with Break. How dare he tell me I have to live in Berkeley? The radio is tuned to a talk station, and I register Joe Carcione, the popular "Green Grocer," instructing the whole Bay Area about choosing pumpkins. Ah, Halloween is coming. Maybe I could revisit Break's office in costume. Witch? Skeleton? Big Bird? Surely some costume could shake him out of his "we all have to live in Berkeley" routine.

With my sheath skirt and matching man-tailored jacket, I'm wearing stockings and high heels. The stockings feel sticky, and the shoes pinch every time I accelerate. How I would love to kick off those shoes. Whoever invented high heels definitely didn't have driving in mind.

I'm getting angrier by the second—at the traffic, which has snarled again; at my gluey stockings and too-tight high heels; and at my own naiveté. But most of all I'm angry at Break. Slowly I begin to understand what people mean when they say their anger makes them see red, because a swelling fury, a deep scarlet anger, now floods the car. The steel frame and glass windows can't contain it, and it bursts onto the road like a flaming oil slick—a torrent sliding over the bridge's girders and thundering across the bay.

As the lights of San Francisco begin to flicker against the darkening sky, I feel a flicker of light within myself. I become a feminist on the Bay Bridge. The anger and enlightenment of that day will energize the rest of my life. They lead me to become one of the creators of a new academic field and new institutions to study sexism and fight it.

It's the morning after my meeting with Break, and I'm exhausted from lack of sleep. Sam was on duty at the hospital last night, so I couldn't debrief with him—and by the time I got Jason and Liz to bed, it was too late to call my East Coast friends. (Since we've just moved to Palo Alto, I have no friends here yet.) So I spent the evening pacing back and forth trying to figure out next steps, and after midnight my dreams endlessly replayed the meeting.

At 9 a.m. sharp, I'm on the phone.

"I need another appointment as soon as possible," I tell Break's secretary.

"One moment, please. I'll check his calendar."

Long silence.

"He says he can't see you until early November."

"That's more than a month from now."

"Yes, I know. He's very busy."

Busy! *He's not busy*, I think to myself, *he's just a coward*. I'd like to punch his secretary right through the phone line, but I put on my best party manners.

"Well, thank you very much. I'll see him then."

❖

What does an academic do when she's mad? Research! Armed with new-found rage, I begin to spend every spare moment in the library.

Libraries soothe me. Vast, quiet, orderly, calm, an escape from routine racket and discord. I've spent so much time in libraries—the public libraries of my childhood in Brooklyn, then the university libraries at Cornell, Tufts, MIT, and Harvard. I've had the privilege of delving into some of the finest collections in the world. So many hours reading the wisdom and foolishness of those who have gone before.

My Berkeley ID gets me into Green Library at Stanford, and I feel my usual awe in the presence of so much scholarship. The library at Trinity College Dublin has busts of all the great (male) philosophers looking down on the reading room. But even without a physical likeness of the authors in Green Library's collection, I feel their presence.

On this day, however, I'm not in search of male wisdom. I'm on an entirely different mission: purposely searching out the writings of *women*, trying to understand why a woman with all the right training and credentials from top-notch schools is not treated the same as her male peers.

Green Library has that authentic library smell—musty books, furniture polish on the big wood tables and card catalogs, and the accumulated sweat of generations of academics. I feel at home. All morning, I thumb through the card catalog. Then, after a quick sandwich, I climb the stairs to the stacks to match the call numbers on my pad with those on the shelves. Sitting on the floor, I page through potentially promising volumes.

I'm surprised to find how much women wrote in the nineteenth and early twentieth centuries, and chagrined that I've never heard of such women as Elizabeth Cady Stanton and Lucretia Mott. I've had more than twenty years of education, and the only feminist name I recognize is Susan B. Anthony's. The sole feminist cause I know about is suffrage.

I'm also appalled to see how little contemporary material there is on women, and particularly how little by economists. I have a second major insight only a day after my first: the almost fifty years since women won the vote in the 1920s have been a wasteland for efforts on women's behalf. As I write this memoir, I've come to understand that historians think there *were* important efforts to improve the situation of women in the mid-twentieth century, but on that day at Green Library,

I can't find a trace of it—not in my own knowledge base, and not in the card catalog.

My greatest delight is finding the Declaration of Sentiments, the manifesto that Elizabeth Cady Stanton wrote and presented in 1848 to the first women's rights convention in Seneca Falls, New York. Modeled after the Declaration of Independence, it begins by listing grievances, and the injustices concerning work resonate powerfully with me:

He has monopolized nearly all the profitable employments ...

He closes against her all the avenues to wealth and distinction which he considers most honorable to himself.

As a teacher of theology, medicine, or law, she is not known.

Aha, I think. Economics is like theology, medicine, and law—occupations men have monopolized, where they don't want women. I'd always thought there were so few women economists because women didn't *want* to be economists. But now I think perhaps the scarcity of women in my field is created not by women's preferences but by men's power. Somehow I squeezed through the system and got my PhD, but now George Break and company are fixing their mistake. I'm being closed out.

As an economics student, I learned a great deal about the evils of monopoly. Monopolists (think Standard Oil, Alcoa, U.S. Steel) restrict production, charge higher prices, and amass greater profits than they could if they faced competition. They serve only their own interests. Even conservative economists, who oppose government intervention in economic activity as a matter of principle, support regulation of monopoly power.

My studies also taught me that there could be monopoly in the labor market: so-called monopsony, when, for example, a single employer in a company town hires fewer employees and pays lower wages than that employer would if it had to compete for workers. In fact, one of the arguments in favor of labor unions is that they counteract employers' monopsony power, increasing employment, raising wages, and lowering profits.

But I had never thought about monopoly or monopsony power in academe. I'd never thought about it concerning women and men, and I'd certainly never thought about it as an explanation for my situation. Stanton gives me an entirely new way to think about my meeting with Break.

I hardly have time to take pleasure in learning how to name the problem of women's exclusion and relate it to what I know about monopoly when, just a few pages later, Stanton's Declaration of Sentiments moves to the solution. Fight! The last sentences of the document are an inspiring call to action:

... the speedy success of our cause depends on the zealous and
    untiring efforts of both men and women, for the overthrow of the monopoly.

"OK, Mrs. Stanton, I'm with you," I call back across the almost 150 years that separate us. "Count me in for the fight."

I feel a great affinity with Stanton. As I sit reading her words in the Stanford library, I am only slightly younger than she was when she penned them. She was already a mother, and so am I. And we both came to the fight for women's rights through experiences of personal discrimination.

Early in her marriage, in 1840, Stanton and her husband attended the first international antislavery conference in London. Women delegates were segregated into a special seating area and not permitted to speak. One of the first motions of the convention (offered by a man) would have given women full rights as delegates. But in the debate on the motion, those opposed argued that it was unseemly for women to speak out in public, and the motion was overwhelmingly defeated. Stanton later pointed to that defeat as the spark that ignited her fight.

At the London convention, Stanton met Lucretia Mott, a powerful and intelligent Quaker more than twenty years her senior. Quakers not only permitted women to speak in public, they encouraged it, and Mott was a well-known orator. She became Stanton's mentor, and it was in 1848, when Mott came from Pennsylvania to visit Stanton in Seneca Falls, that the idea for a woman's rights convention was born.

In the library, Stanton becomes *my* mentor. It doesn't matter that she's been dead for almost seventy years. My isolation diminishes. I don't have the word for it yet, but what I feel is sisterhood.

Real-time sisterhood soon follows. Shortly after I discover Stanton and Mott, my interdepartmental mail includes a notice of a noon meeting of women lecturers at Berkeley. On the day of the meeting, directly after my morning class, I walk across campus to the faculty club, a large building with lovely shrubs on the exterior and handsome wood paneling inside.

Never have I seen so many academic women in one place. We are all in skirts or dresses, all wearing jackets. Our hairstyles are conservative, and many of us, though not I, wear glasses, perhaps an occupational hazard from years of nonstop reading. Some of us are short, some tall. We are in our thirties or forties and in good physical shape. Every one of us is Caucasian.

At the door, we fill out small tags with our names and departments and paste them on our jackets. We represent numerous fields, even the sciences. Some of us will turn out to be well known, including Alice Stone Ilchman, a lecturer in political science who will become president of Sarah Lawrence College. The faces are uniformly friendly, and conversation is easy. Two of my new acquaintances ask me to sit with them at lunch.

I can't remember who chairs the meeting—perhaps anthropologist Laura Nader, sister of Ralph and one of the few women faculty members on the tenure track. Most of the attendees already know what the chairwoman is about to announce, but to me, it's all new. She begins with some history.

"You all remember last spring, when we worked with the Women's Equity Action League to file a complaint of sex discrimination at Berkeley with the Labor Department?"

"Oh, yes," sounds a chorus of voices.

"Well," she continues, "I have good news. The Labor Department has decided to investigate, and they're sending a team from the Office of Federal Contract Compliance in a couple of weeks, definitely before the end of the quarter, to do a whole lot of interviews. They want to find out what's going on here."

A jubilant buzz follows her announcement, but I'm puzzled.

"What's this all about?" I ask the woman next to me.

"Well, about five years ago, President Johnson issued an executive order that prohibits discrimination, including sex discrimination, by federal contractors, and in the last couple of months, the Women's Equity Action League has filed a whole bunch of complaints with the Labor Department on behalf of women at major universities saying that universities are engaging in sex discrimination. Nobody quite got it before that universities are federal contractors too, and that, just like businesses, they shouldn't be allowed to discriminate against women."

I guess I still look blank, because she continues.

"You know, almost all women faculty at Berkeley are lecturers. We want equal access to the tenure track. And we want to earn the same salaries as men. That's why we helped to file the complaint."

My heart starts to race. OK, OK. So this whole travesty is not just about me. I have company. Not only that, I have fighting company. Filing a complaint with the federal government must surely qualify as one of Stanton's zealous and untiring efforts. I walk back to my office humming, something I haven't done since my meeting with Break.

❖

One of the people conspicuously absent from the women lecturers' meeting is Margaret Gordon, the other woman lecturer in economics. Not that I know what she looks like—I've never met her. But when they see "Economics" on my nametag, several women tell me that I am the only representative at the meeting from my department. Before I go to my follow-up appointment with George Break, I figure I should have a talk with Margaret.

"Call me Peg," she says when I enter her office several days later.

Hard to do. The woman sitting behind the desk is imposing. Heavyset, with her hair pulled back into a bun, she exudes "no nonsense." My mother would have called her a battle-axe, but I see more femininity than that term allows. She has sensual hands that flutter when she speaks, as well as a soothing, resonant voice. I wonder if she might be a singer.

The main reason I can't easily call her Peg (I can barely call her Margaret) is that she is the mother of one of my MIT classmates, Bob Gordon, a new assistant professor of economics at Northwestern. In fact, everybody in Margaret's family is an economist. Her husband, Aaron Gordon, is a professor of economics in my Berkeley department, and her youngest son, David, is a doctoral student in economics at Harvard.

In just a few minutes of conversation, I come to see that Margaret is not altogether dissatisfied with her situation as a lecturer, which probably explains why she wasn't at the recent meeting. And by the end of our meeting, I'm positive she didn't sign on to the sex discrimination complaint.

Margaret tells me she is a lecturer rather than a professor not because she is a woman, but because she is the wife of a member of the economics department. Huh? Isn't discrimination against wives sex discrimination, I ask her? No, she says—her problem isn't sex discrimination but the university's antinepotism rule, which prohibits two people who are related (through marriage or otherwise) from having tenure-track appointments in the same department. Aaron had his faculty appointment first. If she'd had an appointment first, then it would be her husband who would not be able to be on the tenure track.

I can't believe she seriously imagines such a scenario. If her husband couldn't get a tenure-track job, wouldn't they move somewhere else? I can't quite picture Aaron as a lecturer. But I don't give voice to my skepticism. I just listen. Being a lecturer has served her well, she says. She works closely with Clark Kerr, former chancellor of the university, and has published numerous books and papers with him. And she doesn't have to worry about supervising dissertations, having a full teaching load, or attending faculty meetings. She can just do her work and teach a few undergraduate courses.

"What about employment security?" I ask.

Not an issue, she assures me. Clark Kerr is not going to run out of funding anytime soon, and as long as there's money for the bulk of her salary, the department is happy to pay her to do some teaching. She says she can see that I might not be happy with an arrangement such as hers. I will probably want to get research grants in my own name, which one can't do as a lecturer. But she concludes with a warning.

"It'll be tough to get what you want, Myra. The last time a woman was hired on the tenure track in the Berkeley economics department was 1928. Emily Huntington. She retired in 1961. And since then, there've been no women on the regular faculty."

After speaking with Margaret, I feel judgmental. How can she possibly be satisfied with her situation? She's not a real go-getter. But writing some forty years later, as I'm closer to the age Peg was when we first met, I understand and admire what she did, making a career as a fine teacher and researcher and learning to be content with not getting the recognition she deserved. When her sons were young, she probably appreciated not having the pressures to publish to achieve tenure; and once they were grown, she found she had created a comfortable niche. She had no allies for fighting against Berkeley's nepotism rules, which were similar to those at numerous other universities. She and her husband were ensconced in the Berkeley community with no desire to go on the national job market to find new positions at different universities in some other city. She took what she could get, and she didn't beat herself up.

In many ways, she paved the way for women like me to fight for more. She was living proof that a woman could teach successfully in Berkeley's economics department, raise children, and carry out significant economic research. That was important to me. It was also important that she wished me well.

A few days after my session with Margaret, I have my second meeting with Break.

"Professor Break, I've come to ask you the same question I asked you last time. Why am I being treated differently from Richard Sutch and Tu Jarvis? We all got our doctorates from MIT. We were classmates. Now we all have the same teaching responsibilities."

My host leans back in his chair, clasps his hands behind his head, rests his feet on his desk, and sets his pipe in his mouth. I glance around his office. Academic décor, circa time immemorial. Floor to ceiling journals and books, *American Economic Review, National Tax Journal,* numerous copies of his new book, *Agenda for Local Tax Reform.* And paper everywhere, manuscripts covering every possible surface in neat and not-so-neat piles, some spilling onto the floor. One small corner of the desk is manuscript-free, cluttered instead with framed photos of people I assume are his family. Musty smell, stale combination of old paper and years of tobacco.

Slowly Professor Break takes his feet down from his desk, leans slightly forward on his chair, lights his pipe, and takes a few leisurely puffs—all the while staring at me. Can he see how nervous I am? After a few seconds, he inhales deeply.

"Do you want me to be frank?" he asks.

Well, I think, *at least more than a month of cogitation has led him to the possibility of an honest response.*

"Yes, please be frank."

"It's because you have two young children, one not even a year old. We just don't know what's going to happen to you."

"Happen to me? I'm not asking you to give me tenure now. I'm asking you to put me on the tenure track and give me a chance to prove myself. In six years, we'll all be able to see what happens to me."

"No," he says, shaking his head vigorously, "No, I couldn't possibly sell that to the department."

Wait till I relate *that* comment to the Labor Department investigators, I think as I leave his office. Mister High-and-Mighty Department Chairman, what you just told me is quintessential sex discrimination. If I were a man with two young children, one still an infant, you'd *never* say what you just said. You'd be falling all over yourself to make sure I could support my family. And you know what else? With the Office of Federal Contract Compliance in the picture, I think you're going to be in the position of *having* to sell me to the department.

As I get into my car, I can't help contrasting my mood with the way I felt last time I left Break's office. Thanks to Elizabeth Cady Stanton, the Labor Department, and the other women lecturers, I've swung from despondent to ebullient. Margaret may be right that it will be a tough fight, but I'm beginning to think I just might win.

Even though I'm teaching the same courses I taught at my previous job at the University of Maryland—labor economics and macroeconomics—the students at Berkeley are so much more intellectually sophisticated that a lecture that was good for an hour at Maryland lasts for only twenty minutes or so at Berkeley. I try to write the additional lectures in my office, between classes, but there's never enough time: unlike students at Maryland, who rarely came to office hours, Berkeley students fill every available slot with questions. What do I think about the costs of the war in Vietnam and their effects on the macroeconomy? Can inflation and unemployment occur at the same time? Why do blacks have so much higher unemployment rates than whites?

I love the way students light up my office with challenging and perceptive queries, but I hate the dreary space itself, with its far from ergonomic chairs, a metal desk with random dents, and walls that look like they came straight from a cement truck. Barrows Hall, which houses the economics department and the other social sciences, is a huge concrete building completely devoid of architectural charm, and the sterility of my office is enhanced by my unwillingness to fix it up. Given my sense of impermanence, decorating feels like a waste of time. I'm also not sure *how* to decorate, because after my conversation with Break, putting out family pictures or anything remotely "feminine" feels self-defeating if any colleagues should stop by.

Eventually, though, after several months without a single colleague visit, the echo of emptiness impels me to haul my books from home—a small box each day—and fill one of the bookcases. I also cover the walls with some gender-neutral posters (no flowers) from a shop on Telegraph Avenue, and I display a University of California coffee mug prominently on my desk. Somehow or other, that mug gives me a sense of belonging.

❖

When I first came to Berkeley, I planned to do research on unemployment, but now that project is on permanent hold. Instead, I'm reading about feminism and women's work. Every Tuesday and Thursday, the days I don't teach, I settle in at Jackson Library at the Stanford Business School. Like Stanford's Green Library, where I discovered Elizabeth Cady Stanton, Jackson has the right ambience and scents. And in contrast to my Berkeley office, it has lovely wood tables and superbly comfy chairs. It also has a reference librarian eager to help me. At Dewey, the MIT business and economics library, I learned that some women librarians wished to be particularly helpful to women students, and now I find that same penchant at Jackson.

I'm anonymous at Jackson. I talk to no one but the librarian. My shoes off, I sit on a soft chair near the second-floor stacks, my feet tucked under me, and absorb new ideas into my brain for hour after uninterrupted hour.

I start with *The Feminine Mystique* by Betty Friedan. When it was first published in 1963, my father's cousin gave me a copy, but I never read it. I was too busy learning economics. Now I devour it. Friedan talks about the problem with no name, the dissatisfaction and depression that educated women feel when they stay at home raising children full-time. To end their depression and find fulfillment, she argues, educated women need to work for pay outside their homes.

Ever since high school, I'd planned to work when I had kids. My mom always worked, and the mere *thought* of staying home all day seemed depressing. But once my children were born, although I still loved my work and knew I needed it to feel whole, that perspective began to strike me as unusual. I never thought my working would harm my children, but I still saw myself as something of a freak for finding fulfillment beyond raising them. Reading Friedan's book, I begin to feel proud instead of freakish.

Even so, the book raises many questions. Friedan argues that women can have both jobs and children by hiring other people to handle their housework and childcare. But surely there is a great deal that cannot be hired out. Unless you're the queen of England, you're not going to delegate someone to go to your child when she's ill or calls for you in the middle of the night. And only the super-rich are likely to hire out the *management* of their household and children: figuring out when and where household items need repair or replacement, for example, or which doctors and dentists your family should use.

Besides, not everybody can afford Friedan's hiring-out solution even for less complex tasks. My babysitter, Margie, has a young child and a job. When she comes to my house to work, other women in her family take care of her children for free. If Margie wanted to enroll her pre-school-age son in group childcare, how would she pay for it? Maybe families like Margie's need a childcare subsidy from the government. But what would be the economic rationale for that?

I also begin to have questions about Stanton's Declaration of Sentiments. What will this fight that she calls for look like? The notion of overthrowing the oppressor is reminiscent of Marx—perhaps not coincidentally, given that the Communist Manifesto and the Declaration of Sentiments were written at almost the same time—but I see a big difference between workers' oppression and women's oppression. Workers don't live with the employers who oppress them. Women not only live with men, they love them. How can you love somebody who oppresses you? By the same token, how can you turn against someone you love? It also seems puzzling that Stanton thinks men should be part of the fight. How can men become allies in a fight to overthrow a monopoly that benefits them?

Simone de Beauvoir's *The Second Sex*, the book I read next, complicates the picture even further. Friedan's book is often cited as the publication that initiated the modern women's movement, the so-called second wave (Elizabeth Cady Stanton's generation being the first wave). But de Beauvoir published her book in France in 1949, and Alfred Knopf published an English translation in 1953—ten years before Friedan's book.

My brain bursts trying to follow the seven hundred densely written pages of de Beauvoir's analysis. I have lived on a steady diet of social science for the past eight years, and philosophy feels like a foreign language. I can't skim anything. I need to read every word. I'm not familiar with the structure of the arguments, and I'm not able to discern their quality easily. I didn't know it then, but struggling to read de Beauvoir was my first lesson in the difficulties of interdisciplinary academic work.

Nonetheless, de Beauvoir's underlying message is clear. In every society and all throughout history, women have been secondary to men, always the "other." To change women's position at work requires changing their position in society at large. Slogging through her arguments, I see that the fight Stanton calls for is bigger than I first thought. *Everything* will have to change if women are to have equality at work.

Sisterhood Is Powerful, the 1970 anthology edited by Robin Morgan, fills out de Beauvoir's message. Inequality in housework and childcare are high on the list of things that must change to enable gender equality in the workplace. Pat Mainardi's article "The Politics of Housework," which reviews the many clever means men use to subvert the idea of sharing housework, reinforces my growing sense that the fight for equality is going to be exceedingly tough.

When I look for current social science publications about women's work, I find only two books, one by the economist Glen Cain and one by the sociologist Valerie Oppenheimer, both about the rise in women's participation in the labor force. I uncover no discussions of differences in men's and women's earnings and occupations. It will be another year before the economist Juanita Kreps's book *Sex in the Marketplace: American Women at Work* takes up those matters.

Thanks to Jackson's reference librarian, I do find a series of statistical publications put out by the U.S. Department of Labor's Women's Bureau. Despite all my years of reading the department's publications in graduate school, somehow I'd never come across these gold mines. But combing through Jackson, I find a whole section devoted to them, and they show me exactly how unusual I am.

I learn that in 1970, only 40 percent of married women are employed or actively looking for work. The equivalent statistic for married men is 80 percent. Years later, when many more people become interested in these matters, the Department of Labor will release statistics showing that the labor force participation rate in 1970 for women like me (age thirty with an infant) was even lower, less than 25 percent.

I also discover that white women are paid far less than white men, about sixty cents to the dollar, and that black women earn just slightly more than fifty cents for every dollar a white man earns. Much of this discrepancy results from men's and women's different occupations—about two-thirds of all female workers (or an equivalent number of male workers) would have to change their occupation for the occupational distribution among women and men to be the same—and men's occupations tend to pay considerably more than women's even when their educational requirements are similar. All these facts will eventually become common knowledge, but in 1970, even most social scientists could not have given you the numbers.

One day, the reference librarian says she thinks I ought to go over to the government documents section at Green Library and take a look at a new publication, *Discrimination Against Women*, just issued by the House Committee on Education and Labor's Special Subcommittee on Education. A ten-minute walk leads me to a second treasure trove: more than 1,800 pages of testimony and backup papers from seven days of hearings that took place a few months earlier. Not only am *I* learning for the first time about discrimination against women, it seems the government itself is just beginning to learn.

The purpose of the hearings was to gather testimony on behalf of Section 805 of H.R. 16098, a bill that would extend federal antidiscrimination legislation to higher education. The person who introduced the bill and was in charge of the hearings was Edith Green, one of only ten women in the House of Representatives at the time. In the Senate, there was just one woman.

As I look over the table of contents, the testimony of Bernice Sandler catches my attention. It lists more than fifty universities against which the Women's Equity Action League has filed complaints with the Department of Labor on behalf of women. The names read like a *Who's Who* of higher education—Harvard, MIT, Tufts, Columbia, Michigan, Minnesota. And the article notes that not just Berkeley but every branch of the University of California is named, as well as all the California state colleges. I thought I'd found compatriots when I went to the meeting of women lecturers at Berkeley, but poring over Sandler's article and others in the volume, I see that I have more company than I ever imagined. The problem I face is not only mine and not only Berkeley's. It's everywhere. And thanks to the Women's Equity Action League and Congresswoman Green, it's finally being addressed!

It's not long before my emerging feminist consciousness about sex discrimination in the workplace spills over into a new discontent with the division of labor in my own family. I am *living* the inequality that feminism theorizes. Although Sam encouraged me to get a doctorate, we've never discussed which chores each of us would do at home. Like others of our generation, we simply fell into traditional roles when we were first married, and even after Jason and Liz were born and I had a job, I continued to do the lion's share of housework, childcare, and managing our household.

One evening, after a particularly grueling commute, putting the kids to bed, and cleaning up the kitchen, I come into the living room to broach the subject of housework and childcare. Sam is on the couch reading a medical journal. He looks tired, and my heart goes out to him. But he's awake, and I need to take advantage of that.

"You know, I'm beginning to feel that how we divide the work at home is just not fair. I do all the shopping and cooking and washing dishes, plus all the care of the kids. By the time I drive to and from Berkeley, teach, make dinner, clean up, bathe the kids, and prepare lectures, I'm exhausted. I get up at the same time you do, but I go to bed long after you're asleep."

"Well, I don't exactly have a life of leisure either," he replies, still holding his journal open and clearly not relishing this conversation. "I'm on call three or four nights a week and every other weekend. I'm taking care of extremely sick people, I'm tired, and I'm trying to squeeze in some time for lab work."

"But what about the weekends when you're off? How about splitting cooking and helping to take care of the kids those weekends?"

"I need those weekends to write grants. And I need Sunday mornings for tennis. I've got to have *some* time to relax."

I can see that Sam is getting agitated. But I'm irritated, too, and my voice gets louder.

"And what about me? When do *I* get to relax?"

My shouting wakes Jason. "Mommy," he calls out, "I need a glass of water."

I get him a drink and take a few minutes to soothe him back to sleep. When I return to the living room, I'm even angrier than before. Sam's back to reading. I stand directly in front of him, arms crossed. There's no mistaking my body language.

"So, what's your answer? Is it ever my turn to relax?"

"Listen—first of all, stop shouting at me. I don't like to be shouted at. Second, nobody is telling you to run yourself ragged. If you need more time to relax, cut back at Berkeley. Work half-time."

"I don't want to cut back at Berkeley," I say, lowering my voice and sitting down. "You know yourself there's no such thing as a part-time career in academia. I'm trying to get a tenure-track job, not go part-time."

"Well, I don't know what to tell you. It's fine with me if you have a career. But I can't take on any more at home."

My fury is back. What right does he have to decide how much he will or won't take on? But I realize that I'll never get what I'm aiming for unless I keep my voice down. I also don't want to wake Jason again. So I use every bit of energy to speak softly.

"How about a little give-and-take here? I'm getting about five or six hours of sleep a night, and that works OK, but I need a couple of extra hours when you're here on Sunday mornings. How about taking the kids for a few hours before you go to tennis, so I can sleep in?"

Sam has clearly had enough. He picks up his journal. "OK. You win. I'll watch them when I'm here early Sunday mornings."

"Well, thank you. That's good. But could we please continue? I'm not done. Could you wait to read until we're finished?"

"I need to finish what I'm reading before I go to bed, and I'm getting pretty tired. Can't we talk tomorrow?"

"No, you won't be here tomorrow. You'll be at the hospital."

"How about this weekend? Let's talk then."

I agree. Do I have a choice?

On Sunday night, I raise the topic again. As before, I've put the kids to bed and Sam is reading. This time I sit down and ask if this is a good time to talk.

"As good as any other."

"Well, I want to talk about the fact that you think I should cut back to part-time at Berkeley. It doesn't seem that you think much of my paycheck. And you don't seem to care much about my success. When we first talked about my getting a PhD, you were the one who quoted John Stuart Mill about the importance of everyone fulfilling their aspirations. You encouraged me to teach at the college level. What's happened?"

"Of course I appreciate the money you earn. But it's not worth your driving yourself into the ground. I have an extremely difficult job, and it's going to stay difficult for many years because I want to get tenure at Stanford. If you want to be successful at Berkeley, you're going to have to figure out how to do that and still do the housework and take care of the kids."

"What about John Stuart Mill?"

"I don't know. He seems very far from the issues you're bringing up."

The buzzer's ringing on the dryer. I've put a load of diapers in so Margie will have fresh ones for Liz tomorrow.

"OK," I say getting up to fold the laundry. "I guess we're done."

The net result of our conversation is that little changes. I bring up the subject frequently, but the situation remains the same. I'm increasingly furious, but I have no place to take that fury. Letting it out at Sam feels counterproductive, so I keep it contained. I have no one to talk to about it. I have no friends who are trying to do what I'm trying to do, and no model of a professional couple that shares housework; no way to say to Sam, "Look at so-and-so couple, they're doing such-and-such." Although my parents always shared housework, their situation was so different from ours. Their earnings were about equal, and they both had nine-to-five jobs. Sam and I have demanding careers, and as a professor of medicine, he is going to earn far more than I will as an academic economist.

My circumstances are complicated further by the fact that I want academic success for Sam as much as I want it for myself. I love him and care deeply about his happiness. Moreover, I know that his success will redound to my benefit—that if he has a prominent career, I will share in both the prestige and the economic gain. As Gary Becker and his feminist critics will point out many years later, in a loving relationship, a husband's well-being is subsumed in his wife's utility function (and vice versa).

Perhaps if I'd believed that my work was as important as Sam's, I would have pushed harder for equality. But I felt that his career—making life-and-death decisions for critically ill patients—was of far greater consequence. I had thoroughly internalized an East Coast Jewish culture that saw physicians as second only to God, and American culture seemed to concur. In the 1970s, the Duncan Socioeconomic Index, which measures occupational status, gave medical doctors a score of 92 out of 100 possible prestige points.

❖

Feminist theory also affects my work. The main questions I want to answer are about occupational segregation: Why are women and men in different occupations? Why do men's jobs pay more than women's? *How* do men monopolize the better-paying jobs? Would women really like to have men's jobs, or do they prefer jobs traditionally performed by women? Why might they prefer jobs that pay less?

What I want to do is teach a course on women and work. But to do that, I need the approval of Lloyd Ulman, the senior man in labor economics, who interviewed me for my Berkeley job. If Lloyd likes the idea, he could make it happen.

Lloyd is not only a professor of economics but also the director of Berkeley's Institute for Industrial Relations (later renamed the Institute for Research on Labor and Employment). Housed in a large, gracefully proportioned old home on Channing Street, the institute is just a few blocks from campus. Lloyd spends most of his time there, and I often run into him at the institute's library. He's a short man with neatly combed hair and impeccable clothes, often set off by a colorful bow tie, and he's always quick with a joke.

As the institute's director, he has a much wider range of colleagues than most economists, including labor union officers, labor arbitrators, and California legislators. He appreciates my background in labor relations, and we agree about the importance of the "real world" for labor economics. I find him *much* easier to talk to than George Break. Still, I'm wary of approaching him about the new course, unsure what his reaction will be. After all, it's not even settled yet that I will teach at Berkeley next year. I won't know until spring.

One afternoon in January, I meet Lloyd walking on Channing Way. Though the calendar says it's winter, the sun is bright, the camellias are in bloom, and both Lloyd and I are carrying our jackets rather than wearing them. He asks how my research on unemployment is going. I take a deep breath and seize the opportunity, telling him about my new interest in women's employment and my desire to teach a course on the subject next year. This could be the end of my career at Berkeley. Without Lloyd's support, I'll never be rehired.

"A whole course on women? Is there enough material for a whole course?"

"Yes, I think there is," I say, wondering to myself if that's the case. While there is a great deal of material, little of it is in economics.

"Well, I can't imagine that, but if you say so, I'll take your word for it. But you know if you teach a course on women's employment, then I'll have to teach one of your other courses."

"Yes, I know."

He thinks quietly for a moment, then gives me one of his signature smiles. I can tell he's thought of a joke.

"Tell you what," he says. "I'll teach your labor economics course next year if you'll give me the Susan B. Anthony Award."

"OK, Lloyd," I chuckle, "you've got yourself a deal."

As I drive home that evening, I can hardly stay on the road. I tend to speed anyway, and my Chevy takes it in stride, but this evening I have to lighten my foot multiple times. I feel like Big Blue is about to fly, and I'm more optimistic than I've been in months.

II

1950–1970

2

Banished to the Balcony, 1950–1953

My grandpa, Morris Scharer, is definitely not handsome. He's completely bald, and his eyes seem fuzzy behind his thick glasses. He's not rich, either. He's a waiter at a nonkosher restaurant in lower Manhattan where his salary and tips are low, and his only wealth is the tiny house we're in right now, a one-story bungalow on East 88th Street in the Canarsie section of Brooklyn. But what Grandpa lacks in looks and money, he makes up for in respect. Although none of his adult children or their families are Orthodox, we all attend his Orthodox *shul* and keep kosher out of regard for him. And his neighbors, boss, and co-workers, who are not Jewish, admire him as well—he is a kind man, and his commitment to his religion is unwavering.

No one sings to God like Grandpa. He's a short, lean man, several inches shorter than Baba (my grandmother) and at least twenty pounds lighter, but the volume of his chanting belies his size. Last night I slept over at Grandpa and Baba's house, and now that he's ready to begin his morning prayers, I have a front-row seat.

Grandpa's prayers begin in his bedroom, where he puts on his *tefillin*. He won't let me try on the *tefillin*, but he's happy to tell me what he's doing and what his prayers mean.

"First I put this black box on my arm, way up here, right across from my heart."

"What's in the box, Grandpa?"

"A small piece of parchment with words from the Torah. Just like inside a mezuzah."

Grandpa takes the black leather straps attached to the box and wraps them around his arm.

"What are you doing now?"

"I'm binding myself to God. I'm telling God that I love Him with all my heart."

Next he takes out another black box with straps. He puts that box just above his forehead and ties the straps behind his neck.

"What's that for?"

"This box also has parchment with words from the Torah. So when I bind it to my head, I show God that I love Him not just with my heart, but also with my mind."

After the explanations, Grandpa recites the *Shema* and the *V'ahavta*.

When he finishes, I have more questions.

"What do those prayers mean?"

"*Malkale, Malkale, du bist a gerichtike Malkale.*"

I laugh. "*Ich bin a gerichtike fragerle.*"

Grandpa is referring to my Hebrew name, Malka, which means "queen"; Malkale is a little queen, and he thinks of me that way because I ask so many questions. In response, I tell him I'm a genuine little questioner. Usually, Baba and Grandpa don't like it when I speak Yiddish. They want me to be "modern." "English, English," they insist. But this time, Grandpa seems to get a kick out of our sparring.

"You are like a yeshiva *bucher*, who sits all day with his books and questions every word on the page," he says. "I think you'll go far with all these questions, my Malkale."

Then he explains: "The *Shema* is the most important prayer of all. Just one sentence. It says there is only one God and that all people have the same piece of God inside them."

"And the other prayer?"

"The *V'ahavta*. It says that you should love God and remember all through the day to be kind to every single person, since each one of them has the very same piece of God in him that you have."

He takes off his *tefillin* and puts them back in their case. Then he begins *Shacharit*. For twenty or thirty minutes, I sit on his bed while he walks around the house, swaying from side to side, eyes half-shut, face serene, earnestly bellowing his prayers. He needs no book, for he knows the words and the melodies by heart. When he prays, he goes to a place of peace, and I travel there with him.

As I look out the window, it begins to rain, a light April shower that polishes the green buds just sticking up their noses. The whole scene feels blessed, as though in response to Grandpa's prayers, God has come down personally to water his garden. Does God really hear people's prayers? Does God hear my sister Alice and me fight? We fight a lot. I'm nine now, and she's only seven, but she knows how to get my goat. She doesn't like my being the older sister. She says I'm bossy. But if we both have the same piece of God in us, I need to be kinder to her. I've tried before, but I need to try harder.

When Grandpa finishes perambulating and singing, he gets ready for work. On his way out, he gives me his signature goodbye: he puts his hands around my head, leans me gently toward him, and kisses my forehead.

"*A leben auf dein keppele,*" he murmurs. A blessing on your little head.

On the back porch, he stops at the six or seven *pushkes,* little metal boxes for various Jewish charities that sit on the windowsill, pulls some nickels and dimes from his pockets, and carefully places one coin in each open slot. Then, shouting to Baba that he's off, he's out the door.

Once Grandpa is gone, Bessie Scharer comes into her own. Although she's bigger than Grandpa and has a powerful personality, she plays a secondary role when he's around, and especially when he's praying. But now she strides purposefully to one of the kitchen drawers, takes out a small screwdriver, and expertly jimmies the locks on the undersides of the *pushkes.* Then she removes Grandpa's coins, puts them into her apron pocket, and relocks the boxes.

"Why did you do that, Baba?" I ask, slightly horrified that anyone could annul an action of Grandpa's.

She laughs. "Your Grandpa, he's the big *macher,* always thinking of the unfortunate. It's fine that he wants to help them, but I'm the one who has to buy food, Malka."

Baba likes to call me Malka because it was her mother's name. I'm Baba and Grandpa's eldest grandchild, so I got what they regarded as the prize name. Baba and her siblings revere their mother, Malka Greenberg, and tell me stories about her whenever they see me.

Malka was from a ghetto in Kiptchenitz, a tiny town in a depressed rural area of what was then Austria-Hungary. But although she was illiterate and widowed early in life, she somehow managed to survive, get herself and her five children to the United States, and launch them into new lives. When she came to New York, she started a kosher restaurant with Baba and Grandpa where she was not only the primary chef but also the manager. I have a small brooch with a picture of Malka that I keep in my top drawer, and when I look at it, I'm reminded how formidable she was. I'm proud to be named for her and feel I have big shoes to fill.

Baba puts away her screwdriver, sits down at the kitchen table, and motions me to climb onto her lap. She squeezes me tightly and covers me with kisses.

Baba gives me my first lessons in the power of the powerless. She raised seven children—six daughters and one son—and although they often fight with each other and with Grandpa, they rarely argue with her. She is a phenomenal listener who exercises her power quietly. She loves people unconditionally, and her children and grandchildren adore her. Even her daughters' boyfriends loved her. Aunt Rose told me that she always tried to be ready to go when a man came to pick her up for a date because if he talked to Baba while he waited for Rose, he became more interested in staying to talk to Baba than in leaving the house.

My sister Alice has been learning how to read in school, and I've been watching with fascination as slowly, letter by letter, word by word, she learns to decode paragraphs on the page. She enters a whole new world, "meeting" people she'll never see in real life and sharing their adventures. I'm awed by her transformation, and one day after school, while Baba is talking to her sister, Tante Annie, in the kitchen, I get an idea.

"Alice, let's teach Baba and Tante Annie to read!"

I feel bad that Tante Annie and Baba can't read. I'm not ashamed *of* them; I'm ashamed *for* them. Grandpa can read, write, and speak seven languages. While Tante Annie and Baba went out to work as maids in the old country, Grandpa not only went to *cheder* (religious school) to learn to read prayer books and the Torah, he also went to secular school, where he learned German, Polish, and Hungarian. Then, when he ran away to Italy to flee army conscription, he learned Italian. And when he got to New York, he learned English. What an incredibly different experience he had compared with Baba and Tante Annie!

Alice says she likes my idea of teaching Baba and Tante Annie to read, and together we rush out of our bedroom to tell them our plan.

Baba and Tante Annie are in their seventies, but they're in excellent physical shape, probably because they do so much walking, and so much schlepping of grocery bags. Baba is a few years younger than Tante Annie, and she's taller and more *zaftig* (full-figured), but they wear the same clothes: laced-up, sensible shoes; loose-fitting cotton print housedresses (short-sleeved in summer, long-sleeved and covered by a long sweater in winter); and heavy stockings, rolled down above the knee in warm weather and hooked to a girdle when it's chilly. Their hair is also similar—long, gray, and pulled into a bun at the nape of the neck.

They speak English with a pronounced Yiddish accent (as does Grandpa), and when they have something particularly emotional to express, they lapse into Yiddish. But I don't mind. I'm fascinated by their old-fashioned ways. I also love that they're superb cooks and bakers; spending time with them ensures delicious meals and yummy desserts. Right now, Tante Annie is making mushroom barley soup and Baba is rolling out dough for rugelach, a crescent-shape pastry with a croissant-like crust.

"Why should I learn to read?" Baba asks. "Every night, Grandpa reads me the *Fovitz* [the *Jewish Daily Forward* in Yiddish]. I like when he reads to me."

Tante Annie is a better prospect.

"Tante Annie, if you could read, you could read all about the Rosenberg trial. You could learn more than you can from just listening to the radio," I say.

Julius and Ethel Rosenberg are on trial for espionage, and Tante Annie, like most Jews, is both repelled and riveted by the allegations.

"OK, so teach me," she challenges. "Teach me to read."

So we three sit at the kitchen table: two skinny girls in matching blue dresses, with the blondest hair imaginable and fair skin that burns at the slightest hint of sun, and a white-haired woman who has stopped her cooking to learn to read more than a half century after she should have.

"Here, Tante Annie," I say, getting a pencil and paper from the drawer where Dad keeps his pads for keeping score in gin games, "I'm going to write your name, ANNA. See, it starts with an A and it ends with an A, and in the middle there are two N's."

"*Oy vey iz mier* [woe is me]," says Baba. "I have a headache already."

"Baba, don't say that," I tell her. "Tante Annie doesn't have a husband to read her the paper. She needs to learn how to read for herself."

"OK," Tante Annie says, "two A's and two N's. What does that mean?"

"It means that when you see ANNA on a piece of paper, you know that's your name."

"OK."

"So you see, you learned how to read your name. Now you can learn how to write it. Here's the pencil. Just copy what I wrote."

Tante Annie takes the pencil, but she doesn't know how to hold it. She grabs it like she's getting ready to stab an intruder.

"No, don't hold it like that," Alice says. "You look like you're going to kill somebody."

"*Oy, shayna maydele* [pretty little girl], how should I hold it? I can't hold it. I'm too old to hold it."

"OK," I say. "Forget about writing. We'll just do reading. You already read ANNA. Now let's read 'dog.'"

"*Oy vey iz mier.* I don't like dogs. I don't want to read about dogs."

"What do you want to read about?"

"*Oy, oy, oy,*" Tante Annie takes a handkerchief from her apron pocket and rubs her eyes with exhaustion. "I'm sorry to tell you, I don't want to read. I don't want to read anything."

Alice and I both feel bad that we failed in our efforts. But when we tell Mom about our experience, she tells us a story. Mrs. Smith, my cousin Natalie's other grandmother, a woman only a few years younger than Baba and Tante Annie and also initially illiterate, learned to read and write in a class she took during World War II. Why? She had four sons serving in the armed forces and wanted to be able to write to them and read the letters they sent home. Alice and I weren't successful with Baba and Tante Annie, Mom explains, because they had no strong reason to want to learn.

Today, well into the twenty-first century, there are 775 million illiterate adults across the world, two-thirds of them women. And even though there are hundreds of literacy programs to provide grown men and women with established curricula and teachers far more experienced than Alice and I, adult learners often fail. My heart goes out to each and every one of them—and I'm angry, just as I was about Baba and Tante Annie, that these adults were not taught to read when they were children.

❖

Tante Annie is Mom's substitute in every way. She comes to our house five days a week and not only cooks, cleans, and takes care of Alice and me but also serves as our family's designated housewife. Mom is the only woman on our block who works for pay. When she was a few months' pregnant with me, she took maternity leave from her job as an elementary school secretary, but once I was born, she found it tedious to care for an infant and do housework all day. After a few months at home, she told Dad she wanted to go back to work. He agreed that Mom didn't seem suited to full-time childcare and housework, and he was enthusiastic about having her salary again.

When they asked Tante Annie if she would take care of me, she agreed readily. She'd never had any children of her own, but she loved helping to raise all of Baba's children, and she welcomed the chance to care for me. When her husband died, he left her without any savings. Her only income was a small monthly welfare check, so she also welcomed meals at our house.

When Alice was born, Mom took another short maternity leave, then again returned to work. Nobody on our street ever teases Mom about working, but some of the men make disparaging remarks to Dad.

"Whatsamatta, Jules? Gotta send the little lady to work?"

Dad laughs. "If only they knew," he tells Mom. "If only they knew that I don't 'send' you anyplace."

From early childhood, I understood that Mom's working set us apart from other families, but I never felt something was missing. I had plenty of mothers—Mom, Tante Annie, Baba, and Mom's sisters—and I could see that Mom loved working. I could also see that our family was far better off because she brought in a paycheck. I didn't know until later that she actually earned more than Dad, but I knew early on that a woman could be a good mom and also work for pay.

Spending so much time with Grandpa has instilled a keen Jewish identity for me, and I love to go to High Holiday services each year in his *shul*. On the mornings of Rosh Hashanah, Dad and I usually get to services around 10 a.m. Grandpa gets there at 9—he pretty much opens up the place—but Dad and I never get there *that* early. After Dad puts on his *yarmulke* and *tallis* (prayer shawl), we walk down the aisle to Grandpa, who smiles and motions for me to sit next to him.

Grandpa sits right up front on a bench that's acknowledged as his, and he shares it with his son, sons-in-law, and grandchildren. But even if you didn't know which bench belonged to Grandpa, it wouldn't be hard to find him. In the same way that his voice fills his house when he prays *Shacharit* at home, it fills the *shul* at the High Holidays.

I spend the next hour or so enthralled, fingering the fringes on his prayer shawl and soaking up his songs. I understand nothing. The prayer book is in Hebrew with a Yiddish translation. I've learned to read Hebrew at Hebrew School, but I can't even begin to follow the prayers, and interrupting Grandpa to ask questions is not possible. So I just sit there and take it all in. For me, Grandpa's singing and swaying brings God directly into the building.

When I tire of sitting and listening, I'm free to wander upstairs to the balcony where Baba and Tante Annie sit with all the other women. Unlike Grandpa, Baba and Tante Annie don't pray out loud. They rest their open prayer books on their laps, but since they can't read, they have no idea what page they should be on. They simply sit and think. And I do the same.

Sometime around noon, close to the end of the service, Mom and her sisters arrive. As soon as I see them coming, I go back downstairs to Grandpa. I love these women dearly, but I find them annoying as they gossip back and forth, delighting in the attention they draw as heads turn to see their stunning new hats. Some look like giant sombreros, some like half an airplane. They're the perfect accessories for their stylish dresses.

But one Rosh Hashanah, when I am twelve, just as Dad and I are about to leave for services, Mom drops a bomb.

"When you get to *shul* this morning," she tells me, "you are *not* to sit downstairs with Grandpa. You are to go upstairs and sit with Baba and Tante Annie."

"What?" I shriek. "Why?"

"Because you might distract the men who are praying."

My fury rises quickly.

"Distract them? I'm very quiet when I'm down there. It's you and your sisters who distract everyone with your noise and your fancy hats, and you do it from upstairs."

"Yes, well, be that as it may, you can't sit downstairs anymore. You're a woman now."

I ask Dad about Mom's pronouncement. "She's right," he says. "You're too big now to sit downstairs."

I'm utterly crushed and start to cry.

"It'll be alright, cookie," he says hugging me. "You're not a little girl anymore. You're my big girl now."

I push him away.

I go with Dad to *shul*, but I don't go inside. I wear my new dress, a soft navy blue wool with a slim skirt and a Peter Pan collar (what a waste of time buying *that* dress!), but I spend my time out on the street playing stickball with my cousins. My shiny new Mary Janes feel odd, but I can still run around the bases.

When Aunt Bimi arrives and notices I'm not at services, she comes out to where we're playing and takes me aside. Aunt Bimi is Mom's youngest sister, and, like Mom, she works as an elementary school secretary. She and Mom are the only two of Baba and Grandpa's children who are college graduates. While Mom is serious and bossy (being the eldest of seven children had its effect), Aunt Bimi is sunny and affectionate.

"I know how you feel," she says. "I remember when Mama told me I couldn't sit downstairs with Papa anymore. But really, darling, you're a big girl now, and you can't. Someday when you have a daughter, you'll have to give her the same news. But it's OK. There are lots of compensations for being a woman."

I know Aunt Bimi is trying to comfort me, but I don't want to hear her, so I just run back into the game. On that day, stickball and my young cousins are my salvation.

A few days later, I try to bargain with Grandpa.

"Even though I couldn't sit with you for Rosh Hashanah, can I sit with you for Yom Kippur?"

Grandpa is adamant that I cannot, and right after Yom Kippur, I come to understand that having to sit upstairs in *shul* is just the beginning of my problems.

When Hebrew School starts up again for the fall term, my best friend there, Billy Green, tells me he's preparing for his bar mitzvah. Billy is almost exactly my age, so I ask my Hebrew teacher if I can start preparing for my bar mitzvah (nobody has taught me that girls have a bat mitzvah instead).

"Certainly not," he says. "Bar mitzvahs are for boys."

"But why? My Hebrew is as good as Billy's. I'll work hard. I promise, my reading will be perfect."

"It's absolutely not possible."

"Billy and I are the two top students in our class. He gets to have a bar mitzvah and I don't? That's not fair," I tell Mom.

"It's not about fairness," Mom says. "Women and girls simply can't read Torah or Haftorah from the *bima* [the raised platform in front of the ark that holds the Torah]. My Hebrew is better than most men's, and I understand exactly what the Hebrew says, but I've never read Torah or Haftorah from the *bima* either."

I appeal to Grandpa. "Where does it say in the Torah that girls can't have a bar mitzvah?"

His answer is one of exasperation: "The Torah is filled with different commandments for men and women. You're a woman now. Enough with the questions."

His message is clear. When I was a young girl, he found my questions charming, but now that I'm a young woman, they're unwelcome. I want to remind him that he was the one who told me all people have the same piece of God inside them, that surely my piece of God warrants a bar mitzvah for me as much as Billy's piece warrants one for him. But I know I will be greeted with stony silence. I never stop admiring and loving Grandpa, but after this conversation, our relationship is never the same.

No one seems persuaded by my arguments about fairness. In one form or another they all say the same thing: *This is what it is. Accept it.* But I'm enraged, and I can't.

In 1970, the economist Albert Hirschmann wrote that voice and exit are the two productive responses to dissatisfaction, be it the dissatisfaction of a worker, a customer, or a citizen; and that when voice is closed off, exit is the only remaining choice. Workers strike or look for a new job, customers shop elsewhere, and citizens leave their political party or country. When I am denied a bar (or bat) mitzvah, I take the only path open to me: I exit.

"I'm never going to Hebrew School again," I tell Mom.

And that's the end of my childhood Hebrew education. It's also the end of my friendship with Billy. I don't even attend his bar mitzvah.

My family and my Hebrew teacher didn't seem to be aware of it at the time, but there were in fact bat mitzvah ceremonies for Jewish girls in the 1950s in non-Orthodox congregations. In New York City in 1922, thirty years before I made my request, Judith Kaplan—the daughter of rabbi

Mordecai Kaplan, the founder of Reconstructionist Judaism—was the first girl to have a bat mitzvah. Still, although Ms. Kaplan got up in front of her father's congregation on a Saturday morning and read that week's Torah portion in Hebrew, she didn't read from the Torah scroll itself.

Although it was not until after my meeting with George Break in 1970 that I became consciously aware of my feminist leanings, I clearly had feminist inclinations much earlier. But I was a child and a product of the 1940s: I exited from uncomfortable situations when I could, but basically I accepted a gendered reality and did what I was told. However, as my adolescence advanced, so did my rebelliousness. Like Baba, I learned I could jimmy locks.

3

A Boost Up, 1954–1958

In the mid-1950s, like millions of Americans whose incomes are rising, Mom begins dreaming of moving to a better neighborhood. She calls Canarsie "geographically undesirable" and thinks the school Alice and I attend is not as good as those in more middle-class neighborhoods. She has high ambitions for her two daughters and realizes that achieving them depends on the quality of our schooling.

When Mom was young, she had her own high ambitions, but circumstances forced her to lower them. She was an excellent student in high school, and several of her teachers encouraged her to go to law school. (In the early 1920s, you could go directly to law school from high school.) But Baba's oldest brother told her that getting more schooling would be selfish; that, as Grandpa and Baba's eldest child, she needed to go directly to work and help out by giving her parents a portion of her weekly earnings. She felt ashamed that her uncle saw her as selfish, and she never talked to her parents about what he'd said. Instead she looked for a job and found one as a secretary. It wasn't until many years later that she enrolled at Baruch College, part of the City University of New York system, at night, and it took her seven years to complete a degree in business. When she finally graduated, it was with honors.

She wanted to be a high school teacher of stenography and typing, and passed the New York City written exam for high school teachers with an excellent score. But in 1935, in the midst of the Great Depression, the New York City Board of Education had more teacher applicants than teaching jobs, and they flunked Mom on the oral exam. Her voice was too gravelly, they told her, too hoarse. Students might have trouble understanding her.

Mom was sorely disappointed. Had she put in seven years of study only to continue working at an insurance agency? But then she learned that with a college degree, she was eligible to work as a school secretary. She passed that exam easily—no oral exam required—and began working as an elementary school secretary in Brooklyn. She liked the work, the short commute, the children, the summer vacations, and, perhaps most of all, having college-graduate colleagues. She also liked the salary. She earned about a third more than Dad. Such was the power of a college degree.

What Mom would really like is to buy a house in an upper-middle-class neighborhood in Queens. Jamaica or Forest Hills would be perfect. But Dad is afraid that if he loses his job, he'll be unable to pay the mortgage. So they compromise and rent a two-bedroom apartment in the Flatbush section of Brooklyn, at the edge of an affluent neighborhood of one-family houses.

We move in February 1954, right in the middle of my eighth-grade year, and Mom registers me at Hudde Junior High School. I know only one person at Hudde: Eileen Stringer, a friend from Pine Lake, a modest bungalow colony with a day camp in Peekskill, New York, where our family spends summers. Fortunately, she's just the right person to know. Beautiful, popular, and very much wanting to help, she pulls out all the stops.

"This is Myra, my friend from camp," she tells her many friends. "She's going to be part of our group now."

And so I am. Within a month, I have at least six new girlfriends who all live close by. Unlike my old friends, these girls live in large homes and have plenty of spending money for bowling on Friday nights, shopping on Kings Highway on Saturdays, and trips to Manhattan for theater. I feel indigent compared to them and am constantly asking Mom and Dad for more allowance. I visit their houses but almost never invite them to our apartment.

Mom turns out to be quite right about Hudde. It's much more intellectually challenging than my school in Canarsie, and I have my first experience with the sad fact that upper-middle-class kids have far better schools than their working-class cousins. Our classes are smaller and our homework assignments more creative, especially in social studies. But most important, the classes are run with more discussion and less lecture, and the other students' comments are stimulating.

Late twentieth-century research on the economics of education shows time and time again that the ability of peers is one of the most important inputs to education success. I witnessed that daily at Hudde.

The highlight of eighth grade is when my English teacher introduces us to *Gone with the Wind* by taking our class into Manhattan to see the movie. We talk about it at length in class—slavery, race relations, the Civil War, Reconstruction, choosing marriage partners, integrity, and deceit. I find the story inspiring, and as soon as school is out I spend every free hour at Pine Lake reading the novel: all one thousand-plus pages. I admire both the young heroines—I want to be kind, like Melanie; and determined and shrewd, like Scarlett. And like all my friends, I'm madly in love with Rhett Butler.

When I enter ninth grade, and my friends and I form a chapter of B'nai B'rith Girls (BBG), my boy-girl social life takes off. During parties in my friends' large finished basements, I meet boys almost every weekend, and many of them ask me out—to the movies, bowling, school basketball games, plays in Manhattan, and more dance parties.

Interestingly, I never date a single boy from any of my classes at school. I talk a great deal in class, my teachers usually praise what I have to say, and somehow this combination doesn't attract my male classmates. It's a bit puzzling to me, because I talk a lot at parties also, but somehow that's different. Maybe it's that I don't really think much about boys as potential dates while I'm in class, so they don't think that way about me; or maybe there's just less boy-girl competition in social situations where the teacher and her praise are absent.

Although Mom and Dad enjoy going out on Saturday nights, and Mom takes time to play the piano while Dad reads, they both work hard at home and never ask Alice or me to do any housework. Our job is to study hard and get good grades.

My friends don't do housework either—not because their parents are pushing them to get good grades, but because they have household help. One of the downsides of adopting all of Eileen's friends is that I don't make friends with girls who are paying a lot of attention to school. Not until my senior year, when I'm in Advanced Placement (AP) classes, will I meet and become friendly with girls who are more like me—less wealthy and more academically motivated.

Once we move to Flatbush, Tante Annie no longer comes to our house every day. Alice and I are now old enough to care for ourselves after school, and Tante Annie is becoming frail. She spends her days taking care of her own small apartment and talking with Baba and the other women on her street. Without Tante Annie, Dad does the vacuuming and the dishes and takes the laundry down to the washer and dryer in the apartment-house basement. But everything else falls to Mom—shopping, cooking, dusting, window washing, clerical work, mending, folding clothes, and ironing. There are no permanent press fabrics and all our cotton shirts need ironing, to say nothing of tablecloths, aprons, and handkerchiefs.

On weeknights, Dad goes to bed by 10 p.m., but Mom stays up until at least midnight to iron, pay bills, and catch up with the newspaper. Since I'm also beginning to stay up late, I'm delighted with Mom's night-owl habits. Especially when she's ironing and her mind is free, we have time to talk.

"How will I know when I love somebody?" I ask her.

"You'll know. You'll feel you want to spend your whole life with him, every single day. You'll feel peaceful but also excited. You'll feel like he understands you and you understand him."

"How did you fall in love with Dad?"

Mom met Dad when she was at Baruch College. A fellow student of Mom's who was also a childhood friend of Dad's introduced them. Dad was intelligent, read voraciously, kept up with politics, and had friends who were either college graduates or in the process of getting their degrees at night. Mom just assumed that Dad was a college graduate, and Dad never said otherwise. It was a great shock for her to learn that Dad didn't have a bachelor's degree and was too tired in the evenings to go to night school. But by then, she was in love with him.

"You know, I had another boyfriend besides Dad," Mom says.

"You did? At the same time?"

"Yes."

Wow, I think to myself. *This is really getting interesting. If Mom had made a different decision, I wouldn't be me.*

"Who was the other boyfriend?"

"His name was Sam, and he was a lawyer. He proposed to me just about the same time that Dad did."

"Really? You had two proposals?" My admiration for Mom has just gone up several notches. "How did you decide on Dad?"

"I was at the theater with one of my friends, and I decided in the very first act. The heroine was in exactly my situation. She had two proposals. One was from a lovely man who had no college degree and would never be rich, the other from a fellow who was already rich. She loved the poor one but chose the rich one. As soon as she did, I could see she made the wrong decision. I didn't want to make her mistake."

Mom smiles dreamily, remembering it all. But then she comes back to being Mom.

"But you know, I'll tell you something, Myra. It's just as easy to fall in love with a rich man as with a poor one. You just have to meet a lot of rich men. I didn't do that. I met mostly poor men. I want it to be different for you. I want you to fall in love with a doctor or a lawyer. I want you to have an easier life than I've had."

Although Mom expects that I'll marry (and hopes I'll marry well), she also expects me to have a career, and she often asks what I field I think I might want to pursue.

"Always remember," she tells me with some frequency, "marriage is not the be-all and end-all of life. You must be prepared for a rainy day."

Mom never identified particularly with women's issues (she was too young to be a suffragette, and the women's movement was not prominent in the United States for a while after that), but what she instills in me year after teenage year accords perfectly with the crux of feminist teaching: "You have to be able to support yourself. You can't rely on a man for your economic security."

Mom is so firm about my economic independence that she demands I take two years of shorthand and typewriting. We're both planning for me to go to college, but she wants me to be able to earn my own living in case she and Dad can't afford to keep me there. I'm the only girl in my stenography class getting an academic diploma.

This rekindles Mom's desire to teach those subjects, and one day she asks me if I think she should retake the exam and try to get a license. I'm astonished at her question, as I know she would never be able to hear the students in her class, but I don't want to use her own infirmity to dash her dreams.

"I don't think you'd have much fun teaching stenography and typing," I say instead. "The girls in my classes are pretty rough, and my teacher constantly has to discipline them."

I don't know whether Mom is put off by my description of what her job might be like or if she realizes herself that she could not pass an oral exam, but she never mentions the possibility again, though she frequently tells us how overqualified she is to be a school secretary and how if she were principal "instead of the jerk I work for," the school would be far better run. Mom's frustration with her job and her inability to fully use her skills are powerful factors in her constantly pushing Alice and me to achieve.

I never fight with Mom about taking stenography and typing. I'm annoyed, but I feel she has my best interests at heart. However, by the time Alice is in high school, I lobby hard for her. Between my arguments and Alice's determination that she will never be caught dead taking those courses, Mom relents.

As I look back now, I'm sad that Mom's fears that I might not finish college for economic reasons exacted such a high price. Thanks to stenography and typing, I took only two and a half years of math and one year of science—no advanced algebra, no trig, no analytic geometry, and no chemistry or physics. It also seems unfair that my friends could take whatever courses they wished, and I—who was more academically oriented, with a mother who was much more interested in her daughter having a career than their mothers were—wound up with a less intellectually challenging curriculum. There's a lesson here: the rapid social and economic change that takes place between generations makes it likely that parents' well-meant advice is often out of date.

My favorite course sophomore year is European history. The teacher, Miss Rundback, is statuesque, beautiful, and brilliant. Every day she brings European royalty, popes, and peasants to life. My most astounding insight from her class is that not all that long ago, Europe was organized by feudalism. At Hebrew School, I learned about the nomadic wanderings of the Jewish patriarchs and their families, but that was ancient history. It is truly exciting to learn that a fundamentally different way of organizing society existed even after the American Revolution—from a historical perspective, barely yesterday. After a few months with Miss Rundback, my future career is clear: I want to be a high school social studies teacher.

The following year, I have another sensational social studies teacher, Max. A rumpled man with an unruly mustache, he's far more radical politically than Miss Rundback. He teaches American politics and asks us to call him by his first name, a rarity in the 1950s. Max makes students think during every minute of class.

"Miss Hoffenberg, what do you think about the Supreme Court decision in *Brown v. Board of Education*?"

"Miss Hoffenberg, what do you think about the Army-McCarthy hearings?"

I learn that I have strong opinions and know how to express them. I argue with Max almost every day, and one day he takes me aside.

"You're a terrific student," he says, "and you have a talent for social studies. What are you going to do with your life?"

"I'm going to be just like you. I'm going to argue with students and make them think."

These classroom discussions play out at home, too. My parents and Alice also have a penchant for history, economics, and politics, and our dinner conversations are filled with the issues of the day and their origins.

"Why do workers need to be in unions?" I ask.

"Workers need unions so they can bargain with their employers," Mom answers. "Employers have vast power, especially the power to fire any worker they don't like. But a worker who is fired has no power except the right to look for a new job. And if he's fired because he was trying to get a higher wage or a fairer workplace and he's labeled a troublemaker, he can't get a new job. So then where is he? Out on the street. Hungry. His family is starving. By joining a union, he gets stronger. If all the workers go out on strike together, and if the strikers picket and other workers respect their picket line, then the power between the employer and the workers gets a little more even."

"Are you in a union, Dad"?

"No, salesmen don't have a union."

"What about you, Mom?"

"No, I work for the Board of Ed. We're not allowed to have unions."

"Can't you start a union?"

"Oh, it's very dangerous to start a union. The first thing the employer does is fire the people who are starting the union."

I ask Max about this.

"Your parents are right. It takes very brave and committed people to start a union. And for public employees, it's especially risky."

Little did any of us imagine that less than a decade later, there would be a strong teachers' union in New York City, and both Max and my mother would be members.

One of the highlights of Midwood High School for me is singing as an alto in mixed chorus, and when Alice starts at Midwood, she is accepted as an alto in that chorus, too. From then on, we sing together regularly—at home, in the car, on the street, whenever we're in the mood. Neither of us is really a soprano, but Alice enjoys "searching" for the high notes while I love hearing my own lower voice against the melody.

But although we sing harmoniously, we fight furiously. Part of our discord stems from sharing a room. I like the room tidy; she doesn't care. I like darkness and quiet when I sleep; she can sleep with lights blazing, and when she puts her good ear into the pillow, a live orchestra could play three feet away without disturbing her. However, most of our fights stem from the differences in our personalities and our mutual intolerance. I like to rebel quietly; she likes to make a show of it. I like to smoke behind my father's back; she likes to enrage him by smoking where he will find her. She thinks I'm far too interested in being "well-behaved" and regularly calls me "goody two-shoes," while I fault her for needlessly distressing our parents. I find Judaism spiritually enriching; she's not at all moved by it. We have frequent truces, and we both know we love each other, but our daily lives are filled with petty and not-so-petty arguments. Sometimes our parents intervene and succeed in lowering the volume of our hollering, but most of the time they let us go at it.

In early 1956, Grandpa is diagnosed with colon cancer, and in mid-August, he passes away. On a hot, sultry morning, our whole family and Grandpa's neighbors and co-workers set out for the funeral home. After the service, the cortege stops in front of Grandpa's *shul*. We exit our cars and stand quietly while the rabbi ascends the steep front stairs and opens the synagogue's carved wooden doors.

"Moshe Menachim Mendel," the rabbi intones, "this is your time to say good-bye to your *shul* and your *shul*'s time to salute you. You have served it well. May you rest in peace."

We stand for several minutes in sweltering silence until the rabbi closes the doors and returns to the street. This *shul* stirs up so many memories—my delight in sitting next to Grandpa and listening to him pray, but also my anger when Mom and Dad prohibited me from sitting next to him, and my fury and frustration when I learned I could not have a bat mitzvah here. The opposing memories jostle painfully, and my tears, born of sorrow and regret, also bear intense resentment.

When we return to our cars, we begin the procession to the cemetery in Staten Island. There is no Verrazano Bridge yet, and the fifteen cars in our cortege are all loaded onto the Staten Island ferry. The crossing provides a welcome breeze, but once we get to shore, suffocating humidity envelops us once again, and our steps toward the cemetery are measured. Baba grasps Uncle Nat's arm, and Tante Annie leans on Dad. Both women carry large black umbrellas to block the sun.

Because Aunt Bimi is pregnant, Jewish law prohibits her from coming to the gravesite. She sits in a shaded grove nearby, and I join her.

"It's the end of an era, Myra," she says. "Nothing will ever be the same again."

She's right. Two years later, Tante Annie dies, after losing her mind and being confined to Bellevue Hospital. And two years after that, when Baba dies of stomach cancer, Mom sells Baba's house. Baba and Grandpa's children each join different Conservative synagogues near their own homes, and while small subgroups of the family get together for seders, the whole clan never gathers again. Grandpa, Baba, and Tante Annie bound us tightly to them and to each other. Without them, we scatter like chaff before the wind. I miss Grandpa, Baba, and Tante Annie exceedingly, but most of all I miss the outpouring of massive family love.

Not long after Grandpa's funeral, I decide to talk to Dad about college. He's reading on the couch, and I move to a chair next to him.

"Daddy, I have something I want to talk to you about."

No answer.

"Daaaaaddy."

Still no answer.

I tiptoe up to where he's reading, peer over his book, and nudge his shoulder.

"Earth to Mars, Myra to Julius, hello?"

Dad laughs. This isn't our first such interaction. Dad reads mysteries all the time, several a week, to and from work on the subway and on the couch at night. They're a good escape from a job he dislikes more and more.

"I'm sorry, cookie. I just get so absorbed. What can I do for you?"

"I want to talk to you about college."

"What about it? It's still years away."

"I know, but I'm not happy about you and Mom saying I have to go to Brooklyn College."

"What's wrong with Brooklyn College? It's a good college, it's close by, you can live at home, and it's free."

Dad works as a salesman at J. Weinstein & Sons, a small company that buys woolen fabrics from textile mills and sells them to men's suit and coat manufacturers. His second cousins own the company, and he's been working for them for twenty-five years, ever since he graduated from high school. He never expected to stay that long, but when the Depression hit in 1929, he was glad to have the job—and he's never had the confidence to look elsewhere. He worries frequently about losing his job, should his company "go under," and as I begin to understand the situation, I worry, too.

"Brooklyn College is a good college," I tell Dad, "but it's not a great college. I want to go to a great college. And I don't want to live at home while I go to college. I want to go out of town."

"Yeah, but we can't afford for you to go out of town. We're happy we can afford to send you to college during the day. Mom worked during the day and went to college at night, and I couldn't go to college at all."

"I know, I know. You've told me a million times. I should be grateful. I don't have to trudge to school for miles through the snow, like Abe Lincoln."

"Listen, getting bratty isn't going to help you."

"OK, what's going to help me?"

"To me, Brooklyn College seems like a dream come true. You don't have to go on the subway to get there. It has a beautiful campus, and it's free. Explain to me what's wrong with it."

"To go to Brooklyn College, all you need is an 85 average. I can get an 85 average without ever opening another book. I want to go to a college where you need a 95 average, where there are really smart people. And I want to live in a dorm."

"Fine. Why don't you go out and find some new parents, some really rich ones?"

"Now who's being bratty?"

"Sorry."

"Listen, Dad, I understand that you can't afford tuition and room and board. That's not what I'm asking. I'm asking you and Mom to agree that if I get a scholarship that pays for all of that, you'll let me go out of town."

"I don't like the idea of your living by yourself."

"I won't live by myself. I'll live with two hundred other girls."

"I still don't like it."

"OK, Dad, now I'm really mad. You know what? If you and Mom don't let me try to get a scholarship and go out of town, I'm not opening another book. I'll get my 85 average, and that will be that."

My father looks alarmed.

"Oh, my," he says. "You'd *do* that?"

"I would," I say, and leave him to his book.

That evening, I hear him reporting our conversation to Mom. She says she can't believe I'm not satisfied with Brooklyn College. Who do I think I am? But when Dad tells her about my threat, she changes her tune, and a few days later, they agree to let me try to get into an out-of-town college and compete for a scholarship.

"But only in New York State," Mom says.

"Why only in New York?"

"Because you'll be eligible for a New York State scholarship, and we wouldn't want you to have to turn that down."

"But what if a college in some other state gives me enough money that I don't need the New York State scholarship?"

"Listen, we're letting you go out of town, but in New York State. That's enough for today."

Well, I think to myself, *that's pretty good. Not perfect, but pretty good.*

"Oh, and one more thing," Mom says, "no matter how many scholarships you get, it's going to cost us more money to send you to out-of-town college than it would if you went to Brooklyn College, so we want you to start working after school as soon as you're sixteen. With your typing and steno skills, you should be able to get a good job."

❖

I have no problem with working after school, and the following March, when I turn sixteen and can get working papers, I get a job in the office of a dry cleaner just a few blocks from our apartment. I work five afternoons after school and no longer get an allowance. Then, in the fall of my senior year, I get an even better job working for Stanley H. Kaplan—yes, *the* Stanley H. Kaplan, whose little company will grow to be the largest test preparation corporation in the world, eventually bought by the *Washington Post* and becoming the Post's most profitable division.

When I work for Kaplan, the business is almost twenty years old, but it's housed in the basement of a modest house near Madison High School. I take the Nostrand Avenue bus to get there and spend the late afternoon taking dictation, answering the phone, and helping with filing. I enjoy working with him and get a kick out of the fact that he made up his middle initial. (He says it stands for "higher scores.") But I never talk with him about my own college plans, and he never asks. I'm merely the girl Friday. It's strange: here's a man who helps hundreds of thousands of high school students improve their chances of being accepted at the colleges of their choice, but he doesn't talk about college aspirations with the one high school student who works for him.

Instead, mentorship for college application comes from my next-door neighbor, Jacob Loft, a professor of economics at Brooklyn College; and Margaret Bradshaw, the college counselor at Midwood. Although I've known the Lofts for almost three years and their daughter is a friend of Alice's, I've had almost no contact with them before. But once Mom and Dad give me permission to apply to out-of-town schools, Mom insists that I talk with Professor Loft. She's now fully committed to my leaving Brooklyn, and she wants to take a trip in the spring of my junior year to look at colleges.

"We have to figure out which ones you might apply to, so we know which ones to visit," she explains.

"I already know which ones I want to apply to."

"Listen, Miss Know-It-All, it wouldn't hurt you to get a little advice. Just ring their doorbell."

I hate the idea of what I now know is called a "cold call," but I follow Mom's instructions. It feels like she's taken over the whole application process, but I do as she wishes.

Professor Loft turns out to be exceedingly helpful. After he listens to my interests, he suggests that I investigate Cornell University's School of Industrial and Labor Relations (ILR).

"It's a really fine place," he says. "Small. They only take about sixty students a year, but the faculty is terrific. I think you'd like it. Write to them and ask them to send you their materials."

When the materials come, I agree that the school fits my interests well. I ring his bell again to thank him, and Mom and I put Cornell on the list of places to visit.

My interactions with Miss Bradshaw don't end nearly as pleasantly. A fearsome "old maid" with stringy gray hair in a severe bun at the nape of her neck, dowdy clothes, sensible shoes, and a permanent pout, Miss Bradshaw runs the college application process with an iron hand. Midwood has about a thousand students in each graduating class, but only about 250 apply to college. At the beginning of senior year, Miss Bradshaw compiles the GPAs of those 250 and informs them of their numerical place in the rankings. My magic number is eighteen.

She then calls in the top students, one by one, and tells each of us which selective college she will permit us to apply to. The number one girl may apply to Radcliffe, the number two girl to Wellesley, and so on down the Seven Sisters line. The boy with the highest rank may apply to Harvard, the boy with the second-highest rank to Yale, and so forth. My assigned school is Vassar. Somehow or other, Miss Bradshaw has agreements with admissions directors at all the top schools—if only one student from Midwood applies, that student is accepted. And, in fact, all the top students at Midwood in the year I graduate are accepted to the schools she designates for them.

Although Cornell Arts and Sciences is regulated by Miss Bradshaw's system, Cornell ILR is not, so I am able to apply. It's exceedingly competitive, especially for girls. Of the sixty students it admits each year, only fifteen are female.

By early April, I learn I've been admitted to the four schools where I applied: Brooklyn College, Cornell ILR, Syracuse University, and Vassar. (Another of Miss Bradshaw's rules is that no student may apply to more than four schools). Vassar offers me a full scholarship, courtesy of the Vassar Club of Brooklyn.

Mom is overjoyed, and I hear her talking to Aunt Bimi on the phone.

"Can you imagine? *We* are going to have a daughter at Vassar. And *you* are going to have a niece there."

But I don't want to go to Vassar. I want to go to Cornell. I'm in love with Cornell's beauty—the gorges and waterfalls, the hills in the distance, massive Cayuga Lake. And I love the hugeness of the place, the fact that it has a football team, and majestic libraries. But most of all, I love that it has boys. I don't want to go to an all-girls school. I want to discuss history, politics, and economics with boys *and* girls. My experience in high school classes is that the genders often have very different opinions on these matters. Besides, I just like being around boys. I don't want to see them only on weekends.

Somehow or other, I have to tell Mom that I want to go to Cornell. And somehow I have to tell Miss Bradshaw. Both conversations feel formidable.

I start with Dad.

"Oh, boy," he laughs. "That's my girl."

"You think it's OK?"

"Listen, cookie, it's your life. Of course it's OK. They'll both be mad, but so what?"

Miss Bradshaw is stunned. I've ruined her whole system, she tells me. And Mom is equally devastated.

"How can you give up Vassar? How can you do this to me? How can you do this to Miss Bradshaw? I knew we shouldn't have visited Vassar during their reunion. At Cornell you saw all those handsome guys, but at Vassar you saw nothing but old biddies. What a shame."

Miss Bradshaw never forgives me, but Mom does.

"You can go to Cornell on two conditions," she finally says. "First, I want you to understand that if Dad loses his job, you will come back to Brooklyn College right away. There's no way we could keep you at Cornell, if Dad lost his job, even with free tuition. Second, I want you to promise that you will use your electives to take all the history classes and all the education classes you need to be eligible to take the exam to become a high school social studies teacher in New York City. I want you to be licensed to teach. In case of a rainy day, I want you to be able to support yourself."

I fully understand my family's anxiety about the possibility that Dad might lose his job. Indeed, my own apprehension about Dad's becoming unemployed is one factor that leads me to study economics. In some irrational way, I believe that if I could understand the economy, I could help him keep his job.

I also understand Mom's wanting me to be a teacher. So I promise to take the requisite education courses, and I keep my word, even though many of those classes turn out to be truly uninspiring.

Today, as an educator, I often think about my college application experience. I still don't quite understand how Miss Bradshaw was able to do what she did, but when I think about her "system," I am awed by Mom's prescience at moving our family into the Midwood High school district. Mom wanted to give Alice and me an education "leg up," and she certainly knew how to do it. I am forever grateful to her.

I also wonder if a liberal arts Vassar education would have been more useful than the highly specialized education I received at ILR. But I also think, just as I thought back then, that no matter how fine the education, at Vassar I would have been deprived of diverse classrooms. There is a great deal of evidence now, much of it cited in Supreme Court cases on affirmative action, that diversity is a major asset in the classroom; that research is about race, but my experience in academe tells me that gender diversity changes classroom conversations significantly. It doesn't surprise me that today only 2 percent of female college applicants say they would prefer to go to an all-women's school.

On the other hand, in recent years I've had the privilege of serving on the Board of Trustees of Mills College, an excellent women's college in Oakland, California, and after being part of the college for almost a decade, I've concluded that a single-sex education might in fact have been ideal for me. Mom may have been right, and I sometimes wonder how my life might have been different had I accepted Vassar. But I never get very far in my imaginings, partly because I had such a wonderful time at Cornell and partly because so much of the way my life turned out stems from having gone there.

❖

The summer after I graduate from high school, I'm at our bungalow colony at Pine Lake as the archery counselor, and my friend Helen Goldzimer is the music counselor. Helen is tall, graceful (she's a fabulous dancer), and a talented musician. She has a wry sense of humor and a delicious laugh, and our friendship has been building for many years. The summer before, we became particularly close when we were senior and junior counselor for a group of girls and wrote the whole script for *Color War Sing*, taking popular songs and changing the words to make them about Pine Lake.

Much to my delight, I also become close to Helen's brother, Eddie, whom I've known for many years as well. Just a few summers before, Eddie and I had raced each other down the road to see which of us could sprint faster, but now we are powerfully attracted in a totally different way. Eddie makes me happy. He laughs easily, and I laugh with him. We also sing together and talk endlessly about Cornell, for it turns out that he is already a student there, about to start his sophomore year. Perhaps because we've known each other for so long, or perhaps because we realize that we'll be together at college, we get serious pretty quickly.

But Mom is afraid I'm going to be hurt.

"You need to be careful about falling for Eddie. I've known his mom for years, and many's the time she's told me that she wants her son to marry a rich girl. I don't think he would ever ask you to marry him. He'd have too much opposition from his parents."

I'm crushed. I'm sure Mom is right. Although Helen and Eddie's mom has been friendly to me in the past, I now find her a bit cool. I don't feel I can tell Eddie what Mom said, but I talk with Helen.

"I don't think it's about money so much," Helen says. "I just think my parents don't want Eddie to have a serious girlfriend right now. They want him to concentrate on his studies and figure out what he wants to do after college."

As the summer goes on and I'm more and more in love, I begin to feel I have to protect myself. One night, as we sit on the lifeguard bench and watch the stars reflected in the lake, I tell Eddie that when we get to Cornell, I think we should continue to go out with each other but also date other people. He says he doesn't like the idea at all and points out that such an arrangement will be very awkward, especially when we're at the same party, each with another date. But I insist. I cannot imagine my life without him, but if he's not ready to commit to me, I want to be free to explore.

Looking back more than fifty years later, I see more clearly what happened. Mom and Dad wanted me to be engaged by the time I graduated from college, and I came to want that, too. Why were we all in such a rush? Part of the answer is that the median age of marriage for American women in the 1950s was 20.3 years. Never before and never again has it been that low. Both the reality and the cultural expectation had shifted toward early marriage, and we all went along with it. If you weren't married by at least the age of twenty-five, you feared you'd be shut out, that everyone worth having would be taken.

It is also true that for most couples, being in love and playing the field simultaneously was unusual. Dating multiple people was seen as a prelude to falling in love. In Mom's day, it might have been possible to date many men at the same time and get multiple marriage proposals, but in the 1950s and '60s, a marriage proposal was usually preceded by a declaration of love and going steady. When I told Eddie I loved him but wanted to play the field, I was violating a social norm; but he was violating one when he said he loved me and wanted an exclusive relationship but didn't want to commit to eventual marriage. The upshot of these multiple violations was heartache.

4

Into the Sanctum, 1958–1964

Built to resemble Henry VIII's Hampton Court Palace, my freshman dorm, Risley Hall, is breathtaking—a gigantic fairytale castle. And inside it's equally grand—common rooms filled with artwork and antique furniture, a wood-paneled dining room modeled after the great hall at Cambridge's Christ Church College. How can I possibly fit in here? I've never seen such luxury.

And besides, I'm really scared of being on my own. Mom and Dad and Alice have driven up to Cornell with me, and I don't want them to leave. I've never been away from them before. I know I'm going to miss them terribly.

"My God," Alice says, "you'd think we were leaving you in Africa or something. Take it easy. You'll be home for Thanksgiving in a couple of months."

The dorm houses two hundred women, and my corridor-mates include a girl from Mississippi who's never seen snow, along with several girls from farms in upstate New York. They're friendly, and we talk early on about how we're going to share the one phone in the hall among the sixteen of us.

To save money, I requested a double single, a room meant for one person but housing two with bunk beds, so my space, especially my closet, is tight. But as I visit the rooms of my corridor-mates, I see that some are extraordinarily spacious and include an outdoor balcony. My roommate is a woman I know slightly from high school. She wanted a double single to save money as well, so we decided to bunk together. Fortunately, she meets a boyfriend soon after we arrive and spends hardly any time in the room except after curfew.

After several hours of unpacking, the whole dorm gathers in the living room for orientation. Sitting on the gorgeous but singularly uncomfortable chairs (and on the floor—much more comfortable), we listen to our housemother, a mousy woman with stringy gray hair.

We're in training to be ladies, she explains, and our residential experience will be a course in "gracious living." We must dress "properly" for a sit-down served dinner every evening, and wear a dress and stockings for Sunday lunch. We are to converse quietly during our meals, and, when finished, we are to fold our napkins neatly before leaving the table. Later in the week, we will have instruction in the proper way to pour tea. Every week, a maid will clean our rooms and change our bed linens.

I simply can't absorb this. I think of my Tante Annie's stories of her trip from Hamburg to New York in steerage, and only two generations later, I'm being groomed to be a lady? As Baba was fond of saying, "only in America."

After our housemother's speech, we hear from the president of the Women's Self-Government Association (WSGA), who recites a list of mind-numbing parietal rules. Some of my dorm-mates seem to know these rules already, but to me, they're brand-new, and I think about how laughable it is that my father was afraid to send me away to college. I had more freedom at home than I'll have here.

The most significant rule is that all women must live in a dorm reserved exclusively for women. None of the dorms are coed (nobody even dreams of such an arrangement), and although men may live in apartments, women may not. In her 1977 book *Women at Cornell: The Myth of Equal Education,* Charlotte Conable will argue that although Ezra Cornell founded his university in 1865 as a coeducational institution, the university administrators who followed him were not nearly as keen on enrolling women students. They kept the number low by requiring women students to live in women's dorms, but never built very many of them. During my time at Cornell, women made up only 25 percent of undergraduates.

To further protect a woman's "honor," the parietal rules decree that she may not visit a man's apartment alone; she must be accompanied by at least one other woman. And if a man wants to visit a woman in her dorm, he has to jump through numerous hoops: he must be announced by a receptionist, who phones the corridor of the woman he is visiting and asks her to come down to the living room to meet her "caller." A man can go to a woman's room only on special days, and then the woman's door must remain open and at least three of the couple's four feet must be touching the floor. Seriously.

Curfews are strictly enforced: if a woman goes out in the evening, she must sign out when she leaves and then sign back in by 11 p.m. on weekdays, midnight on Fridays, and 1 a.m. on Saturdays. If she wants to go away for the weekend, she must obtain approval from her parents. The penalty for violating these rules more than once is suspension from the university.

But the most surprising rule is that women cannot wear pants to class unless the temperature is less than 20 degrees F. We actually check the temperature in the morning before going to class.

The WSGA, elected by women students, is the judicial body that enforces these rules. That was striking to me when I was a student, and I often think about it today. Even now, across the world, women are generally the ones who enforce gender restrictions. It interests me that institutions make women responsible for policing their own subordination.

In my four years at Cornell, I frequently hear women complain about the parietal rules, but I never see an organized protest against them. Mine was the transition generation. Two years after my class graduated, in the midst of social change throughout society, most of the rules were completely abolished, though it was not until the mid-1970s that pants became acceptable work attire for professional women.

During my first months at Cornell, I continue to feel out of place. I had some practice in junior high and high school with girls whose parents had much more money than mine, but this university really feels too rich for my blood. I also have frequent bouts of homesickness. I'm happy to be out of Brooklyn, but I really miss Mom and Dad. Still, I'm unreservedly in love with the campus's beauty—the freshness of the fall air and the omnipresent waterfalls, including one right outside my dorm—and I thoroughly enjoy my classes.

The most unusual class by far is Bus Riding 101. Every week we take a daylong trip to some different work site—a coal mine, a steel mill, an IBM factory, a pajama factory, and so on—to interview representatives from management and labor and tour the workplace. After each visit, we write a comprehensive paper on significant issues in that industry and firm. For the coal mine tour, the school has to get special permission from the

United Mine Workers to allow women underground, something miners consider bad luck.

Eddie and I talk on the phone several nights a week and go out every other Saturday night, but otherwise each of us is free to see other people, and I begin dating several different guys. The only trouble is, most of them are in Eddie's fraternity, and, as he anticipated, things get sticky when we each arrive at his fraternity's parties with someone else. Eddie keeps wanting us to date each other exclusively, but I'm unwilling to unless he's ready to make a firm commitment. And he's still not. I'm beginning to feel less in love with him. Trying to negotiate complicated arrangements, then explaining them to others, seems like more and more of a hassle. Still, I really enjoy being with him when we're together.

By the end of first semester, I've conquered my homesickness, and begin to feel part of Cornell. A few months later, I apply to be a resident assistant (RA), an upper-class woman who lives in one of the freshman women's dorms and helps first-year students adjust to Cornell life. Given the difficulties of my own adjustment, I would really like to help some of next year's freshmen women if I can.

My application is accepted. Just before the beginning of sophomore year, when I go back to Cornell a week early for RA orientation, I meet Judy Berman, who will be the RA on the corridor adjacent to mine at Risley. It's warm and sunny, the kind of glorious fall weather that often comes to the East Coast in September, and Judy and I find we have entered a several-day blast designed to endear us to our alma mater for all time. Cheerleaders teach us fight songs for football games; Cornell a cappella singing groups come to serenade; we eat large quantities of barbecue chicken with secret sauce, and we dance into the night.

I can see from the first that Judy knows how to have fun—to sing, cheer, and joke, and especially to dance. Her delight in life is irresistible, and by the end of orientation we are close friends. But once school starts, I learn that Judy relishes the life of the mind as much as she does enjoying herself. We take European history together and share our class notes. Before midterms and finals, we sequester ourselves for hours in an out-of-the-way classroom in the chemistry building, Baker Hall, and talk about the course material. Our friendship-long habit of conversing about politics (national, academic, and family) is forged in the bowels of Baker.

Although we're exactly the same age, Judy is a year ahead of me, and both she and her roommate, Judy Silverman, whom I'm also getting to know, are members of Sigma Delta Tau (SDT). In the rush season that begins in January 1960, the two Judys propose my name as a potential member, and with their sponsorship, I pledge the sorority.

One evening, we invite Professor Andrew Hacker to the sorority house for a lecture. He's relatively young, only about ten years our senior, and one of our favorites. Nonetheless, when one of my sorority sisters asks him what careers he thinks we should prepare for, he suggests only traditionally female professions: teacher, nurse, and librarian. All of those will be intellectually challenging, he says, and will allow us to follow our husbands wherever their careers might require.

Many of us take Hacker's advice, but quite a few of us eventually obtain graduate degrees, and two of my sisters become judges. And although there is more chatter at the sorority house about weddings and silver patterns than I prefer, several of my sisters remain some of my closest friends.

My sorority is specifically Jewish. All of Cornell's numerous fraternities and sororities are segregated by religion, and there are very few "crossovers": men or women who are Jewish in a non-Jewish fraternity or sorority. About 25 percent of Cornell's students are Jewish, but there is not much interaction between Jews and non-Jews. In the Ivy Room in the basement of the student union, where I frequently play bridge, tables on one side of the room are "reserved" for Jewish students, while those on the other side are for non-Jews. We call the dividing line the Gaza Strip.

Cornell has an active Hillel, and I attend Rosh Hashanah and Yom Kippur services there. One year I accompany my roommate at the time, Linda Gilinsky, to Yom Kippur services at her family's synagogue in Binghamton, New York. These Reform and Conservative services are completely different from those at Grandpa's *shul*. Women and men sit together, and the much shorter prayer book is in both English and Hebrew. The sermon is in English (not Yiddish), and I understand it fully. But critical elements are missing—Grandpa's voice, first and foremost, and the earnestness of his prayer, but also the sense of awe of the other congregants. As I look around, people seem to be going through the motions, but there doesn't seem to be much passion in their prayer or singing, and when I try to seek God's presence during the service, all I get is static. Later in the day I pray by myself, in my own room, with no prayer book at all, and finally peace and connection flood my soul.

❖

My roommate sophomore year is a woman in my ILR class, Betty Lefko-witz. We're both on scholarship and both of us work at Cornell—she as a waitress and I in the ILR library—but Betty's need for money is greater than mine, and she wants to spend the following summer working as a waitress in the Catskills, a job that gets excellent tips. Betty and I are at a fraternity party on a Saturday night, and I see that she's in deep conversa-tion with one of the brothers. When they finish talking, she rushes over to tell me that Jerry Seigman has offered to drive her down to Grossinger's the following morning (he wants to apply for some jobs, too), and she wants me to come with them because she doesn't want to be alone with him.

I agree to "chaperone," and the next morning, much earlier than I would like, Jerry picks us up at the dorm. When we get to Grossinger's, Betty goes in for an interview but Jerry says he doesn't want to apply there. The tips are outstanding, but the work is too hard. He knows some places where he thinks he'd be happier, so we proceed to three other hotels where he has interviews. Finally, when he's satisfied that he's likely to get an offer, he asks me where I want to apply.

I'm about to say that I don't want to apply anywhere, that I'm bored and hungry and really just along for the ride, but Betty's eyes shoot daggers.

"Oh," I stammer, trying to think quickly. "Well, maybe I could get a summer job as a secretary."

"Ah," says Jerry. "Perfect. I know just the place. The Windsor Hotel, and it's really close by."

This is crazy, I think to myself. But Betty looks at me pleadingly, and I continue the charade.

The Windsor turns out to be lovely, and I have a pleasant interview with Theresa Sussman, the office manager and one of the hotel's owners. She's impressed with my ability to take dictation and type, and she tells me she'll be in touch in a few weeks.

Almost two months pass, and in the meantime I'm accepted to a sum-mer program at Oxford University with a scholarship. But I don't com-mit. Although I don't need money the way Betty does, I feel it would be good to earn *some* during the summer.

Finally, a letter comes from Theresa. She'd like to hire me. I'll take dictation, be responsible for typing up the daily menus, and help at the switchboard during busy hours. The pay is low, but I'll get a free room and three fabulous meals a day. Betty thinks I'll have a grand time and urges me to go. Eddie, who will be at ROTC training for most of the summer, also encourages me to take the job. He says he can at least visit me there at the end of the summer, but he wouldn't be able to visit me in Oxford.

Mom is super-enthusiastic. "Just think of all the money you can save," she says.

So I tell Oxford I'm not coming, and when school is out, Mom and Dad drive me to the Windsor.

George, the bellhop who helps me with my suitcases, is gregarious, tall, hefty, and blond. But my eye catches a different bellhop. Shorter and much thinner than George, he has olive skin and dark brown curly hair. Drop-dead handsome, he reminds me of my longtime crush, Clark Gable. George doesn't know how fast my heart is suddenly beating, but he does see me staring.

"Oh, that heartbreaker?" he chuckles. "He's my fraternity brother at Columbia. Sam. Sam Strober."

Sam and I quickly become an item. We see each other every day, at all three meals, and often in between to play tennis or take a swim. And every evening, we either take a long walk on the road toward town or attend one of the shows at the hotel. In addition to telling each other our life stories, we gossip about the characters at the hotel (the three owners, the chefs, the camp counselors, waiters, receptionists, and bellhops), and particularly colorful guests, who are far wealthier than either of us can imagine. We learn each other's views on politics, economics, history, religion, and philosophy, and we find out that we're both interested in bringing our children up to understand and appreciate Judaism.

Not only do I love Sam's looks, I love how smart and articulate he is. I love how he listens to what I have to say. I love that he likes that I'm smart. Pretty soon, I realize that what I love is simply him. And not long thereafter, he tells me he loves me. I'm happy in a way I've never experienced, and I recall my conversations with Mom about love. She was right: when you're in love, you just know.

Sam and I have quite similar families—one sibling plus untold cousins from our mothers' huge numbers of sisters—and our parents are politically liberal, lower middle class, and live in Brooklyn about a twenty-minute drive from each other. My mom is the only college graduate among them, but all four want their children to finish college. Sam also wants to go to medical school, and his parents are enormously enthusiastic about that aspiration (as are mine, when I tell them).

At the end of August, we each have visitors. Eddie is finished with summer ROTC and comes to see me, and Sam's parents visit to find out what this new girlfriend he's been talking about is like. The visit with Eddie is short and only modestly painful. He says he's sorry we won't be dating anymore, but we're both relieved.

The visit with Sam's parents is fun. They both have a good sense of humor, and I don't feel any of the coldness I'd felt from Eddie's mom. Sam tells me his parents like me a lot, and that his father thinks I will "save him money over the long run."

In other words, "He doesn't think you're a gold digger."

I understand what Sam's father means, and I admire him for understanding me so quickly. I don't covet the kind of fancy jewelry that I see women guests wearing at the hotel, and I'm very much committed to finding work that I love and earning my own living. On the other hand, I'm certainly pleased that if I marry Sam, we're likely to be well-off.

Two years after my experience applying to college, it's Alice's turn, and she is the beneficiary of my victory in the out-of-town college wars. Mom and Dad have no hesitation in allowing her to apply to schools other than Brooklyn College, and indeed, when Miss Bradshaw tells Alice that she may apply to Mount Holyoke, Mom and Dad agree, no longer insisting that their daughter confine her applications to schools in New York State.

But Alice also disappoints Mom and Miss Bradshaw. She has visited me at Cornell and has also fallen in love with it, so she applies to the School of Industrial and Labor Relations. When she is accepted to Mount Holyoke with a full scholarship, she turns it down to go to Cornell ILR. Miss Bradshaw calls Mom in. It's lucky that they have no other children, she says, because Mom should rest assured that Miss Bradshaw would never lift a finger to help any other Hoffenberg child with college admission!

When Alice arrives as a first-year student at Cornell at the beginning of my junior year, I'm living at the sorority house, and many of my sorority sisters who've never met her before tell me they saw my sister on campus.

"She doesn't exactly look like you, but you walk the same way and you look like sisters."

I'm happy that Alice has the chance to be at a place I love so dearly, but we actually have very little contact. Although Mom tells me that it's my responsibility to look after her, Alice neither wants nor needs looking after. She says she's never homesick, and quite quickly she begins dating a non-Jewish man in her class at ILR. We never meet for coffee or a walk, and the parties she and I attend are completely different. Each of us has our own friends, and we rarely run into each other, even at the ILR library, where I still work. She's considered a legacy by my sorority and receives an invitation to pledge, but she declines, saying she finds the sorority too segregated and Greek life too narrow.

I spend far more time writing to Sam than talking to Alice. The highlight of my week is his phone call, and I relish his letters. Over Thanksgiving vacation, we agree that our relationship is "for keeps." He gives me his fraternity pin, and we agree not to date others.

The following months are a whirlwind, as Sam applies to medical school and is admitted everywhere, including Harvard, where he decides to go. Then, after his graduation from Columbia, we both return to the Windsor Hotel, and once again we have a magical time—more delicious food, wonderful weather, and endless evenings to talk.

But this summer ends quite differently. The hotel's kitchen and grounds workers, poorly paid and badly treated, form a union. They look to the "college boys" to help them, and Sam, who strongly supports their cause, signs on. But he's a part of their effort for only a short time. As soon as the hotel owners learn he's involved (he thinks they have a spy among the workers), they fire him and order him to leave their property.

At Cornell, I've studied the techniques managements use to discourage unionization, and now I witness them firsthand. Of course, I leave with Sam, and we return to our parents' apartments in Brooklyn. A few weeks later, I go back to Cornell for my final semester, and Sam begins his first year of medical school.

❖

When I get to school, I find a message from Donald Dietrich, ILR's dean of students, who has summoned me to his office. *What the devil does he want?* I wonder as I dutifully make my appointment. His secretary is no help at all, absentmindedly shrugging her shoulders when I ask why he wants to see me.

I've exchanged pleasantries with Dietrich several times in the three years I've been at Cornell, but I've never talked with him one-on-one. As I enter his office—casual, with comfortable furniture designed, no doubt, to put students at ease—he rises to greet me. Tall and jovial, he's a John Kennedy look-alike.

"Several faculty have recommended you for a Woodrow Wilson Fellowship for graduate school," he says as he pumps my hand animatedly. "Are you planning to go to graduate school?"

"Uh, no, I don't think so. I'm planning on being a high school social studies teacher."

"Are you sure? You're number one in the class. You'd make a great professor."

"Well, thanks, but I've never thought about being a professor."

"Fair enough. Why don't you take some time to think about it? You can let me know in a couple of weeks."

I leave his office astonished. Faculty have recommended me for a Woodrow Wilson? They think I ought to be a professor?

My plans have not been going in that direction at all. Sam hasn't given me an engagement ring yet, but marriage occupies my mind. Yes, I love my studies; and yes, I'm a very good student; but what I want most is to set a date for our wedding.

In a few weeks, I'll be keeping my promise to Mom and taking the New York City exam for a license to teach high school social studies. I'm sure I'll pass. And then, if all goes well, Sam and I will be formally engaged. What more can I want? I'm on a good path. I'll just ignore what the dean had to say.

But despite my best efforts, I keep thinking about the possibilities Dietrich raised, and when I go to visit Sam in Boston, I relate the conversation.

"Why don't you do it?" he says. "Instead of being a high school teacher, you can be a college teacher."

In one sentence, he reduces the difference between the two careers to a mere modifier.

"You know," he says, "I'm really a believer in what Mill had to say about all of this."

As an undergraduate at Columbia, Sam took a first-rate contemporary civilization course that included John Stuart Mill's essay on liberty. To this day, it gives me pleasure to think that Mill was indirectly involved in my decision to get a PhD.

"What did Mill say?" I ask. I've read some Mill, but I can't recall its relevance to our discussion.

"He said that everyone should have the right to develop their potential. He said that most constraints on people are not natural but socially imposed, and that the good society is one that eliminates those social constraints."

I'm thrilled at his comment and pull him close for a huge hug. I can't believe my good fortune. This is the best of all possible worlds. I've found a man who is very smart and very likely to be successful. That's important to me, because despite his intelligence, my father has never been financially successful. But because Sam is confident in his intellectual abilities, he isn't threatened by mine. He wants *me* to succeed, too. I haven't experienced many men who react that way.

Years after Sam's and my conversation, Judith Stiehm will write an article on smart women who choose a husband they think is even smarter, then spend the rest of their lives feeling inferior to him. She called the phenomenon "invidious intimacy." I fit her description perfectly.

But now my practical side kicks in.

"How will we live?" I ask. "If I work as a high school teacher, I can support us. If I'm in graduate school, what will we do for money?"

"I don't need you to support me," he says, annoyed. "Just support yourself. I already have a fellowship, and if you get a Wilson or some other fellowship, it'll all work out fine."

"And we can still get married?"

"Why not?"

I don't know any married women professors. In fact, I only know one woman professor altogether, Alice Cook, and she's divorced. Can I really be a married woman and a professor? Sam is saying I can.

Recalling this conversation more than fifty years later, I can see that neither Sam nor I had the slightest idea what we were getting into. In terms of career demands, teaching at the college level, particularly at a research university, is not at all like being a high school teacher. We had absolutely no understanding of what would be required to combine two demanding careers with raising children, and we said not a word about how we planned to do it. On the other hand, perhaps it was lucky that I made the decision to get a PhD with what economists call "imperfect information." If I'd really understood what it would take to be a successful college professor, I doubt I would have followed that path. And I would have missed out. I would have missed out extraordinarily.

On the way back to Ithaca, my thoughts race with excitement. If I get accepted to graduate school, I can take classes and study for four more years. With a fellowship, I can get paid while I do it. How amazing! I can't wait to see the dean again.

But first I need to call my parents.

"What does Sam say?" my father asks.

"He likes the idea."

"He likes it?" my mother asks, incredulous. "And he'll still marry you?"

"Yes."

After that, I just listen while they talk, and somehow or other, in a matter of a few minutes, they convince each other that they can get on board.

"Well," Mom finally says, "if it's OK with Sam, then I guess it's OK with us."

"You always have surprises for us," Dad says, and across the phone line, I can visualize him shaking his head and smiling. "Good luck, cookie."

I'm disappointed by Mom's lack of enthusiasm, but a couple of years later, when my friend Judy Berman decides she wants to go back to school for a PhD, her mother's reaction makes me appreciate my mother's mere lack of enthusiasm.

"If you get a PhD, you'll have to find a husband who has *two* PhDs," Judy's mother says.

❖

Dietrich is pleased with my decision and asks what field I will go into. I haven't thought about that. My undergraduate degree will be in industrial and labor relations, but I don't want a PhD in that field. It feels too narrow. Let's see ... how about history or economics? I have taken a lot of history courses in preparation for being a high school social studies teacher, as well as quite a few courses in economics. I find both fascinating.

About an hour or so after leaving Dietrich's office, without ever talking to a history professor, I decide to become an economist. My reasoning, seriously deficient in retrospect, seems quite straightforward at the time. *How*, I ask myself, *can I become an expert on all history, for all time, in all places?* I'm smart, but not *that* smart. Despite all the history courses I've taken, I have no notion that historians specialize in particular countries and particular periods. Becoming a historian, I conclude, would be just too tough. Economics would be much more manageable.

So I go to talk with M. Gardner Clark, the professor at ILR who teaches us economic history. Like Dietrich, Clark has a comfortable office. I particularly love the large Ithaca-area photos on his walls: waterfalls, gorges, rolling farmland, and snowy hills. He's very supportive, tells me I'll make an excellent economist, and offers to write letters of recommendation. We also talk about whom else I ought to ask to write for me, and where I should apply.

"My fiancé is at Harvard Medical School," I tell him.

At the word *fiancé*, my heart begins to pound; the combination of the white lie and my anticipation of eventually legitimately calling Sam that is intoxicating. I can barely maintain my train of thought.

Taking a deep breath, I make my point: "I need to confine my applications to the Boston area."

"Well, that's OK. Harvard and MIT have the two best doctoral programs in economics in the country. But you should also apply to Tufts, just in case. They have no PhD program, but they have an excellent small MA program, and they give MA students money. You could do a lot worse than spend a year studying economics with Frank Holzman at Tufts."

I leave Clark's office jubilant. PhD Economics. Harvard. MIT. Hardly able to contain my excitement, I rush to Dietrich's office to leave him a message about my plans, then to my room to begin typing requests for applications.

❖

When I'd realized, a year or so earlier, that by the end of my senior-year fall semester I would be finished with all my required courses and units, I decided to graduate early. I didn't really want to leave before June; there were a lot more courses I wanted to take, but I felt I needed to save my parents the additional money after all the sacrifices they'd made to send me to Cornell, and I knew I'd feel guilty staying another semester when I didn't really need to. My plan was to go to New York City in late October to take the high school social studies teacher exam, then spend spring semester teaching in Brooklyn and helping my mother plan my wedding. But since Sam has yet to give me an engagement ring, there will be no wedding in June. And since graduate school is now in the picture, I begin thinking that instead of moving back to Brooklyn, I'll look for a job as a research assistant in Boston or Cambridge for the spring and summer. That way, Sam and I can at least live in the same city, even if we aren't married yet.

My conscience tells me that my promise to Mom means I have to take that New York City exam, graduate school or not, but my body won't cooperate. On the day I'm supposed to take the train to the city, I come down with the flu. A week later, though, I take the *junior* high school social studies teacher exam instead, and at Thanksgiving I can virtuously report to Mom that I've passed the exam and received a license in the mail.

The teachers' exam is a lot easier than the Graduate Record Exam (GRE), which I also take that fall. The morning part of the GRE is just an upgraded SAT test, but the afternoon test is on economics, and while I've boned up for several weeks, I don't think I've done particularly well.

The Woodrow Wilson oral exam goes even less successfully. I sit in an imposing room, the lone candidate on the long side of a huge table. The room looks like a hall for signing international treaties. On the opposite side of the table are three men, all between the ages of seventy and ninety (or so it seems to me).

"I see on your application that you're interested in unemployment," says the graybeard in the middle.

"Yes," I respond in a voice meant to be confident, but sounding just plain loud to my apprehensive ears.

"What is unemployment?" he asks.

"It's when people who want work can't find it."

"And what is the cause of unemployment?"

"Well, there are several types of unemployment. They all have different causes."

"No, no," says my second tormentor. "That's not what we're interested in. What do the *theorists* have to say about unemployment?"

"Oh, the theorists. Well, Keynes thought that unemployment occurs when there isn't enough demand for goods and services in the economy as a whole."

"Yes, and the others?"

"Which others?"

"That's what we are asking you?"

Oh, boy, I think. *Somehow or other, I have to figure out what they're looking for.*

"Well," I say mustering all the confidence I can summon, "Keynes was arguing with the classical economists who thought that unemployment was caused by wages being too high. But Keynes said that while lowering wages might cause a *particular* employer to hire more workers, for the economy as a whole, lowering wages would cut aggregate demand and that would lead to more unemployment rather than less."

"It sounds like you are very taken with Keynes."

"Well, yes, I think his arguments are persuasive."

"So you don't think that unions and minimum wages cause unemployment by keeping wages higher than they should be?"

"No, I don't."

"I see," says my inquisitor, while the other two write carefully on their pads. "Let me ask you something else. Do you think that government should be responsible for lowering unemployment?"

"Very much so."

"And what should government do?"

"In times of high unemployment, it should increase spending."

"On what?"

"In some sense, it doesn't matter. It was government spending for World War II that got us out of the Great Depression. I'm not advocating war as a way of increasing employment, but government spending on roads, schools, research—those all help."

"Aren't you concerned that government will get too big?"

"When the economy improves and unemployment falls, then the government ought to decrease its spending and let the business sector take over."

"Yeah, that'll be the day," laughs one of the examiners, the other two chortling along.

"What about monetary policy? Don't you think the government can take care of unemployment though monetary policy?"

"No, I don't. Monetary policy works well to slow down the economy, but not to recharge it."

"Well, thank you, Miss, for giving us your ideas," he dismisses me.

"They certainly have converted them all to Keynesians around here," one of the examiners tells the others as I quietly close the door.

As soon as my last final is over, I fly to Cambridge. My goal is to find a research assistantship with one of the professors at the Harvard Business School who studies unions and industrial relations. But I never get to see a single one. Each of their secretaries tells me the same thing: "Any RA positions the professors have, they give to their own students."

So it's back to crowded, noisy Brooklyn, the place I've worked so hard to escape. And even though my parents go out of their way to make me comfortable, their two-bedroom apartment seems even smaller than I remember. Still, dinner conversations are lively, and Dad makes it clear that the curfew I had in high school is no longer in effect.

My job search is tougher than I'd expected. There are no vacancies for junior high school social studies teachers except in Bedford-Stuyvesant, a high-crime neighborhood that is mostly black ("Negro," we said then), but I feel too young and inexperienced to control rowdy black boys. What Brooklyn badly needs are science teachers, and to my amazement, even though I didn't take a single science course in college, I'm offered five jobs to teach science. I turn them down, unable to imagine how I can possibly learn enough science on my own to teach it to others.

I'm about ready to give up and turn to my trusty shorthand and typing skills when my mother discovers from a handbook she has been browsing that with a junior high school license I can teach fifth and sixth grades. After making some inquiries through her school-secretary network, she learns that there is a vacancy for a fifth-grade teacher in an elementary school near Coney Island, filling in for a teacher on maternity leave. I call the principal and go for an interview; the following morning, I'm teaching forty-two fifth-graders.

I feel completely unprepared. My education classes at Cornell were mostly theoretical, I've never done any student teaching, and the few practically oriented classes I've taken have been about teaching high school history, not fifth grade. What am I to do with these forty-two children, each looking at me expectantly?

My savior is the fifth-grade teacher in the room next door, Miss Goodman. A year older than I, she has three semesters of fifth grade under her belt.

"Groups," counsels Miss Goodman, "the first thing you have to do is listen to every child read and assign each one to a group."

Miss Goodman soon becomes Nancy. She teaches me how to do lesson plans, teach long division, and quiet the troublemakers.

❖

In late March, right around my birthday, I have news about graduate school. The letter from the Woodrow Wilson Foundation says "Thanks, but no thanks," and Harvard and MIT have similar news. Both say they don't think I've had enough economics to start a PhD program. Both suggest I take more economics and apply again.

I'm angry. I hadn't originally been looking to get a PhD. Why did that dean get my hopes up, only to have them smashed? But I do get a consolation prize. Tufts accepts me into its MA program with a fellowship that covers full tuition and living expenses. They recommend I come and meet the faculty before I decide.

There isn't much to decide. I have only one choice. Feeling blue, I go up to Boston to visit the school. I'm pleasantly surprised: in addition to Frank Holzman, I meet Dan Ounjian and John Cornwall, all three welcoming, smart, and interesting. And all three promising that if I do well, I can count on them for letters of recommendation when I reapply to Harvard and MIT.

A few weeks later, when Sam comes home for Passover, I get a second surprise.

"I'd like you to come with me and my parents to choose a ring," he says. "I'd like us to get engaged."

I am beyond excited, and once I get the ring, I can hardly concentrate on my teaching; every time my hand moves, the diamond shimmers in the reflected light.

❖

The semester teaching fifth grade ends uneventfully, and when I leave for Boston in late June, I'm jubilant. Sam and I are finally going to live in the same city! I move into an apartment a few blocks from Harvard Square, on the first floor of a large home, and share it with Judy Berman, who is finishing up an MA in teaching at Harvard.

Strange as it seems all these years later, Sam and I never discuss the possibility of living together despite our engagement. It's unthinkable to us, and surely unthinkable to our parents. Sam remains at Vanderbilt Hall, the Harvard Medical School dorm, and I live in Cambridge. Only two years later, social conventions will unravel like a yoyo, never to be rewound. But in 1962, no one could predict that. And certainly no one could act as though they had already unraveled.

To support myself before I begin Tufts, I take a summer job as a secretary at Harvard's Russian Research Center. My work is easy, and I enjoy walking to work along Cambridge's tree-lined streets and sitting in our grassy little yard in the early evening. Most of all, I love seeing Sam with some frequency instead of being apart, as we have been for most of our relationship.

We take weekend trips to Marblehead and Plum Island for sailing and swimming, and many evenings we drive to the Arboretum or Walden Pond for long walks and discussions. In addition to the topics we've always chewed on, we add a new subject—Sam's immunology experiments. Although I have no background in science, I find it fascinating to hear the details of his work trying to prevent mice from rejecting skin transplants.

Judy and I both learn to cook that summer, with Sam and her boyfriend as our official tasters, and we have lots of laughs about our many failures and near-failures. At the beginning of September, Judy leaves for Long Island to start her first teaching job, and I move into a new apartment in North Cambridge with two classmates from Cornell.

❖

In late September, Sam and I spend our first Rosh Hashanah together. On the eve of the holiday, we attend services at a magnificent Reform synagogue on Beacon Street, Ohabei Shalom, not far from the medical school. The congregation is the oldest in Massachusetts, and the rabbi gives an interesting and erudite sermon analyzing some of the writings of the famed Protestant theologian Paul Tillich. The Byzantine building is awe-inspiring, and the sermon is intellectually challenging. But I don't find any soul in the service. It feels like a cross between an organ concert and a scholarly lecture.

The next day Sam feels he can't skip classes, so I go to synagogue myself. I choose a small Conservative *shul* in Brookline and sit in the back. I find the English in the prayer book distracting, so I close it and pray from my heart, just like Baba and Tante Annie used to do. The Conservative *shul* is more to my liking than the Reform service the night before, but I'm lonely. In my Canarsie *shul*, I had family and friends. Here nobody reaches out to me, and I miss the sense of community that I associate with Rosh Hashanah. I'm still searching for a spiritual home.

❖

The Tufts MA program in economics is small—there are only five of us, and I'm the only woman. Most of our courses are with undergraduates, who are extremely bright, but we also get special attention from Frank Holzman, who teaches Soviet economics, economic development, and comparative systems; Dan Ounjian, who teaches microeconomic theory and tax policy; and John Cornwall, who teaches macroeconomic theory and statistics. All are superb teachers who put energy into their lectures and time into discussing issues with students after class.

As I learn more economics, I realize how deficient in economics my program at ILR was, and why I'd been unable to answer satisfactorily the questions about unemployment that the Woodrow Wilson Fellowship Committee asked. What I'd learned at Cornell was elementary economics. At Tufts, I take intermediate economics. From Cornwall, a ruddy, pudgy man with a no-nonsense demeanor, I learn about alternative theories to Keynesianism, the role of money in the economy, the classical economists' theories and which of their ideas might deserve further investigation, and the incredible complexities of trying to lessen unemployment. Had I taken Cornwall's course before the Wilson interview, I would never have said that my interest was in unemployment. I would have known that unemployment was simply too vast a topic for a novice to speak on with any authority, particularly at a competitive interview.

From Dan Ounjian, I learn the ins and outs of consumer demand, including the complexities of indifference curves, as well as production theory, and theories of markets. Dan is the most fun-loving of the faculty. Tall, dark, and extremely handsome, he has a twinkle in his eye, even as he teaches some of the most abstruse work in economics—linear programming and input/output analysis.

I love the precision of microeconomic theory and the vast scope of problems in macroeconomic theory, and I admire intensely the minds of the men (and one woman, Joan Robinson) who developed them. The texts and lectures use graphs, algebra, and occasionally some trigonometry, but no calculus—and I have no trouble with any of it, even though I never took a trig or an advanced algebra course in high school or college. My grades in the theory classes are always at the top of the class, and both Cornwall and Ounjian are happy to support my reapplication to MIT.

But my most enjoyable work is with Frank Holzman, a slight, gentle man with a wry sense of humor, whose scholarly work is on Soviet tax policy. I choose the topic of Soviet trade unions for my MA thesis and write it under Holzman's direction. The thesis is not meant to be an original piece of work but rather a scholarly analysis of an important question. My question concerns the role of Soviet trade unions in the lives of Soviet workers, and how that role evolved from the teachings of Marx and Lenin.

I'm fascinated by the process of economic development and find it of great interest that the Soviets have been successful at industrializing and becoming an economic power in such a short time. Although I'm horrified by the violent ruthlessness they use to achieve their goals, I'm impressed by their accomplishments. As an American who has grown up surrounded by Cold War terror, including air raid drills at school, I'm fearful that Soviet-style economic development will take hold in developing countries, to our nation's detriment. I want to understand the Soviet system so I can encourage other developing countries not to use it.

The Cuban missile crisis furthers my interest in these matters, and at the beginning of my studies at Tufts, I think I might specialize in Soviet economics, so I sign up for two semesters of Russian language. But it soon becomes clear that whatever skills I might once have had with foreign language are long gone. It takes great effort to learn Russian vocabulary, grammar, and sentence structure, and each week I seem to forget what I learned the week before. As a result, the sources I use for my thesis are either translated from the Russian or in English to begin with, and by the time I leave Tufts, I'm quite sure that my specialty in economics will be something other than the Soviet Union.

Although the economics department at MIT rejected me for its doctoral program, it accepted my housemate (and former ILR classmate) Vicki Custer, even though she had very little more in the way of economics than I. As I watch Vicki struggle through the first year of doctoral work at MIT, and ultimately decide to drop out of the program, I become grateful that MIT rejected me. My experience at Tufts is much more positive than Vicki's at MIT.

In late fall, I begin my reapplication process to MIT and Harvard, and since I now live in Cambridge, I request a meeting with an economics faculty member at both places. The meeting at MIT with Professor Abraham Siegel is stressful but encouraging. I'm in his office for quite some time as he questions me in detail about my studies at Tufts and my decision to do my MA thesis on Soviet trade unions.

However, the interview at Harvard, with Professor Gary Fromm, is disastrous.

"Are you normal?" he asks me, after shaking my hand perfunctorily.

"What do you mean?"

"Do you want to get married and have kids?"

"Yes. In fact, I'm engaged to be married," I say, probably being too quick to try to persuade him that I'm "normal."

"Well, then," he laughs, "there you go. Why would you want to get a doctorate in economics if you're going to get married and have kids?"

In other words, I'm either abnormal or abnormal.

I leave his office shaking and angry, feeling the same powerlessness I felt when my mother told me I couldn't sit downstairs with Grandpa in his *shul* and my Hebrew teacher told me I couldn't have a bat mitzvah. Who makes these rules? Why can men be married or engaged and also get a PhD at Harvard while I, a woman, can't?

I'm certain that my Harvard application will be rejected, and when only a thin envelope arrives in the mail from the school the following spring, I'm not surprised. But shortly after the Harvard rejection, I receive a fat letter of acceptance from MIT! Somehow or other, the rules there are different.

But now I have a new problem. Sam has decided that he wants to take time off from medical school to do full-time immunology research, and after several inquiries he's arranged to go to Oxford, England, to work with Dr. James Gowans. I'm excited at the prospect of a year in Oxford, but I don't see how such a plan fits with continuing my studies at MIT. Sam says he thinks we can have a win-win solution and suggests that I ask MIT simply to defer my admission for a year. This seems sensible, but when I call to make my request, the economics department at MIT informs me that their policy is not to offer deferments. If I turn down the acceptance, I'll have to take my chances and reapply the following year. With sadness and anxiety, I do turn down MIT. Although Sam and I never specifically say so, our actions make it clear: Sam's career comes first.

❖

As May approaches, I turn my thoughts to exams, my MA thesis, and my upcoming wedding. I try to keep the wedding as simple and low-budget as possible. Rather than pay for a new wedding dress, I borrow the beautiful dress my Pine Lake friend Joanne Gould (now Brody) wore to her wedding. *What's the point of buying a dress that you wear once for a few hours?* I think. And although Sam has invited six of his friends to be ushers, I decide to have only one attendant, Alice. Choosing six bridesmaids from among my many friends seems bound to result in hurt feelings, and none of that seems worthwhile.

But even somewhat simplified, the wedding weighs on my mind. My mother spares me work on all the details. She sends out the invitations and plans the reception and dinner with the caterer, but for weeks I have unsettling dreams about the ceremony. In one recurring dream, I have to walk down the aisle in sneakers, having forgotten my dress shoes at home.

I'm also nervous about Alice's participation in the wedding. A year or so earlier Jon Amsden, the man she'd been dating at Cornell, left to study for a year with a scholarship at Trinity College, Dublin, and shortly after his departure, much to my parents' horror, she'd taken a year's leave from Cornell and followed him. When I wrote asking her to be my maid of honor, she accepted, but I haven't heard from her since. When she arrives home a few days before the wedding, I ask if she's bought a dress.

"No. Where would I get a dress?"

"Ireland has no stores?"

"Of course they have stores, but how would I know what you want me to wear?"

So off we go to get her dress, and within a few hours, we find a dress we both like that fits my budget.

Still, the outing is disappointing. I had hoped for an opportunity for closeness. But Alice is jet-lagged and doesn't seem particularly interested in either me or my wedding. What she wants to talk about is Mom and Dad's chagrin about her following Jon to Ireland, and the embarrassment Mom caused her by contacting Dean Dietrich to try to get him to force her to come back. I see both sides of the yearlong argument: her desire to be free of our parents and their desire to continue to control her while they're paying for her schooling. But she's angry that I'm not 100 percent on her side.

Despite all my apprehensions, the wedding is a wonderful success. Alice is there and wearing an appropriate dress, I don't forget my high heels, the ceremony and dinner go off without a hitch, and I'm a very happy bride. I love Sam with all my heart and can't wait for us to share our lives.

❖

A few weeks after the wedding, we leave for a month's holiday in Europe, and then go to Oxford for the year. Sam begins his research, and I spend the days working on my MA thesis and auditing economics classes— several undergraduate lecture courses and two graduate seminars, all open to the public.

Unfortunately, the Oxford lectures are boring and virtually empty, since undergraduates, busy with tutorials, rarely attend lectures. And the graduate seminars rival each other for dryness, despite being led by illustrious faculty: Sir John Hicks, whose pathbreaking theoretical contributions will win him a Nobel Prize, and Sir Roy Harrod, whose work on growth theory is renowned. One late afternoon, a presentation by one of Harrod's doctoral students is so lackluster that the great professor falls asleep. I take this as a signal, leave quietly, and never return.

Instead I spend my time in the library at Nuffield College, working on my thesis. My days are solitary, and I meet no one with whom I can discuss my work, but Sam turns out to be quite good at integrating political and economic ideas. In the evenings, we enjoy conversations not only about his work on how and why mice reject their skin grafts but also about how Soviet trade unions were shaped by Lenin's ideas.

However, once the weather turns chilly, I become grumpy. Both our house and Nuffield Library are unheated and I long to be warm, at least during the day. First I find a job as a secretary and then as a third-grade teacher. I enjoy the teaching enormously and wonder if I really should get a PhD. I've finished a first draft of my thesis by working on it nights and weekends, and I've been reaccepted to MIT with a full tuition fellowship plus a living stipend. But should I be a teacher instead?

Eventually I decide to go through with my plans for a doctorate. There are so many economics questions I want to answer, and I want a big challenge. Finishing a first draft of my MA thesis has been exciting. I want more of that. I can't believe MIT is willing to pay me for what I love doing—reading, writing, and noodling over economic problems. I'm ready to start.

5

Add Children and Stir, 1964–1970

The morning of my first day at MIT, I'm carrying an armful of Sam's shirts to the laundry. As I step off the curb, I sprain my ankle, so I'm a few minutes late when I limp into Charles Meyers's labor relations seminar. I'm the only woman in the class.

"I think you're in the wrong room, young lady," Meyers says as I sit down.

"No, I don't think so. I'm Myra Strober."

"Oh, you're Myra Strober." He smiles. "Well, welcome then."

The message is clear. In general, women are brushed off, but somehow I'm an exception. I try to puzzle it out. By some means or other, I'm an honorary man.

In my PhD economics cohort of about thirty students, there are three women, and I'm the only one who's married. A few of the men are married, but most are single and a year or two younger than I. My fellow students are cordial and accept me readily into study groups, but I don't become particularly friendly with any of them. I'm starved for female companionship. The secretaries and women administrators see me as odd, and while they greet me politely, they rarely engage me in their conversations. My best chats are with the janitor, a spirited woman with a lively Irish accent and seven children. When we talk mid-morning in the ladies' room, she cheers me on.

"Your mother must be proud of ya, gettin' all this education. Don't ya worry you're the only woman. You'll do yarself proud."

Sometimes, when my desire to interact with women gets intense, I take the MBTA a few stops from MIT to downtown Boston and go to Filene's Basement. The Basement has no dressing rooms, so women parade around in their underwear, trying on blouses, skirts, dresses, and coats, and asking other women what they think of their proposed new outfits. I have no money to buy anything, but I love to try on new fashions, get other women's comments, and help them assess what they're considering.

"No, it's all wrong," I tell one woman. The horizontal stripes make you look fat, and you're not fat."

She tells me: "You're so skinny to begin with, that skirt makes you look like a long drink of water. Try this one. The pleats'll give you some hips."

After an hour or so of good-natured bantering with women I have never seen before and never will again, I'm in a better mood and ready to go back to the library to conquer calculus, the elasticity of substitution, or aggregate production functions.

As a student, I had no idea how male my chosen field was, but in the mid-1960s, women made up only 7 percent of doctoral recipients in economics. I also had no idea how quintessentially male MIT was. Of its more than six thousand students at the time, only four hundred, or a little under 7 percent, were women: about two hundred undergraduates and two hundred graduate students.

Some fifteen years after my MIT experience, Rosabeth Moss Kanter would coin the term "tokenism" for the strangeness I felt at MIT. But during my MIT years, I had no term except the one I coined for myself—honorary man.

Because our programs are so demanding, Sam and I rarely visit our parents in Brooklyn. Instead, they drive up together to visit us every few months. The two older couples get along well, and the six of us enjoy park strolls when the weather is good and museum excursions when it's not. I particularly like being taken out to dinner, something Sam and I can rarely afford on our own. My favorite is Jimmy's Harborside for baked stuffed shrimp, or, on special occasions like birthdays and anniversaries, steamed whole lobster.

The only disagreeable moments during these visits are my mother-in-law's pleas for grandchildren. Taking my arm and moving to be alone with me, she inquires: "So, when will you be pregnant? You've been married already two years. It's time for a baby, no?"

"No, Mom." (Starting about six months after I was married, I started calling her Mom at her request. My own mom said she didn't mind in the least.) "I'm not ready to have a baby yet. My studies take up all my time."

A few months later, she's at it again. "So, are you ready now?"

"Nope. Not yet. Just be patient."

I ask Sam to get her off my back, but either he never does or he's unsuccessful. She raises the issue every time she sees me.

MIT's economics program is highly quantitative, and I find it every bit the challenge I want. But I'm grateful each day that the school didn't admit me straight from Cornell. Even after my year at Tufts, my math background is weak, and I enroll, along with numerous other classmates, in Math for Economists, taught by Karl Schell. Not exactly remedial, the course proceeds at breakneck pace through trigonometry and differential and integral calculus. But while I have to work really hard, I enjoy the material and do well. In fact, I do well in all my courses, although I'm not sure exactly how the microeconomics will help me answer the labor market questions I'm interested in.

Microeconomic theory with Paul Samuelson, arguably one of the most outstanding American economists of the twentieth century, is a highly unusual class. Samuelson's knowledge is deep but eclectic, and he spends the better part of most sessions talking about various tangential subjects that interest him: Karl Marx's childhood, David Ricardo's love life, his own losses in soybean futures. He's funny, almost a stand-up comic, and the class enjoys his long digressions.

But after an hour or so of jesting, everything changes. He looks at his watch, realizes there are only twenty or thirty minutes left of class, and exclaims, "Oh, we'd better get going."

Then, without consulting a single note, he begins scribbling equations fiercely on the board, talking rapid-fire to keep up with his writing. As soon as he fills one board, he rushes to the next, and when he's filled up all three, he erases everything swiftly and continues. Our task is to keep up with him, copying everything without understanding anything. Of course, there's never time for questions. When class is over, he smiles and walks out, leaving us all asking: "What the hell did he say?"

After a couple of such lectures, we realize we have to form small groups and try to figure out collectively what the lectures are about. We're aided by his book, *Foundations of Economic Analysis*, based on the thesis he wrote at Harvard more than twenty-five years earlier, because most of his equations come from there. Eventually we work it all out: why indifference curves are convex, why demand curves slope downward, and under what conditions it's possible to derive social welfare functions. Paradoxically, we spend so much time working on Samuelson's equations and puzzling them out that we learn the material better than we would have had his lectures been lucid, and ever since my experience with his class, I have seriously wondered if presenting highly disorganized material to bright students is in fact a good teaching strategy.

My favorite theory class, though, is Robert Solow's. Solow's subject matter, macroeconomic theory—unemployment, inflation, productivity, and economic growth—is far more relevant to the questions I care about, and beyond that, Solow is a gifted teacher. He is Samuelson's student and friend, as eminent as Samuelson (both will win a Nobel Prize), and equally humorous in class. But that's where the similarities end. Unlike Samuelson, Solow delivers lectures that are clear and comprehensive. His lecture notes consist of a single index card with three or four words written on it, and with those as his only prompt, he explains complicated concepts, many of which he himself invented, and draws the relevant graphs and equations to illustrate his points. He takes questions regularly and never demeans the questioner.

Solow, a follower of Keynes, argues that in a recession it's necessary for the government to run a deficit; but in times of low unemployment, government should run a surplus. He's unimpressed with the power of monetary policy to pull an economy out of a recession and unimpressed with Milton Friedman's theories about money.

"I don't know about Milton," he says. "Everything reminds *me* of sex, but everything seems to remind Milton of the money supply."

I wish Solow had been among the professors who queried me at the Woodrow Wilson interview. He espouses the same Keynesian economics they disparaged, and I realize that had the composition of judges been different, I just might have won that fellowship, even though I did pick an extremely complex topic to discuss.

And today, as I read economic debates in the public media, I wish every commentator had taken Solow's class. There would be far less foolishness, far less drivel about governments needing to balance their budgets in recessions, "just like families." What is required to get out of a depression or recession is more spending. Not counting foreign countries' imports of our goods, there are three main possible spenders: consumers, businesses, and government. It is in the nature of recessions that consumers and businesses reduce their spending: consumers because so many of them are unemployed or fearful of becoming unemployed, and businesses because they don't see opportunities for profitable investments when consumers and other businesses have reduced spending. So if spending is to increase, it has to be done by government. Recessions are *not* the time for governmental austerity. They are the time for public expenditures on repair to infrastructure, education, and so on. But—and here is the important caveat—in boom times, government should curtail its spending and reduce the deficit it ran up during the previous recession. Government spending should be countercyclical, not perennially creating deficits.

Another of my favorite professors is Evsey Domar, a short, slight man with a heavy Russian accent and a twinkle in his eye who loves good jokes, especially his own. Famous for his work on economic growth theory, he wrote a celebrated paper that begins with a quote from the Red Queen in Lewis Carroll's *Through the Looking-Glass*, "It takes all the running you can do to keep in the same place. If you want to get somewhere else, you must run at least twice as fast as that." The paper argues that to maintain full employment in an economy where the population is growing, it is not sufficient to increase the *amount* of investment; the economy must increase its *rate of growth* of investment. In 1964, although it's been almost twenty years since he wrote the paper, he is still delighted by how perfectly the quotation makes his point.

One break that Sam and I take during my first year at MIT is a trip to New York in February for Alice's marriage to Jon Amsden. Earlier, Mom and Dad were firmly opposed to the marriage because Jon is not Jewish, but as they have come to know him, and after much pleading from Alice, they have relented.

Jon is of Irish descent and has the traditional gift of gab, including the ability to remember and tell an amazing number of jokes. He is kind and respectful to Mom and Dad, and they appreciate his pro-labor politics. He and Alice make a stunning couple—he is tall and handsome, with curly blond hair and a winning smile; and she is tall and striking, with straight blond hair and blue eyes that match his.

Alice has asked me to be her matron of honor and I have accepted, but I'm troubled about my relationship with her. As sisters, we know we mean a great deal to each other. But we rarely talk, and when we do, there's no closeness. We love each other but also disapprove of each other, and it all seems particularly odd because our interests are so similar. Indeed, at her wedding, she tells me that she and Jon are both planning to get PhDs in economics at the London School of Economics. Two sisters, both graduates of the same school, both getting PhDs in the same field. But as Sam points out, despite our surface similarities, we have vastly different worldviews and personalities. I'm a liberal democrat; she's a radical. I like peaceful relationships; she likes Sturm und Drang. And so it goes, year after painful year.

When spring comes to Cambridge, I develop an unusual physical symptom and go to the MIT health service.

"My palate itches all the time," I tell the doctor. "I can relieve the itching with my tongue, but then my eyes itch."

"Hmmm," he says. "This is a typical stress reaction. I think your doctoral program is too much for you. I would advise you to pay close attention to these symptoms. They are telling you something."

"What are they telling me?"

"They are telling you to leave this program, and I think that if you do, you will see that they go away quickly."

When I tell Sam about this "diagnosis," we both laugh. "Imagine," I say, "what a delicate constitution he must think I have."

Years later, when these symptoms return and I see an allergist, he finds I'm allergic to feathers. I realize then what happened in Boston. Sam and I had finally saved up some money and I bought two feather pillows. Just think: had I followed the advice of the clinic doctor, I would have dropped out of school because I was allergic to pillows!

During the summer between my first and second years at MIT, I work as a research assistant for Robert Evans. He is doing a project on the role of employment in parole success, and my job is to read parole records at the Massachusetts parole office in Boston and code the material. The works gives me insights into people and a way of life about which I know nothing. In the end, contrary to our hypothesis, we find that employment plays little role in distinguishing between those who successfully complete parole and those who violate it and return to prison. The only variable that separates the successful from the unsuccessful is getting married while on parole. It's my first lesson that social factors are often more important than economic ones.

That summer, I also finish my MA thesis. I had given Frank Holzman a draft when I returned from England and he'd liked it, but he'd raised several points he thought I still needed to consider. So back into the thesis box went the draft, and it's only now that first-year classes are finished that I have time to research these additional matters and hand in the final version.

I also have a bit more time to work around the house. Sam and I never discuss our division of labor at home. As in Oxford, I simply do everything—the shopping, cooking, cleaning, and laundry. My rationale, if I think about it at all, is that Sam works more hours than I do. In Oxford, his lab schedule was demanding and he often went back in the late evening to check on his rats. Now his work is even more stressful— clinical rotations, including nights and weekends, on matters of life or death for extremely ill patients. I don't see how I can ask him to do house-work on top of all that. There's no one I can talk to about our division of labor. I have no married women friends who are in graduate school with husbands in medical school. The wives of Sam's peers do all the house-work, whether they work or stay home with young children, and without thinking about it or talking about it, I do the same.

Looking back, I'm amazed that I didn't question our arrangement or try to change it, especially since Dad did a good deal of housework, and even Grandpa washed dishes after large family dinners. But Dad and Grandpa were not *doctors*. I am married to a man who is becoming a *doctor*. It never even occurs to me to ask him to do housework.

Sam and I are doing well together, but we don't see each other much because of his schedule, and when he's home he's often asleep, exhausted from his demanding rotations. During term time, I have my own work to keep me more than busy, but in the summer, I'm frequently lonely and grateful for invitations from my father's cousins to spend time at their house in Lexington, just a few miles west of Boston.

Even though I'm only in my second year of study, I feel some urgency to get a thesis topic approved, for I realize that I'm going to be in residency at MIT for only three years, not the usual four. Sam will graduate from medical school at the end of my second year at MIT and immediately begin a one-year medical internship at Massachusetts General Hospital in Boston. At the end of his internship, he will serve in the military by doing research at the National Institutes of Health (NIH) in Bethesda, Maryland. Now that the Vietnam War is under way, all physicians are required to do some form of military service, and Sam has opted for the NIH. So I will be moving with him to Bethesda in a little over a year. The possibility that I might stay in Boston to finish my thesis while he goes to Bethesda to do his military service never even enters my consciousness.

In Domar's course on Soviet economics, I figure out the topic for my doctoral dissertation. It will be about the differences in average wages in manufacturing industries across countries, what is known as the manufacturing wage structure. I come to the topic after reading a paper by Stanley Lebergott showing that in developed countries, the same manufacturing industries are all high wage (for example, transportation manufacturing and oil refining) and the same are low wage (for example, textiles and clothing). This is true even in the Soviet Union, which has a completely different economy from the nonsocialist countries in Lebergott's sample.

But when I look at the Soviet manufacturing wage structure when that economy was much less developed, I find that its wage structure was quite different, which leads me to wonder what the manufacturing wage structure looks like in currently developing countries. Do those less developed countries have the same manufacturing wage structure as developed countries, or do they have the pattern that the Soviet Union had before it became highly developed? Also, in developed economies the wage structure is highly correlated with the productivity structure. Is that true in less developed countries as well?

After some digging, I find that the International Labour Organization (ILO) has wage and productivity data for fifteen manufacturing industries in each of fifty-three countries, and I realize that I could use the data to investigate my questions about how economic development is related to wage and productivity structures.

When I tell Meyers about my idea for a thesis topic and also that I will be moving at the end of my third year in the program, he is super-supportive. He likes my topic and thinks that if I work on it for a year, I will be able to finish my dissertation before I leave for Bethesda. He points out that unlike my classmates, I have an MA in economics, so even though I'll spend only three years at MIT, I will have done four years of graduate work. He also thinks I should go on the job market during my third year.

I'm excited. But I still have to go through general exams in late May—written and oral exams in theory and two other fields, in my case labor economics and economic development. I'm nervous about these exams, as are my classmates, and I spend weeks, both by myself and in study groups, going over all the material suggested.

With the exception of making a seder at Passover, I do nothing but study ten or twelve hours every day. But I'm amply rewarded for taking time out for the seder. We invite Ted Pincus, Sam's medical school classmate and fraternity brother from Columbia, and Ted brings his new girlfriend, Diane Eder, a student at Wellesley who is applying to medical school. Medicine has about the same percentage of women as economics, and I'm delighted to meet another woman going into a traditionally male occupation. We bond immediately, with laughter and deep understanding, and begin a close friendship that endures to this day.

When I finally take the written exams for generals, I pass with no difficulty. The oral exam, which I've truly dreaded, is eased considerably by Domar's presence on my committee. The oral exam is not usually about one's dissertation topic, but Domar is so interested in my thesis that he keeps bringing up questions related to it. What do I think about the theory that postulates a relationship between labor productivity and wages? Why do I think that the connection between labor productivity and wages might be weak in less developed economies? What do I think happens in the course of economic development that enhances the connection between the two? Since I've thought a good deal about these questions, the exam is most agreeable, and I can't help contrasting it with the painful Woodrow Wilson fellowship interview several years earlier.

Just a few days after the oral, I'm advanced to candidacy (the technical term for successfully going through the general exams), and a week or so after that, relaxed from months of tension, I realize that I very much want to have a child. It's as though a big blanket has suddenly dropped from heaven and wrapped my entire being in longing for motherhood. I feel an almost physical ache, and my arms suddenly yearn to hold a baby.

Fortunately, Sam wants a child, too (he's been ready for some time now), and we begin talking seriously about timing. We want to wait to have a baby until after he's finished his internship and I've finished my thesis. By then we expect to be living in a slightly larger place than our tiny Boston apartment.

In a few months, I become pregnant. My due date is July 15, just two weeks after we're slated to move to Bethesda. I'm thrilled, but when we call my mother-in-law, she's beyond thrilled. She's ecstatic.

The pregnancy is not easy. I've heard of morning sickness, but my nausea seems to last until after dinner instead of ending at lunchtime. Fortunately, I'm not taking any classes, because I need to make several trips a day to the MIT restroom. I'm also exhausted, sleeping nine and ten hours a night and taking frequent naps in the library. Nothing seems to help— not Saltines (they leave a salty taste in my mouth and a lot of crumbs), not the anti-nausea medicine (it gives me a headache), and not plain hot water sipped slowly (yuck). But many things make it worse, including climbing the four flights of stairs to our walk-up apartment. I just endure it, reminding myself that it's finite and a small price to pay for this incredible life inside me.

After about three months, the nausea diminishes and I decide that I'll announce my pregnancy at school. Each morning, as I drive from Boston to Cambridge, I tell myself that this will be the day. I picture exactly where I'll be and exactly whom I'll tell. But I'm never able to picture positive reactions, so when I get to my designated time and place, I remain fearfully silent. The whole place is so *male*, and being pregnant is so quintessentially *not* male. I'm afraid if I tell them, they'll take away my honorary male status—withdraw their support for my job search or refuse to serve on my thesis committee. Whatever they might do, none of it seems good.

There's no one I can talk to about this. I have no friends in this situation, and I don't know any older women who have preceded me. I think about talking to Mom but reject that idea pretty quickly. She would be far too anxious. I could talk to my Irish janitor friend, but I don't want my professors or fellow students to hear the news from her, so that path doesn't seem sensible. When I ask Sam, he says he doesn't really know what I should do. Finally, I rationalize my silence, deciding that it's probably best to go on the job market without publicizing my pregnancy. As a woman, I'm an unusual candidate to begin with. A pregnant woman might be too much for a prospective employer.

❖

The process of matching MIT economics doctoral students with job openings for assistant professors or researchers in think tanks and government is highly organized, and every year a faculty member is put in charge of the activity. This year, the task falls to Bob Solow, and he is superb! In October, he gathers all of us looking for jobs and gives us his spiel, "Job Market 101." The watchword is "communication" with him at all junctures—before we sign up with recruiters, before we send out letters of inquiry, before we go off to give job market talks.

"Most important, don't accept any job offers without talking to me first," he thunders. "Tell me what they're offering, and I'll help you get a better deal."

He tells us at every opportunity how desirable we are. "They all want you. Your job is to figure out where you'll be happiest."

My geographic constraint makes the search both less and more difficult—less because the search can be limited, but more because I can't investigate several matches that seem potentially very positive. Still, I'm happy. I get interviews with three universities in the D.C. area (American University, George Washington University, and University of Maryland) and two federal government agencies (the Office of Economic Opportunity and the Department of Defense).

With Sam's full support, I arrange to go to D.C. and give job talks on three successive days. I'm five months' pregnant, and I buy a loose but stylish suit for the interviews. I ask the saleswoman if she can tell I'm pregnant. She says she can't. Sam says he can't either. I feel like some kind of espionage agent with my little secret, but I'm really not showing at all. I'm also not at all nauseated anymore. I'm still more tired than usual, but I sleep well in the D.C. hotel and am full of energy every morning when the job talks and interviews take place.

Although I've made only slow progress on my thesis because of my nausea, I still have enough material to present preliminary results. Faculty and students are clearly interested in my work, and nobody seems to have difficulty with my being a woman.

The only interview in which gender is an issue is at the Department of Defense.

"Why did you sign up to interview with us?" my interviewer asks.

"Because I'll be in D.C. next year, and I wanted to see what kinds of jobs you have for labor economists."

"We don't have any jobs for labor economists. And we don't have jobs for women. Do you know what we do? We do cost-benefit analyses of our bombing. Is that what you want to do? Of course not. No woman wants to do that. You should interview at OEO and help in the war on poverty. That's the kind of work women should do."

It's a short interview, and I'm ambivalent about it. Certainly I don't want to analyze the effectiveness of American bombing in Vietnam and Cambodia, and I'm relieved that I don't have to take such a job. But I'm sad that the interviewer thinks it's OK for men to do such work. Although I've not been active politically during the antiwar movement, I'm firmly against the war. I think the threat of communism in Southeast Asia has been overblown, and I don't think we can win. My interview makes me think I should do more in the antiwar movement, but I don't.

In the first months of my pregnancy, it was constant nausea that slowed my thesis progress. But now it's exhaustion. When Sam is on duty at the hospital, I fall asleep on the couch by 8 p.m. and wake up twelve hours later. When he's home, I live it up until 9 p.m., and actually sleep in a bed. But he's dog-tired, too. We're twin sleepyheads.

A month or so after my interview at Maryland, the school makes me an offer. I pass it by Solow, and he approves. The salary and teaching load seem right to him, and I accept enthusiastically. Wow—in a little more than six months, I'll begin my first college teaching job.

But when I phone Mom to tell her, she's appalled.

"How can you sign up for a job that begins in September when you're going to have a baby in July? Are you crazy? What if you decide you don't want a job? What if you decide you want to stay home full-time with your baby?"

"I don't want to stay home full-time with my baby any more than you did. You think I've sweated all these years through an MA, an MA thesis, two years of coursework at MIT, and now a doctoral thesis so I can stay home with a baby? You're the one who must be crazy."

I hang up in tears. I may be a big shot on the phone with Mom, but deep down, I'm scared. Maybe Mom's right. Maybe I am crazy. The people at Maryland don't even know I'm going to have a baby when I start working there. Have I been dishonest?

I talk to Sam about it. "I think it'll be OK," he says. But I know he's so fatigued, he can hardly think.

Eventually, I calm down. Why is what I've done dishonest? Why does Maryland need to know that I'm having a baby? My teaching is not going to be any better or worse for being a mother. They're hiring me for my mind and my teaching ability. And as far as I know, neither is going to be affected by having a baby. No, whatever Mom may think, I'm convinced I'm doing exactly the right thing.

Finally, I begin to show. At first I just loosen up the waistband on my skirts, but after a while I need to buy maternity tops. Nobody seems to notice, not even my janitor friend (although I wonder if she thinks I'm just getting fat and is too polite to say so). As for the faculty, I think the idea that one of their students might be pregnant is so foreign that they can't see my pregnancy, even when it's right in front of their eyes. Or maybe they can, but, like me, can't bring themselves to talk about it.

However, one day when I stand up in front of the labor seminar to give a talk on my thesis, the secret is out. When I'm finished, Abraham Siegel comes up to me.

"I see you're pregnant. Congratulations," he says, in a most straight-forward way.

I sigh with relief, smile, and thank him. But I don't fully appreciate his attitude until years later, when I see women colleagues and graduate students in male-dominated fields berated by male colleagues and thesis advisers for becoming pregnant: "You could have been a star, and now look what you've gone and done." MIT may have had few women, but the faculty in economics supported me all the way.

It's probably not an accident that Siegel is the one who comments on my pregnancy. He is younger than the other full professors, and since his admissions interview with me, he has regarded me as his special student. Once he opens the conversation, that seems to make it safe for the other faculty and students to chime in, and everyone who says something is congratulatory and supportive. And now the women secretaries begin to talk to me. I can hear them thinking: *well, she's a woman, after all.*

My obstetrician is also supportive. When I tell him I plan to work after the baby is born, he looks at me quizzically.

"Of course you do. Why else would you be getting a PhD?"

He suggests I sign up for Lamaze classes to prepare for delivery, saying that even if I decide to use anesthesia, the breathing techniques will be helpful. I take the classes, but I'm chagrined to find I'm the only woman there whose husband is not present. Sam is simply too busy to fit Lamaze into his backbreaking schedule. I understand, but I fervently wish it were otherwise.

❖

Sam's internship ends on June 30, and he's supposed to report for duty at the NIH on July 1. Because we need to drive rather than fly, Mass General lets him leave a few days early. He will technically be a lieutenant commander in the U.S. Navy, assigned to the NIH, so fortunately the Navy pays for both our packing and moving. I'm so pregnant I can hardly walk, let alone pack.

We drive to New York, stay overnight with my parents, and leave for Bethesda the following morning. We've rented a house not far from the NIH and only a short commute from the University of Maryland. In sweltering heat and drenching humidity, we move in. I'm anxious about my upcoming delivery. In just a couple of weeks, I'll have a baby at Bethesda Naval Hospital with a doctor I've never met.

When I do meet the obstetrician, my anxieties worsen. He's distant and old-fashioned. When I ask him about arrangements for Sam to attend the birth, he says he doesn't believe in that.

"Women are not at their best during labor and delivery. It's far better when their husbands see them after it's all over."

"But my husband is a doctor, and I want him to be there."

"I don't care who he is. I don't allow husbands at my births."

I want to tell him that it's *my* birth, not his, but it all seems hopeless. I'm going to deliver in less than two weeks, I don't know anyone in Bethesda who can recommend another OB, and obviously I can't go back to Boston.

Since Sam did not attend the Lamaze sessions, I knew he wouldn't be able to help me with breathing during the delivery, but I was certainly looking forward to having him there for support. Now I would be truly on my own.

When my due date arrives, Mom and Dad come to stay at our house, and two days later, I go into labor. I do well with the Lamaze breathing at first, but when I switch to rapid panting for the second stage of labor, the resident on duty tells me that if I don't stop breathing in that "weird way," he will stop caring for me.

"We don't want you hyperventilating, for God's sake."

Between pants, I tell him that I am not going to hyperventilate, that I am practiced at Lamaze and doing fine. But he and the nurse are adamant: any more panting, and they stop caring for me. Neither of them has ever heard of Lamaze.

So I stop, and five minutes later I'm in great pain and calling for anesthesia. I'd always thought I would use anesthesia—I was not aiming for heroism—but I thought that as long as I could do without it, I would. I feel profoundly alone, but what are my options? I'm in pain, powerless, and furious. The labor lasts for fourteen hours, and when Jason is born, his Apgar score is low. Then I'm really furious, sure that if I'd continued with Lamaze and postponed the anesthesia, his score might well be higher. Still, when the nurse puts Jason in my arms, overwhelming elation trumps every other emotion. I have a son!

After a week in the hospital (standard practice in the late 1960s), I take Jason home. I'm completely drained, hardly able to get out of my chair. We have a traditional Jewish circumcision ceremony, a *bris,* at our house and both my parents and in-laws attend. At the ceremony, Jason gets his Hebrew name: Moshe Menachim Mendel, in honor of Grandpa.

Exhausted, in pain, and still angry about my delivery, I feel Grandpa's spirit filling the room. I can hear him *davening* in my mind, and our conversation after his prayers some fifteen years ago comes back clearly.

"Be kind to everyone. Everyone has a piece of God in him."

"Even those awful obstetricians?" I ask Grandpa's spirit, laughing to myself.

"Even them!"

The day after the *bris,* when Sam goes back to work and my parents and in-laws return to New York, I become depressed. The heat and humidity affect me less now that I'm no longer pregnant, but I have little energy, probably because I'm still sore and getting up every few hours during the night to breastfeed. I sit in the backyard and weep. I feel my life is over. I work a bit on my thesis, but since I'm feeding every few hours, I can't get a good block of time to concentrate. I have a few friends from Boston who have also moved to Bethesda, particularly Diane Eder (now Diane Pincus), but they don't have children and are still working, so they're no company during the day. I feel utterly alone.

The profoundly disturbing fare on TV is no help. Just two days after Jason's *bris*, race riots break out in Detroit. I'm horrified to watch black people loot and burn their own homes and stores, and equally upset at the techniques the police use to contain the mayhem. I watch for days, unable to believe my eyes but unable to turn the set off. After five days, two thousand buildings have been destroyed and forty-three people have been killed.

After a month of sadness and lethargy, I realize that if I'm going to start teaching in a few weeks, I'd better find care for Jason. There are no childcare facilities in the D.C. area in 1967, and certainly no group care for infants. I pull myself together and send the local paper a classified ad for a babysitter.

Only one person responds: Jean, a single young black woman from nearby Rockville, whose experience caring for infants comes from taking care of her younger brothers and sisters. I interview her, find her person-able and kind, and call the one reference she gives me. It checks out, and I hire her on a trial basis. For a week, she comes to the house, and we feed, change, and coo at Jason together.

I like what I see, but I'm terrified to leave Jason alone with her. I'm twenty-six. I've never interviewed anybody for anything. What if I'm wrong about her? What if she and her reference are in cahoots, and as soon as I leave they kidnap Jason? I'm frantic. And I'm still depressed and not thinking terribly clearly. Sam is not much help. He's thoroughly engrossed in his new lab at the NIH. Somehow it seems that finding a caretaker for Jason is solely my responsibility.

What to do? I have a contract to teach. I want to teach. I need to go to campus and prepare my syllabus. Finally, I summon my courage, leave Jason with Jean, and go over to College Park. Within an hour or so of visiting the department, getting the key to my office, and meeting some colleagues, my depression is gone. I'm in familiar territory.

I call Jean. "Everything's just fine," she says. I breathe deeply, head for the library, and think how lucky I am to have an adult life apart from my life as a mother—how lucky that I always knew I wanted to work in addition to being a mom! Never again am I troubled by the feelings of hopelessness and lassitude I experienced that summer. And never do I have an experience as scary as hiring Jean.

Both Mom and my mother-in-law are skeptical about my leaving Jason to go to work, and I get phone calls almost daily asking how things are going. But after a few weeks, when they come to visit, meet Jean, and watch her with Jason, they're reassured. So am I.

❖

Since I've never taught before, I'm beyond busy. I'm teaching labor economics and macroeconomics three days a week, and on the days I don't teach, I'm preparing lectures and grading quizzes, exams, or papers. Most days I'm only one lecture ahead of the students. I need to create a stockpile of lecture notes.

Also, though Jean does some of the housework and laundry during Jason's naps, I'm still responsible for all the shopping, cooking, and cleaning up. Even though Sam and I are both working now, my schedule is more flexible than his, and we don't change our traditional division of labor. We don't even talk about the possibility of changing it. I have fully bought into the idea that his career is more important than mine. He needs to set up a lab. He needs to meet colleagues. He, he, he. And me? I just keep slogging away. Incomprehensible as it seems to me today, I never think to ask him for help.

Many an evening I'm still busy preparing my next day's lectures even after Jason's 10 p.m. feeding. Because I still haven't finished my doctoral thesis, which is sitting in a big box in our basement, my appointment at Maryland is changed from assistant professor to lecturer. I really want that assistant professor title, and I'll get it as soon as my thesis is approved, but, unfortunately, there simply aren't enough hours in the day to even consider working on it.

I love teaching, and I have several colleagues whom I like a lot. Many of them have held policy positions in the government and are articulate and passionate about improving people's material lives. I often have a sandwich with one or another of them at lunchtime and find the conversations stimulating.

But my favorite colleague at Maryland is Barbara Bergmann. For the first time, I have a professional woman to talk to. And what a woman! She's tough and extremely successful. She's fourteen years my senior, but she married late and had a baby only recently, so her daughter and Jason are almost exactly the same age. She's living proof that I can accomplish what I've set out to do—be both a devoted wife and mother *and* a successful academic.

When I tell her that I never told anyone at MIT or at the places I interviewed that I was pregnant, she applauds. Someday the world may be different, she says, but right now, that's the way we have to play the game. She also strenuously nixes my idea of switching to a part-time appointment once Sam becomes an assistant professor and his salary increases.

"One thing I know for sure," she says, "you will never have a successful career if you go part-time."

❖

The summer of 1967 produced riots in Newark and Detroit, but the spring of 1968 generates even more discord and violence. In early April, Martin Luther King Jr. is killed, and almost instantly riots begin in Washington, D.C. African Americans loot and burn hundreds of their own stores and homes and overwhelm local police, and federal troops are called in to maintain order. On the weekend, Sam and I take Jason in his carriage for a walk along the C&O Canal in Potomac, and we watch in horror as plumes of gray smoke rise from the city. The violence lasts for five days, stops just a few blocks from the White House, and results in twelve deaths.

❖

Jason changes incredibly during his first year, and I delight in his development. My favorite time of day is when I return from work. As soon as he hears my key in the lock, he crawls rapidly across the living room, meets me at the front door with *oohs* and *ahs*, and stretches his little arms toward me. Just before he turns one, he takes his first steps, and his walking seems miraculous. On his first birthday, we have a huge party in our backyard. I remember how miserable I was in that same backyard just one year earlier, but with all our new friends, neighbors, and colleagues toasting Jason, I simply can't connect to that former self.

I spend the summer working full tilt on my thesis, but mostly I play catch-up. I wish that when I'd left Boston the previous summer, someone had suggested I annotate everything and leave myself notes about what I'd done and what I was thinking of doing later. It takes me months to reconstruct my earlier analyses and ideas. But once burned.... Now

I carefully note every thought and possible line of argument I plan to pursue.

Toward the end of August, I get a phone call from my thesis adviser, Charles Meyers. It's dinnertime, and I can't quite reconcile talking to him while feeding Jason. We chat for a bit as he brings me up to date on doings at MIT, and then he gives me exactly the boost I need:

"I just wanted to call and let you know that all three of us on your committee are looking forward to receiving your thesis. Keep at it, Myra."

Years later, when I have my own doctoral candidates, I remember how even the smallest bit of encouragement can have a profound effect on a student struggling to complete a dissertation.

In September, I return to teaching and find the second time around much easier. Not only is Jason a year older and reliably sleeping through the night, but now I have a stash of lecture notes. In the evenings and on the days I'm not teaching, I can work on my thesis.

The following March, I realize I'm pregnant again and due at the end of November. Oh, boy—I had better get this thesis finished before the next baby comes! I work nonstop. Fortunately, unlike my first pregnancy, this one has no nausea or exhaustion. I'm able to prepare for class, teach, care for Jason, care for the house, and write. Ah, youth!

In May, I send a draft of the dissertation to all three advisers, and a few weeks later I get the news I've been hoping for. Very few revisions are needed, and almost all of them are minor. I send out the final draft in July, and in August I fly to Boston for the thesis oral, looking as pregnant as when I left two years earlier.

At MIT, there are no outside examiners at doctoral orals, only the candidate and the three people on the reading committee. All three are complimentary about my work and ask interesting questions, and afterward, Meyers takes me to lunch at the MIT faculty club to celebrate. Although it's right upstairs in the Sloan Building, I've never been there before, and it's a wonderfully symbolic initiation into faculty life.

But before I return to the airport and my flight home, I have my own celebration—at Filene's Basement! The old familiar clientele are there, chattering away, and the friendly repartee is as good as I remember. But this time I actually have money to buy what my fellow shoppers say looks good, so I come away with an armload of new maternity clothes. A true economic triumph!

❖

The University of Maryland has no maternity leave policy. (Nor does any other university at the time.) Pregnant faculty are an anomaly, to say the least. If I want maternity leave, I have to do it on my own dime and take a leave of absence for a whole semester without pay. Sam and I talk about it and conclude we can't afford to lose half my annual salary. And in any event, I don't want to leave work for five months. My experience with depression after staying home full-time with Jason makes me want to go back to work as soon as possible after this next birth.

My colleague Bob Knight, also a labor economist, volunteers to take my classes for a few weeks while I recuperate. We figure I'll be out between Thanksgiving and Christmas, then come back at the beginning of January. But my child-to-be has other plans.

In early November, almost three weeks before my due date, I feel cramping and go to the Naval Hospital. The doctor who examines me says he doesn't see any signs of labor and that I should go home. But I refuse to go home. After my birth experience last time, I'm emboldened, determined not to be powerless again.

"My husband is a lieutenant commander," I tell the admitting nurse, "and I want a room here. You'll be very sorry if you send me home and I have my baby there. I guarantee you, if that happens, I'll make sure it hits all the newspapers."

I get a room.

At noon, the ward nurse asks if I want lunch.

"Lunch? Why would I have lunch? I might have a baby today."

"If you say so," she says, rolling her eyes and handing me a small bell. "If you need me, just ring."

A few moments after she leaves, my water breaks. I ring strenuously. She comes running back, examines me, and goes into overdrive.

"My God, you're almost fully dilated," she says.

They put me on a gurney and wheel me into the delivery room, but I never get to the delivery table. I use all the Lamaze techniques I can rally. Good thing, too, since there isn't time for anesthesia. The delivery takes about fifteen minutes.

"If you ever have a third child," the doctor says, "I suggest you camp out at the hospital."

"Maybe so," I say, "but you know, you might want to tell your nurses to pay more attention to women who come in and say they feel like they're going to deliver. I had to pull rank to get admitted."

I'm overjoyed! Because I was outspoken, I didn't have to give birth at home or in the car. Even more important, I have a daughter: a perfectly healthy daughter with a good Apgar score. One son and one daughter. What incredible luck.

I often ask myself *how* I knew I was going to have a baby. All I can say is that having had one before, some feeling deep within my body told me another would soon arrive. That's it.

We name our new daughter Elizabeth and call her Liz, and soon after her birth, on a Friday evening, we take her to a Reform temple where the rabbi bestows her Hebrew names: Batya Esther Hannah. Batya is in honor of Baba, Esther for Sam's aunt, and Esther Hannah for Tante Annie (although she was called Anna in English, her Hebrew name was actually Esther Hannah). It's a joyful evening, but except for the baby naming, the service feels analytic and cold and leaves me dissatisfied.

❖

Because my pregnancy was easy and the delivery so rapid, I'm quickly back to my old self, with no soreness and not even a hint of depression. After a week at the hospital, I stay at home for two weeks, and they're filled with fun—getting to know Liz, taking Jason on outings, and having wonderful conversations with Vera, the babysitter who has replaced Jean. Then, after Thanksgiving, I happily return to work.

One of my junior colleagues accosts me my first morning back. He's incredulous. His wife delivered a baby a month before me.

"What have you done with your baby?" he asks.

"I've left her playing in traffic" is what I want to say, but I stay silent.

"I just left my wife at home," he continues. "She's still in her pajamas. Our baby was up all night. You just had your baby. How can you be here?"

"Don't worry," I tell him. "Your wife's the normal one. I'm a little strange."

It will take me several years to fully accept the life I've chosen and see it as just as "normal" as anyone else's. At the time, I truly do view myself as strange.

After Liz's birth, I talk to Alice nonstop about the joys of children, but despite my pro-natal campaign, she remains uninterested in becoming a mom. She says her relationship with our mom is so strained that she can't imagine "reproducing" a mother-daughter relationship—and besides, she says, she wants to concentrate single-mindedly on her career. Her dissertation is on labor relations in Kenya and she wants to work in development economics, a field that requires a great deal of time away from home. She doesn't see how it would be possible to add motherhood to that kind of career.

As I look back now, I'm ashamed of my strenuous urging. At the time, I told myself I was simply trying to prevent her from making a mistake she might later regret. But now I wonder how much of my lobbying was an attempt to feel less isolated in my own lifestyle. If Alice were also trying to combine a demanding career with children, I'd have had company.

❖

Once I'm back teaching at Maryland, I begin making plans for the following year. Sam's time at the NIH will be up at the end of June and we'll be moving to Palo Alto and Stanford University, where he has accepted a one-year position as a medical resident followed by an assistant professorship, a really excellent offer.

It never occurs to me that Sam and I should go on the job market together and each find assistant professor positions, and nobody suggests such a plan: not any of my thesis advisers or my colleagues at Maryland, and certainly not my parents or in-laws. Not even Barbara Bergmann, who in later years will become a staunch feminist. From my vantage point now, I am appalled at how submissive I was, but Monday morning quarterbacking is useless. The truth is that at the time, there was really no other model of behavior that I knew. Women, even highly educated professional women, followed their husbands. Husbands' careers were primary. I didn't make a decision to be submissive. I didn't make any decision at all. I was able to flaunt the norm that said that women whose husbands earned a good living should stay at home with their babies, but I was not able to flaunt a norm I didn't even realize existed. Sam's and my decision-making process just seemed normal—it was what everyone, including me, expected.

❖

In the late 1960s and early 1970s, some job openings were posted, but a greater number were not. People got jobs through word of mouth. I ask Charlie Meyers if he knows labor economists in the Bay Area whom he could call on my behalf. The senior labor economist at Stanford is Mel Reder, but Charlie says he doesn't know him. However, he does know Lloyd Ulman at Berkeley and says there's a vacancy there for an assistant professor of labor economics.

Charlie calls Lloyd, and Lloyd writes to me saying that he'd like to interview me at the annual meetings of the American Economic Association in New York City just after Christmas. On my own, I also arrange to have interviews for assistant professor positions at San Francisco State, Hayward State, and the University of Santa Clara. Those were the days! The professoriate was growing, and academic job opportunities were plentiful.

When I tell Mom about the interviews, she kindly says that if we bring Jason and Liz to Brooklyn, she and Dad will take care of them while I go into the city for the meetings. In the weeks after the interviews, I hear nothing from Berkeley, but the other three institutions ask me to come out to California and give talks. So in spring of 1970 Mom comes to Maryland to take care of Jason and Liz, and Sam and I fly to San Francisco. We use the opportunity to do some house-hunting, and purchase a small but architecturally interesting house in Ladera, just a few miles from Stanford's campus.

Although all three job talks seem to go well, I never hear back from any of the economics departments. We're moving to California, and I have no job. I decide to call Mel Reder at Stanford. He's friendly and says he looks forward to meeting me when I come to Palo Alto, but confirms that there's no job for a junior labor economist at Stanford.

❖

On April 30, 1970, when President Nixon announces that the United States is invading Cambodia, I have no idea how soon his decision will affect my life. Two years earlier, Nixon campaigned on a platform to end the Vietnam War, but that has not happened. In fact, it comes to light that the United States has been unofficially involved in Cambodia for some time, and after Nixon's broadcast, demonstrations break out at universities across the country.

Although the University of Maryland has not previously been a major site of antiwar demonstrations, only one day after Nixon's speech, students there attempt to take over the ROTC offices on campus and succeed in blocking Route 1 adjacent to the campus, a major thoroughfare into the District of Columbia. The Maryland governor calls up the National Guard, and when I arrive for classes, I find that each classroom, including mine, has a National Guardsman standing outside with a fully loaded rifle. This is chilling enough, but on May 4, when Ohio National Guard troops shoot and kill four students at Kent State University after similar student antiwar demonstrations, the presence of the National Guard on campus becomes truly terrifying. The troops at Maryland remain for two weeks, and I'm shocked at the cavalier way the young men handle their arms, flirting with coeds while they lean on their rifles or twirl them in the air. When the semester ends, I'm more than ready to leave.

One month later, we're California-bound with Jason, almost three, and Liz, just a little over six months. From the very first day, I'm in love with the Bay Area. I'm awed by the drive to Palo Alto on Interstate 280, with nothing but mountains to the west, and I can't believe the ubiquitous palm trees, oleander, and hibiscus. But the biggest plus is the weather—not too hot, not too cold, and blue skies every day. I learn that it will stay perfect until fall; that between June and September, there is no rain at all. No outdoor activities spoiled. No rainy-day alternatives necessary. It seems like Camelot.

Our house is in a community that includes a large swimming pool and playground, and I go there with the kids every day and meet neighbors who also have young kids. *But what am I going to do*, I keep asking myself, *when September comes and I have no job?*

Then one afternoon in August, I open a letter from Lloyd Ulman at Berkeley, forwarded from Maryland. Would I please call him? When I do, he tells me there's a job at Berkeley for me after all. But it's not as an assistant professor. It's as a lecturer. Am I interested? What can I say? I've worked things out so that I have no alternative. Yes, I tell him, I'll take the job. What a shame, I think, I got to be an assistant professor for only one year.

Still, I have little time for self-pity. I need to find a babysitter. Once again, I put an ad in the paper, and once again I get only one response:

Margie, a gregarious and fun-loving black woman from East Palo Alto who has young children herself.

"Don't worry," she assures me, "my family takes care of *my* kids. But we need money. That's why I gotta take care of *your* kids."

This idea that professional women with children need to hire poor women with their own children in order to be able to work strikes me as far from ideal, and although I don't know it yet, it's an idea I will seriously investigate in the work I ultimately do on the economics of childcare and the importance of professional group care for all children. At the moment, however, the reality is the one Margie outlines. I need her, and she needs me.

This time around, I'm much more confident about the interview process than I was when I hired Jean to care for a one-month-old infant who couldn't give me any feedback at all. As I watch Margie with Jason and Liz, I can see immediately that she's wonderful with kids and that they love playing with her. The reference she gives me checks out positively, and I arrange for her to start work while I'm still at home. A few weeks later, I'm teaching labor economics and macro theory again—and making an appointment with Chairman Break to find out why I'm a lecturer and not an assistant professor.

III
1971–2012

6

Where the Rubber Hits the Road, 1971–1972

Loud conversation and peals of laughter greet me as I walk down the Berkeley hallway toward my classroom. It's the first day of my seminar on women and work, and I'm amused by how much excitement can be generated by twenty young women, undergraduates, and doctoral candidates from all over campus. When I enter, the students applaud. (It's clear that I'm the professor—not only because of my ten-year age advantage, but also because I'm the only one in high heels and a dress with a slim-line skirt.)

My word! I've been teaching for four years, but I've never had a welcoming like this! Even Paul Samuelson was not applauded on the first day of class at MIT before he said a single word, before we could even begin to assess the value of what he might impart.

Of course, the ovation is not for the quality of my teaching. It's not even really for *me*, although one doctoral student from anthropology tells me she admires my courage.

"You weren't afraid to ask the *economics* department to offer a course on women," she says. "That's amazing."

Mostly, though, they're clapping to express thanks: someone (it happens to be me) has come to feed them, to sate their hunger for understanding the mind-boggling sex-role tsunami that is changing their lives. For the moment, I'm their Joseph, meting out grain in famished Egypt.

Fortunately, I have enough experience to know that their unadulterated adulation is likely to be short-lived. And sure enough, once I hand out the course syllabus, it's clear that some of the students are only partly pleased with my approach to the class.

Two different strands of thought and action have animated the women's movement of the 1960s and early '70s—liberal and radical—and I'm clearly in the liberal wing, inspired by Betty Friedan and Congresswoman Edith Green, who recently held congressional hearings on discrimination in academe. I'm excited by the inclusion of women in the ban against employment discrimination in Title VII of the Civil Rights Act of 1964, by President Johnson's extension to women of his executive order requiring government contractors to take affirmative action to integrate their labor force, and by the formation of the National Organization for Women and its efforts to get the Equal Employment Opportunity Commission to ban sex-segregated want ads and to pressure governments to create childcare facilities.

However, many of the students are more interested in the radical branch of feminism, the feminism created by women in the civil rights and antiwar organizations of the sixties who became disenchanted with the lack of sex equality in groups such as the Student Nonviolent Coordinating Committee (SNCC) and Students for a Democratic Society (SDS).

One of the texts I've assigned for the course is Robin Morgan's anthology *Sisterhood Is Powerful*, and students see from the syllabus that the chapters I've asked them to read concern women's education, employment, and housework. But the more radical students want more radical feminism. They raise their hands, one after the other, saying that while they're happy to read what I've assigned from the Morgan book, they also want to read and discuss the chapters on the politics of orgasm, lesbianism, the Redstockings Manifesto, witches' covens, and the Society for Cutting Up Men (SCUM). After all, they tell me, this is Berkeley, home of the free-speech movement and monumental antiwar demonstrations. The feminism of Betty Friedan is not enough here.

What have I gotten myself into? I don't know a thing about the politics of orgasm, and I'm absolutely opposed to violence of any type, including cutting up men. Stalling for time, I tell them I "appreciate their input" and will think about what they've said. Then I continue with the introductory material I've prepared—analysis of the increase in women's labor force participation, the pay gap between women and men, and occupational segregation by sex. But as I'm teaching, I realize that unless I get to some of the other issues students care about, the class will never succeed. What to do?

A few hours after class, Maxine Raz, a doctoral student in sociology in the class, slips a note under my office door. She's disappointed in today's session because she thinks that, like all economists, I focus too much on understanding what *is* and not enough on what *could be*. She wants the course to help her think creatively about new systemic and institutional policies.

Her note has a powerful impact. She's absolutely right. It's not enough to understand what exists and theorize about how it came to be. The course needs to focus on change—what we want women's equality to look like, and how to get there. Although Maxine's note has nothing to do with the more radical readings in the Morgan anthology, somehow it brings back the insight I had almost a year earlier after reading Simone de Beauvoir's *Second Sex*: if women are to have equality at work, the whole society will have to change. The radical women in the class are right. If I don't know anything about the politics of orgasm, I'd better learn. And just because I'm opposed to violence doesn't mean I can't teach about women who are not. Indeed, if the focus of the course is to be change, we *must* talk about why violence is a poor strategy.

I breathe more easily. This course is going to be even more work than I had imagined, but it's also going to be more exciting. I'm going to learn a tremendous amount. I'll keep the economics focus of the class, but also examine other disciplines' take on economic issues. When I first approached Lloyd Ulman about teaching the course, I was worried there might not be enough economics reading for a course on women and work. Now I understand that such a concern was unnecessary. To understand women and work *requires* material from outside economics.

I walk to my car with a light step, and on the drive home, my mind turns over a stunning array of possibilities for inclusion in the course. When I pull into my carport, I can't even remember if there was traffic on the road.

❖

My first cross-disciplinary act is to invite psychologist Carol Jacklin to be a guest speaker in the class to talk about her work with Stanford professor Eleanor Maccoby on sex differences in children. (In those days, social differences between women and men or girls and boys were called "sex differences." It was not until a good deal later that we began distinguishing between the biological and the social, introducing the term "gender differences" to refer to the latter.)

I know that a good deal of occupational segregation results from men wanting to keep women out of better-paying jobs, but I want Carol to discuss the extent to which it may also stem from women's and men's own behavior. Are sex differences in children's behavior part of the explanation for sex differences in adult occupations?

I've never met Carol, but when I call to ask if she will speak at my class, she accepts enthusiastically, and on the day she's scheduled to lecture, when I pick her up in Big Blue at the Stanford Oval and she slides into the seat next to me and begins talking rapidly, I know my class is in for a treat. She's funny, irreverent, and wickedly smart.

In the classroom, Carol paces rapidly as she speaks.

"Here's the first thing I want you to remember," she says. "It's a myth that little boys behave one way and little girls behave some different way."

She sits down on the desk facing the students and begins swinging her legs to and fro. She looks like she's getting ready to sprint.

"Parents and other casual observers of kids draw conclusions about sex differences in children from their own kids. But these are exceedingly small samples. In our work, we look at large groups of children—masses of data—and what we find is that there are actually very few childhood sex differences that hold up over multiple studies."

"Not only that," she continues, "but the behaviors we look at are distributed by and large along a normal curve. The curve representing the boys' characteristics overlaps the curve representing the girls' characteristics. So even when there is a statistically significant mean difference between girls' and boys' behavior on some variable, it is also true that *some* girls have more of the characteristic than some boys. Let me give you an example. There may be a statistically significant mean difference in math achievement between girls and boys at a certain grade level. But if you concentrate only on the mean difference, you miss the fact that *some* girls are more talented in math than some boys. Get it?"

Affirmative nodding.

"Which characteristics have means that *are* statistically significantly different across the studies?" one of the students asks.

"One of them is physical aggression. We measure physical aggression by how many feet a child travels in a classroom to hit another child, and boys turn out to walk or run farther to do that than girls do."

Hands shoot up all over the room, and Carol calls on one woman who's waving wildly. This discussion is definitely getting the students going.

"Does the sex difference in aggression explain why men are so much more likely to be managers than women?"

"Whoa, wait a minute! You're making a lot of leaps here. First of all, you're confusing assertiveness with aggression. Assertiveness is what you want in a good manager, not aggressiveness. Aggressiveness leads to crime, to solving problems through physical means rather than talking things through."

As the class comes to an end, Carol gets even more worked up.

"You are here to study the sex distribution of adults across occupations. And I am here to tell you that sex differences in children, even significant ones, have little to do with that distribution. Occupational characteristics are not genetic, and except for purely biological characteristics, like the ability to lactate, human beings' behavior need not be limited by sex differences in childhood. If you want to change the occupational structure, you need to change society's power structure. That's where the answers lie."

Carol's perspective is liberating for both me and the students, and combined with the idea that we will spend our time looking not only at what *is* but what *could be*, my course becomes an interdisciplinary adventure in figuring out what new policies on the part of families, work organizations, and government are needed to change women's economic, social, and political power.

I will teach a course on women and work in one version or another for the next forty years, and indeed, at the time of this writing, I am still teaching one. I've never lost my passion for the class, and it never feels stale. The subject matter changes, the students change, and I change; every year I learn anew. But the learning curve has never again been as steep as it was that first year.

After Carol's talk, we become close friends. We're about the same age, both married, both with young children, and both trying to climb the academic ladder. Finally there is someone with whom I can strategize about combining an academic career with a demanding family life, with whom I can commiserate about how to cooperate with a husband who is unwilling to do much by way of housework or household management.

My personal life this year is far more upbeat than last. Sam is now an assistant professor rather than a resident, and while he's busy setting up his lab and applying for grants, he is no longer on call in the evening or at night. We purchase a subscription to the San Francisco Opera, host some dinner parties, and feel our social drought is over. We also have time for family activities and spend weekends pedaling around campus with the kids on the backs of our bikes, digging sand castles and dodging waves at Half Moon Bay, or pondering the vast size of the elephants at the San Francisco Zoo.

In addition, I have two new friends, Carol Rudoff and Patrice Crever, whose sons are in Jason's class at nursery school and who have bailed me out several times when Margie's had a family emergency. Years later, when the media touts the so-called mommy wars, delighting in the animosity their informants report between mothers who are employed and those who stay home, I recall that my experience was opposite. Neither Carol nor Patrice was employed, but they took every opportunity to show their support for me.

Like my Mom, I'm an anomaly. I know very few mothers who also have jobs. But perhaps because I watched Mom work *and* parent for so many years, the role is beginning to feel familiar. Although I felt "abnormal" at the University of Maryland when I returned to work after Liz's birth, I no longer feel strange about my dual roles. Yet I have plenty of difficulty combining them.

❖

Just as I begin teaching my new course at Berkeley, I get a phone call from a neighbor who would like Liz to join a playgroup she is forming. I like the idea of Liz's joining a playgroup. She's too young for nursery school (no school will take her until she's three), and I think it would be great for her to have some playmates. So I invite the other moms and their children over, and while Margie feeds four toddlers peanut butter and jelly sandwiches in the kitchen, I sit outside with my neighbors, attempting to ease the afternoon heat with some iced lemonade.

When the conversation turns to the proposed playgroup, one of the moms explains that they're thinking of twice-weekly meetings, two hours for each session, rotating among the four kids' homes. That all seems fine,

I say, but since I work, Margie would need to entertain the kids when they play at my house.

"Oh, no, no. That wouldn't work at all," they reply. "We want this playgroup for the children's *intellectual* stimulation, and we're counting on *you* to be there when the kids come to your house."

My heart sinks. What am I going to do with four two-year-olds for two hours twice a month? And how am I going to rearrange my schedule to fit this in? As it is, I barely have time to sleep. In return for allowing me to teach a seminar on women and work, George Break has asked me to teach a large lecture course on the economics of health, education, and welfare. I love teaching that course. It satisfies my desire, born in Pine Lake, to be an actress or a singer. I thoroughly enjoy being on a large stage, pacing about and waving my arms as I make my points. But now I have two new preparations in the same quarter with no store of lecture notes for either. How am I going to find time to be part of a playgroup for two-year-olds?

I talk to Sam, and he says he thinks the whole thing is ridiculous. I should just decline the invitation. I think it's ridiculous, too, but I want to be a good mom and I want Liz to have some friends, so I agree to their terms.

A couple of weeks later, when it's my turn to host, one girl and two boys appear quietly at our door, their moms close behind. But as soon as the moms leave, one of the boys starts to howl. I try to comfort him, but Liz is far more successful. She takes him to Jason's room, and the moment he begins assembling Jason's Lego, he stops squalling. The other little boy likes the Lego, too. I know Jason won't mind their playing with his toys, but neither of the girls has the slightest interest in Lego. They're in Liz's room, playing with her stuffed animals. Will it be OK with the other moms when they find out the boys and girls played separately? Do the other mothers have Lego in mind when they think of intellectual stimulation?

Unfortunately, I have little time to contemplate these momentous questions. The two boys are now clawing at each other over the Lego, and their piercing screams reverberate through the house. I break up their fight and decide we should all have milk and graham crackers. Between their munches, I attempt to make conversation, but I quickly learn that Liz is the only one of the four who can talk. The others can say a few words, but they can't yet form sentences. I chuckle to myself. This could work in my favor. None of these children can report anything back to their mothers. Unless *I* tell them, none of the moms will know about either the sex segregation or the cognitive quality of any of the morning's activities.

Liz sees her new friends' developmental stage as advantageous, too. As the only one who can speak, she delivers animated soliloquys about her stuffed animals, *Sesame Street*, what she had for breakfast, her hopes and dreams—whatever. Not until she has a young child of her own will she have such rapt attention paid to her every word.

For the playgroup's next session, I ask Margie to help me, and she and I supervise an art project that I discover in a parenting magazine at the pediatrician's. I buy colored paper, and Margie and I cut it into the prescribed patterns. Then the kids glue the pieces into three-dimensional objects—pumpkins, witches, ghosts, etc. What a mess. Glue all over the table and chairs. Glue all over the floor. Glue matting the kids' hair. Margie finds all of this hilarious and is good-natured about cleaning things up, but it's the least favorite part of my week. I put *Swan Lake* on the record player and tell the kids to dance while I put my feet up and have a cup of tea. Without a doubt, this is the hardest job in the world, yet childcare workers are paid the same as parking lot attendants.

After several months of these sessions, my patience runs out and I make a deal with Liz. She can have swim lessons instead of playgroup. She's happy. Now that the other children are talking and her days of nonstop monologues are over, she doesn't enjoy playgroup nearly as much as before. But I'm even happier, having regained the equivalent of a half workday every month. And I'm no longer searching parenting magazines for art projects!

❖

At Rosh Hashanah, Sam and I attend Hillel services on campus, and they are unlike any services we've been to. We gather in a shabby room at the Old Union, with no more than twenty or so in attendance. We sit on couches with the stuffing sticking out and use prayer books on the verge of crumbling. But the service is inspiring. Men and women sit together, and because there is no organ or choir, we all sing. For the first time ever, I see women read from the Torah. Rabbi Familant gives a sermon on caring for other people that is scholarly but heartfelt. On Yom Kippur morning, we return and enjoy the service again, but I am shocked at how few people are there. Hillel services at Cornell were at least five times the size. For the first time, I realize how very small Stanford's Jewish community is.

❖

One of the economics doctoral students in my women and work class, Marilyn Power, asks if I will be on her doctoral dissertation committee. She wants to write her thesis on the economics of housework, and she sees from our course that I would be amenable to her using sociological and psychological ideas to illuminate the economics. My discussions with Sam have led me to understand how central the matter of housework is to women's success (or lack thereof) at work, and as I think back to Tante Annie and all the ways in which her labor substituted for Mom's and Dad's, I realize that Marilyn's interdisciplinary study of housework will make a contribution to both economics and feminist scholarship.

Once I accept Marilyn's invitation to be one of her advisers, she gets the necessary permission from the department to have a (mere) lecturer on her committee, and I have my very first doctoral student. I'm thrilled. Serving on doctoral committees and helping to mold students' research is what faculty at research universities do!

Adding to this upswing, some of my colleagues now drop into my office to talk, and a few invite me to lunch. Even better, the economics department announces that it will conduct a national search for an assistant professor in labor economics, the position that I currently hold as a lecturer, and Lloyd encourages me to apply. When I tell him about my conversation with Break a year earlier in which Break told me he could never sell my candidacy as an assistant professor to the department, Lloyd shrugs.

"If you don't apply, he *certainly* can't sell it."

So I apply.

Shortly thereafter, I get a phone call asking me to sit on a panel on labor unions at the annual meetings of the American Economic Association (AEA) in New Orleans in late December. My caller says Lloyd suggested my name.

That evening, I talk with Sam. He's excited for me and thinks I should go to the meetings and discuss the paper.

"You'll be a much stronger candidate for that assistant professor job if you show up at the various sessions and then have dinner with people from the department so they can get to know you. Don't worry. I'll take care of the kids."

I make arrangements to go, but before I leave, I prepare three dinners for three nights and put them in the freezer. "Taking care of the kids" doesn't include cooking their meals.

❖

I've never been to New Orleans before. I love walking through the French Quarter, browsing the antique shops in the late afternoon, and listening to jazz through the clubs' open doors at night. But most of all I love the food, especially the desserts. And Sam is right: dinners with Berkeley colleagues prove useful.

I attend several of the sessions in labor economics and find them modestly interesting but rather dry; contrary to my experience at MIT, I see that few economists are riveting presenters. Fortunately, the papers at the session where I am a discussant are somewhat more thought-provoking. The following May, in the published *Papers and Proceedings* of the meeting, my discussion appears in print. It's my first publication, and I keep it displayed prominently on my office desk.

But the most memorable part of the meetings is a session titled "What Economic Equality for Women Requires"—organized and chaired by Barbara Bergmann, my former colleague at Maryland—where I learn that a caucus will meet later that day to draft resolutions on women economists to present to the AEA's business meeting. The caucus is led by Marianne Hill, Peggy Howard, and Laurie Nisonoff, doctoral students at Yale; and Francine Blau and Paddy Quick, doctoral students at Harvard. They met through the women's caucus of the Union for Radical Political Economics (URPE), and have done considerable ground work in advance of the New Orleans event, including Paddy meeting with John Kenneth Galbraith, incoming president of the AEA, and Marianne, Peggy, and Laurie meeting with Guy Orcutt, a member of the AEA's executive committee.

The caucus meeting is lively, with numerous graduate students (male and female), a few young women faculty, and an even fewer older women faculty, including Carolyn Shaw Bell, professor of economics at Wellesley; Barbara Bergmann; Barbara Reagan, professor of economics at Southern Methodist University; and Margaret Gordon, my colleague at Berkeley. Carolyn becomes the de facto chair and scribe. She is an impressive woman, and her voice and demeanor provide gravitas to our deliberations. She has a large yellow pad and writes energetically as we draft our proposed resolutions collectively.

I am thrilled to see this collection of women economists. I think back to my days as a doctoral student at MIT, where I was one of only two women in my class (we started with three women in the class, but one transferred to another program after the first year), and to my current situation at Berkeley, where there is only one other women economist, neither of us with tenure-track appointments.

I also recall that Elizabeth Cady Stanton worked alone to draft the Declaration of Women's Sentiments, with only Lucretia Mott for support, and that Stanton and Mott had no organized body to which they could present their grievances and proposals. In contrast, our effort in New Orleans is astonishingly collaborative, and if the AEA membership agrees, we will have an already existing association (the AEA) through which to achieve our goals.

The resolutions, which Carolyn later presents to the AEA business meeting, call on the AEA to "redress the low representation of women in the economics profession" and "adopt a positive program to eliminate sex discrimination among economists." They specifically prohibit discrimination against women students and women applying for positions as faculty members or for other jobs, and they call for the open posting of job opportunities and the creation of part-time jobs open to women and men. They also call for the association to offer childcare at the annual meetings—not to pay for it, but to make sure it's available.

Most important, the resolutions propose the establishment of a Committee on the Status of Women in the Economics Profession (CSWEP) "numbering at least eight persons, to be appointed by the President of the Association for a term of three years" to monitor compliance with the resolutions. That committee is to report to the AEA annually, and if it learns of discrimination, it is to provide information so that the association can "present, as *amicus curiae,* in any complaint, remedial action, or suit."

"What makes you think the members will vote for this?" I ask the leaders of the caucus. "The economists I know might not exactly be inclined toward these ideas."

"We think Galbraith will carry the day. That's why we want to bring this up this year, while Galbraith is president."

But the caucus does not rely solely on him. It also does an incredible job of recruiting progressive economists of both genders from URPE to come to the business meeting, and when I arrive at that meeting, the large room is packed. There are several speeches opposing the resolution, but two highly regarded economists, Andrew Brimmer and Robert Eisner, speak in favor, and when Galbraith calls for a vote, the ayes have it.

A few weeks later, I get a call from Carolyn Shaw Bell. Galbraith has asked her to chair the new committee. I met Carolyn only briefly at the New Orleans meeting, but she says she enjoyed talking with me and would like to ask Galbraith to appoint me to CSWEP. She tells me the committee will meet three or four times a year in various venues throughout the country. This seems like a big commitment. I tell her I'll have to think about it.

When I talk with Sam about it, he's not at all in favor.

"You're already complaining you don't have enough hours in the day. This is going to take you away from your work, and it's going to take you away from the kids and me. Why would you want to do it?

"Because I think it's really important. And because it will give me some colleagues in economics."

"Well, I'm not going to argue with you. But I think it's a mistake."

I think a great deal about what to do. Sam is right—my time is extremely tight. But if he would just take over some household tasks, it could be a lot less tight. I'm angry with him, but I don't want to bring up the issue of his share of the housework yet again. It just seems so fruitless. I don't want to go against his wishes, but I really want to join this committee. Back and forth I consider, again and again. Eventually, I decide to join. I'll just have to sleep less, I figure, and hope I'm not straining Sam's goodwill.

But a few months later, when CSWEP meets at Galbraith's home in Cambridge, I'm sure I've made the right decision. The more senior committee members—Walter Adams, Carolyn Shaw Bell, Kenneth Boulding, Barbara Reagan, and Phyllis Wallace—become mentors, and the other junior members—Francine Blau, Martha Blaxall, and Collette Moser—become friends.

And from my perspective more than forty years later, I am proud to have served. Although I eventually came to believe that CSWEP's goals are too moderate, that what economics needs is not simply more women economists but major reform in the discipline's thinking, I am gratified to have been part of the vanguard effort to treat women economists with fairness and respect.

❖

Not long after my first CSWEP meeting, I get another call. Sam picks it up while I'm bathing the kids.

"The dean of Stanford's business school is on the phone. He wants to talk to you."

"Yeah, right—and after that, I need to return that call from President Nixon."

Sam smiles. "No, really, it's the dean. Go ahead. I'll finish the kids' bath."

Unaware of the import of the moment, Jason and Liz continue their whoops and shouts, gleefully spraying each other as I dry my hands and go to the phone.

Dean Miller has a booming, staccato voice. Beyond friendly, it's positively ebullient.

"Myra Strober," he says. "I have your résumé here. Very impressive. We want to talk to you. Can you come in next week to meet with Lee Bach and some of the other folks in the economics group? We're looking to hire a new junior person."

I'm stunned, amazed that my voice still works as I arrange a time for an interview.

I'm pretty sure I know how Miller got my résumé. A few months earlier, as I waited at the playground to pick up Jason from nursery school, I'd met Ruth Franklin, the mom of one of the boys in Jason's class, and we chatted as our sons ran about.

"How come I've never met you before?" she asks.

"Well, I'm not the one who usually picks Jason up. I teach at Berkeley, and I'm not usually here at noon."

She asks why I'm teaching at Berkeley rather than Stanford, and I explain that my thesis adviser had some connections at the former and none at the latter. She says she understands. Her husband is on the faculty at Stanford's law school.

"Send me your vitae," she says. "I know Rita Ricardo Campbell—we're both in the Palo Alto Radcliffe Club—and I know that Rita knows Arjay Miller. I'll give her your vitae and see if she'll pass it on to him."

Rita is herself a PhD economist. She's never been able to get a faculty position at Stanford, but she works as a senior researcher at the Hoover Institution, where her husband, Glen Campbell, is the director, and it's through Glen that she knows Arjay. Ruth and Rita are no-nonsense people, not particularly emotional, and often considered "hard-boiled." Few might have predicted that either would go out of her way to help me get an interview at Stanford. But sisterhood is the watchword in the early '70s, especially in California, and these women, both slightly older than I, whose careers suffered from the nepotism and sexism of the '50s and '60s, take the opportunity to further mine.

Feminism is also part of the reason why the Stanford Graduate School of Business (GSB) is interested in hiring a woman. In its almost fifty-year history, it's never had a woman on its faculty. But the investigation by the Department of Labor in response to the Women's Equity Action League complaint of sex discrimination at Berkeley has caused Stanford to rethink its stance on women faculty.

A week or so after Arjay's call, I have an interview. I meet Lee Bach, the head of the economics group, and several other economists, as well as Arjay himself. They don't ask me to do a job talk, but they do ask numerous questions about my teaching and seem especially interested in the course I'm teaching on women and work. Like Lloyd Ulman, they're astonished that there is enough material for a whole course.

The day is enjoyable, particularly my meeting with Arjay. He is the former CEO of the Ford Motor Company, and we have a lively discussion about labor relations in the auto industry. Much to my surprise, his view is that the United Auto Workers (UAW) is in fact a help to the auto industry on the people side of its operations.

A few weeks later, I get an offer to come to the GSB as an assistant professor. At about the same time, I receive an assistant professor offer from Berkeley. George Break and Lloyd Ulman tell me that as members of the department have come to know me and reviewed my doctoral dissertation and teaching evaluations, they have decided that I am just the right person to fill their labor economics position. I'm pleased about their change of heart, but I suspect that the Labor Department investigation has as much to do with their offer as my own credentials.

I would really prefer to teach in an economics department than a business school, but what tips the scales toward Stanford is the fact that it's only ten minutes from my house, so I can save almost a whole day each week by not commuting. I accept the GSB's offer.

❖

The summer provides a welcome rest from commuting, and my parents and Sam's each visit us for a few weeks. Jason celebrates his fifth birthday and looks forward to starting kindergarten in the fall, and Liz will begin nursery school then. We take advantage of the summer weather to do some entertaining on our deck for other friends who have young children, and in the evenings we host dinner parties for Sam's new colleagues at the medical school and their wives.

I spend my days back at Jackson Library, starting a research project on the economics of childcare. I want to understand why there is such a dearth of affordable, high-quality group childcare, and I carefully review the mass of congressional hearings in connection with the Comprehensive Child Development Act of 1971.

One day at Jackson I run into an economic historian from MIT who is spending the summer at Stanford. I never had a class with him, but because I was one of only two women in my cohort, the entire MIT economics faculty knows me.

"Myra, what are you doing here? Are you getting another PhD?"

At first I think he's joking. But then I see he's genuinely perplexed.

"Why would I be getting another PhD? I'm going to start teaching at the GSB in the fall. I'm going to be an assistant professor here."

"You are? Oh, I see. I mean, that's great. Yeah. Great. Well, good luck."

That's my introduction to the problems I'm about to face. MIT faculty were extremely supportive of me—as long as I was a student. But the idea that I'm now a faculty member at one of the top-ranked business schools in the country is another matter entirely.

7

Ninety Men and Me, 1972–1974

A few weeks before I start teaching at the GSB, I get a call from Stanford's Office of Public Affairs. They would like me to participate in a press conference in San Francisco with two other new women assistant professors at the university—Barbara Babcock, the first woman ever to hold a faculty position at the law school, and Lili Young, a new faculty member in the School of Engineering.

"We want to show off our women," my caller says, "show the whole world that Stanford has done the right thing."

I ask Barbara what she thinks we should wear to this press briefing.

"We can wear whatever we want," she says. "*We* are the dress code."

She's right. A study the year before found that women make up slightly less than 5 percent of all tenure-track faculty at Stanford, and only 2 percent of all full professors. Of almost a thousand tenure-track faculty, only forty-seven are women and only nine are women full professors.

At the GSB, I learn that I will have some female faculty company. They've hired a newly minted PhD in social psychology, Francine Gordon, who also comes from Brooklyn and went to Hudde Junior High School and Midwood High, although several years later than I. We don't know it then, but the experiences Francine and I are about to have for the next five years will bond us for life. Together, she and I are slightly more than 2 percent of the business school faculty—ninety men and us. The percentage of women students at the GSB is even lower. Since the school was founded, in 1925, there have never more than five women MBA candidates in a class of about three hundred.

A year ago, three women in the first-year MBA class made a slide show titled "What's a Nice Girl Like You Doing in a Place Like This?" Now they show Francine and me their slides, which portray vividly the difficulties of living in a virtually all-male world.

Negative comments from classmates: "You really shouldn't be here. You're taking the seat of a man who might need this education to support a family."

And from job recruiters: "Are you on the pill? Do you plan to have children?"

They also describe more informal discrimination, such as the extra scrutiny from faculty and classmates when they speak up in class.

But the slide show is not merely about problems. It also shows the opportunities for women in the business field and urges women who are considering a business career to apply to the GSB and help change its male culture. And, in fact, the GSB is quite interested in recruiting more female students. Members of its Advisory Board, high-ranking officers of major corporations, tell Arjay they are under pressure from the federal government to hire women managers but can't find any. It's time for the GSB to begin training women, they say.

In 1972, the GSB does begin recruiting women, and Francine and I are part of their effort. But we recruit for only one year, because as soon as word gets out that the GSB welcomes applications from women, women begin to apply on their own, and throughout the 1970s, the percentage of female students increases.

The GSB is not alone in increasing its percentage of women students. In 1971, among the nine leading graduate schools of business, women make up less than 8 percent of total enrollment; but by 1975, women account for between 13 and 33 percent of MBA candidates in these schools, a phenomenal explosion in such a short time.

A few weeks after I join the faculty, Lee Bach asks me to give a seminar on my research. This is a critical invitation. Because I was not asked give a job talk when I was interviewed for my position, I've never really met most of my economics colleagues at the GSB, and they've never heard me speak. I want to make a good impression. In fact, I want to do more than that—I want to wow them, show them that they've hired a really superb thinker.

Since I've spent the whole summer working on the economics of childcare, I decide to speak on that. I know childcare is one of the most controversial subjects of the day, but I feel the topic gives me an opportunity to convey innovative thinking and show my ability to think like an economist. I work on the talk for several days, carefully considering each word. The first part explains why the childcare market is not working well, and the second presents an economic argument in favor of government subsidization. The talk feels solid, and I rehearse it over and over. On the appointed day, I dress carefully—my most conservative summer suit with high heels and stockings—and look forward to what I expect will be an interesting exchange of views.

I introduce my lecture by saying I intend to argue that good childcare produces numerous external benefits (benefits beyond those accruing to those who receive the service) and that because of those external benefits, there is a powerful economic case for the government to subsidize childcare, much in the way it subsidizes education. But I never get past the first three minutes of what I've prepared. The set-up is akin to a Greek tragedy in which the protagonist is unaware that her doom has been sealed before the play even begins.

My colleagues, fifteen conservative white male professors of economics and finance, are aghast at my ideas and begin sputtering in unison. They have the same view as President Nixon, who, less than a year earlier, vetoed a bill that would have provided federal funding for a comprehensive childcare system. Nixon's reasoning? Such a system would "weaken the family."

My argument is outrageous, my colleagues proclaim, and they spend the next fifty minutes cataloging the evils of government intervention in general and intervention in childcare in particular. Bach, who is ostensibly chairing the seminar, never intervenes to restore order, and I'm too inexperienced and cowed to do it myself. Finally, blessedly, it's 1 p.m., and the men who were supposed to be my audience leave.

I knew that many of my economist colleagues were conservative, but I didn't think I would be the only progressive in the room, or at least the only one speaking up. Now I see that I'm a double minority at the school—not only the first woman economist, but also the first liberal economist. I'm alarmed and walk back to my office trembling, as I did after my first interview with George Break. Now what? How can I possibly succeed in this place?

I'm not the only one who recognizes that the seminar was a disaster, and in the days following, three of my colleagues come individually to my office to advise me solicitously to stop doing work on topics such as women's employment or childcare.

"Wait till you get tenure to do that kind of work," each suggests. "Once you get tenure, you can do whatever the hell you want. But for now, do some mainstream stuff."

I don't follow their recommendation. I can't. I'm fired up about the economics of childcare, about the effects of women's earnings on their family's spending patterns, about the value of unpaid labor in the home—and, most of all, about the fact that some occupations are predominantly female, while others, the more lucrative ones, are predominantly male.

You know, I think to myself, *you people are not paying me enough to sell my soul.* If I'm not going to be able to do research on the questions I care about, I'm going to get a better-paying job. I'll go work for Wells Fargo or Bank of America. If I'm going to stay in academia, I'm going to keep working on women's issues! I make a pact with myself. No more trembling. I'm in charge of my life and my career. If I don't like it here, I can leave.

The GSB has a lively social scene and an active faculty wives group. Every year, the school publishes an attractive pamphlet listing the names and addresses of faculty and their wives, and several times a year there are wives' events. Now that Francine and I are on the faculty, our husbands' names are listed in the pamphlet, and the wives ask them to join their group. Sam says he truly has no time for such events and would feel out of place at teas, knitting circles, charity events, and so on. Francine's husband replies that he is game, but, somehow or other, his invitation is withdrawn—just another manifestation of the awkwardness we all feel.

Sam and I are invited to numerous dinner parties at my colleagues' homes, where sex segregation is prominent both before and after the meal. My colleagues are interested in talking to Sam and learning about his work, and their wives are interested in talking to me. Some of them see me as a curiosity, but many are supportive and wish me well. At first, these parties present an uncomfortable quandary. I enjoy talking to my colleagues' wives, and I don't want to insult them by ignoring them, but I also don't want to squander the opportunity for my colleagues to get to know me informally. Eventually, I learn to play it both ways: spending time with the women at the outset, then walking over to join the men. If

Francine is present, she does this as well, but no other woman does, and not a single man "crosses over" to be with the women.

It's hard for me to square my colleagues' friendliness to me at social events with their hostility toward my work. I talk with Sam about it, and his answer is straightforward: they like me as a person, but they're really not interested in having me as a colleague. I'm not deterred. I love my work and expect that someday, my colleagues will see its worth. I only hope that day comes before they have to vote on me for tenure and promotion. Sam wonders whether all my stress at the GSB is worth it, and each week, when I have new tales of some difficulty, he asks if I'm sure I want to stay. But I never think of quitting. I'm committed to entering their club, to breaking down the male monopoly. I know I've got a Herculean challenge, but I'm not giving up.

From their names, I know that several of my colleagues are Jewish, but I learn that they're "closet Jews." When Sam and I go to Rosh Hashanah and Yom Kippur services at Stanford Hillel, none of them is there. Nor do they participate in any of the Jewish community's fundraising efforts, and when I raise matters of interest to the Jewish community with them or with their wives, they make it very clear that they are not interested.

Sam's and my experiences with his medical school colleagues and their wives are quite different; those who are Jewish take pride in their heritage and participate in Jewish events. All in all, socializing with Sam's colleagues and their wives is much easier. The sex segregation at dinner parties is the same, but in this context Sam and I are in our traditional roles, and there's no need for either of us to "cross over." I may be a pioneer at work, but my social life is conventional, and I'm grateful for that. Pioneering in one realm is enough for me. Eventually, we begin to make friends with couples where the husband and wife are both faculty members at the university, but that doesn't happen for several years, after more women faculty are hired.

Alice's experience of social life is quite different from mine. Because she's married to a man in her own field, all their friends are economists, sociologists, or historians, and many of them are married to scholars in the same or adjacent fields. As a result, Alice is never "just a wife" in social settings. She's an integral part of a radical intellectual group.

Nonetheless, she has an even harder time starting her career than I do. Not only does she encounter sex discrimination, but because her degree is from the London School of Economics, she has fewer former professors who are well connected in the American academic network. When she returns to the United States with her doctorate, she, too, becomes a lecturer at the University of California—first at UCLA, then at Irvine. It's not until the late 1970s that she receives an offer to become an assistant professor at Barnard College.

Although we sympathize with one another about breaking into the economics profession, our relationship remains distant. Shortly after her thesis is published as a book, she and Jon are in a serious motorcycle accident in Holland. They both have broken bones, and Alice needs reconstructive face surgery. Mom and Dad want to go to Holland to see her, as do I, but she doesn't want any of us to come. Fortunately, she receives excellent medical care, but I feel even further estranged from her. I wish she would let me show that I care about her. I love her, but the feeling doesn't seem to be reciprocated.

Before Francine and I joined the heretofore all-male GSB faculty, they held their faculty retreats at the Family Farm in Portola Valley, a beautiful site affiliated with the all-male Family Club, similar to the more famous Bohemian Club. Now the retreat venue will have to be moved, and many of our colleagues are unhappy. Some complain only to each other, and their grumbling stops midsentence when Francine or I walk into the faculty lounge. But others gripe directly to us.

"I suppose you realize you've managed to ruin our faculty retreat."

"Maybe we could put you in big burlap bags and smuggle you in?"

"Maybe we could dress you as men for the day?"

Francine and I take Arjay aside and ask how he thinks we should respond to these bizarre suggestions.

"They're a bunch of big babies," he tells us. "Pay them no mind. And don't worry. We can't get you into the Farm this year, but I'm working on it for next year."

One year, the annual faculty retreat is actually canceled because there is so much grumbling about not being able to go to the Family Farm. By the time Arjay's efforts are successful and the retreat returns to the Family Farm, Francine is no longer at the GSB. Joanne Martin, also a social psychologist, has been hired to replace her, and it is Joanne and I who finally enter the beautifully landscaped and impressively built hallowed male ground in Portola Valley. Arjay has seen to it that one of the bathrooms—with a small toilet off the kitchen and a temporary "women" sign scribbled on the door—has been "reserved" for Joanne and me, and once again I have the same strange feeling of being an honorary man that I had my first year at MIT.

"Overage fraternity boys still struggling through adolescence," I whisper to Joanne as we look through glass cases filled with photos of grown men dressed in costumes, including women's clothes, for various plays. But while we laugh at the snapshots, we realize that they testify all too seriously to the exclusion of women and the restrictions on women's access to critical informal networks. They forcefully reinforce my sense of being "other," an outsider.

As a result of Stanford's press conference for new women faculty, there are articles about me in both the *Stanford Daily* and the *Palo Alto Times*. Not only does the GSB have women faculty members for the first time, they say, but imagine this: there's an economist there doing research on women!

One woman who reads these articles is undergraduate Cynthia Davis, and a couple of months later, she comes to see me during my office hours. Cindy has been taking a course called Cross-Cultural Perspectives with two new faculty in anthropology, Jane Collier and Shelly Rosaldo, and she and some of the other women in that class have been meeting at the newly opened Women's Center to think about how to connect faculty at Stanford who are interested in women's issues, and, more generally, how to bring ideas related to women to the forefront of campus discussion.

Cindy is refined and soft-spoken, but decisive about her mission: "We don't want to create a place for consciousness-raising," she says. "We already have that at the Women's Center. We want to create a research center, maybe something like the Radcliffe Institute at Radcliffe College."

I have heard of the Radcliffe Institute, started in the early 1960s by Radcliffe's dynamo president, Mary Bunting, and I know that it is not an institute for research on women.

"Oh, well, then *not* like the Radcliffe Institute," Cindy says. "We don't really care. We want an institute for research on women."

"That's a terrific idea, Cindy. What can I do to help?"

"We need faculty members to start it. Can you help start it?"

I laugh as the memory of the recent debacle at my childcare seminar comes to mind, and I think about what my economist colleagues might say if they learned I was trying to start a research institute for women.

"What's so funny?"

"I'll tell you: assistant professors don't start research centers. You need senior faculty for that. I support you 100 percent, but I have to support you from the sidelines."

A few months later, when winter quarter begins, I start teaching my course on women and work, and although it's a GSB course, there are only a handful of GSB students interested in enrolling, so I open it up to Stanford undergraduates and graduate students in other programs. Two of my students, Beth Garfield and Susan Heck, have the same idea as Cindy: each wants to start a center for research on women at Stanford.

Beth is a junior, planning to run for student-body president in the spring and to go to law school when she graduates, and Susan is a first-year doctoral student at the School of Education (SUSE). Both are outspoken and funny. Beth has an infectious laugh and a mass of curly black hair that surrounds her with vibrant energy. Susan is tall, blond, and sophisticated. They don't know each other, but they meet in my class and I tell them of their mutual interest in starting a center. I also put them in touch with Cindy, and a few weeks later, the four of us meet in my office.

I reiterate that junior faculty don't start research centers and encourage them to brainstorm about senior faculty they know who might be helpful. Susan says she'll talk to organizations theorist James March and sociologist Elizabeth Cohen, both in SUSE. Cindy says she'll try to get an appointment with psychologist Eleanor Maccoby, and Beth agrees to set up a meeting with Leah Kaplan, dean of women, whom she knows from her work in student government. Beth is currently assembling her campaign materials for the presidential election happening in a few weeks, and she is putting into her platform the idea of starting an institute for women's studies to establish fellowships, seminars, and women-related courses within departments.

A few weeks later, the three students and I meet with the four senior faculty and staff the students have corralled, and in the course of the meeting, Eleanor and Jim agree to be cochairs of a planning committee including all those at the meeting. They also agree to send a joint letter to the Ford Foundation requesting a small planning grant of $25,000.

When we discuss a name for our organization, Cindy reports that several students want us to be called the Stanford Center for Research and Education of Women, or SCREW. We laugh and quickly veto that idea. But we have a long and serious discussion of the name Beth has used in her campaign literature the Institute for Women's Studies. Eleanor argues persuasively that we should *not* use "women's studies" in our name, that the women's studies programs that have recently opened in several colleges and universities across the country are *teaching* programs. She thinks Stanford's comparative advantage is in research, and that our name should make clear our emphasis on developing new knowledge.

The majority agrees about "women's studies." But should we call ourselves an "institute"? Most of us feel that given our small numbers and absence of funding, the term is too grandiose. "Center" seems more comfortable. So we name ourselves the Center for Research on Women. None of us is excited about the acronym, CROW, but it seems far better than SCREW.

The first activity of our unofficial center is the spring 1973 Thursday noon lecture series, which I organize. The topics are diverse, reflecting some of the key research issues of the time. Cindy designs a poster with a logo and the names and affiliations of the speakers and posts it all over campus. The audience is huge—a few students, a few faculty, numerous staff members (mostly secretaries), and many women from the community—and it overflows the lecture room I have reserved at the GSB.

Eleanor Maccoby leads off with a talk on sex differences to an audience seemingly starved for her information. The second lecture, by law professor Barbara Babcock, is titled "The Current Struggle for Sex-Role Equality," and the audience is even larger. I'm afraid that going beyond the legal capacity of the classroom will attract the attention of the university fire marshal, and that my colleagues will soon have additional grounds for complaints about me. But, fortunately, the fire marshal is none the wiser.

The third lecture is a debate between Anne Miner, Stanford's newly appointed affirmative action officer, and Sidney Hook, an eminent philosopher who has become quite conservative and is in residence at the

Hoover Institution. In contrast with my unsuccessful attempt to have a reasoned discussion on the economics of childcare at the GSB, Miner and Hook have a lively but quite civil debate on the pros and cons of affirmative action, with the audience asking questions of both presenters, and I'm proud of our nascent organization's furtherance of academic freedom.

The fourth lecture is by Jean Lipman-Blumen, a sociologist who is a research director at the National Institute of Education. She talks about the effects of crisis on women's roles, particularly the effect of World War II in catapulting women to economic importance. And the final lecture of the series is by Professor Bridget O'Laughlin, a Stanford anthropologist who discusses the role of women in systems of bridewealth exchange in Africa. She teaches us that whereas in many Western societies, the bride's family provides a dowry to the groom, in some African societies the situation is reversed, and it is the groom who pays the bride's family for the privilege of marrying their daughter.

The field of women's studies is being born. There's no balkanization yet. Everybody is interested in everything—history, psychology, philosophy, anthropology, even economics. The lectures are energizing, and Beth agrees to organize a similar series the following year.

At the same time that I'm working to start a center, my own research agenda is moving forward. In early 1973, my first published article, based on my doctoral thesis, comes out in the journal *Industrial Relations*. I'm also writing up my ideas on the economics of childcare for presentation at a conference at Columbia, then publication in a book.

In addition, I'm beginning an empirical research project on differences in expenditure patterns between husband-wife families where only the husband is employed versus husband-wife families with two earners. I ultimately present this work at the American Economic Association's meeting, and it is published in the *American Economic Review*. My analyses show that if we hold total family income constant, those families whose income comes from only one earner save more (spend less) than those who need two earners to earn that same level of income. This is because additional costs are accrued by the second earner—particularly for transportation, clothing, and childcare. Also, holding total family income constant, the one-earner families have higher assets than the two-earner families, probably because they have been able to save more for some period of time. In other words, despite the equality in their income levels, families with two earners are economically less well off than families who have only one earner.

In the course of doing this research, I become quite friendly with two junior colleagues at the GSB, both of whom are interested in family expenditure patterns: assistant professor of economics Bill Dunkelberg and assistant professor of marketing Chuck Weinberg. Their offices are down the corridor from mine, and we enjoy the opportunity to visit back and forth.

Although my research is going well, my teaching is not. I have five years of university teaching experience, and my teaching ratings have always been excellent, but now, in my spring quarter class in macroeconomics, I face new challenges. At the very first meeting, as I walk in to begin teaching, one particularly tall male student gets up from his seat, walks to the door, and loudly proclaims: "I'm not paying this kind of tuition to take an important required course from the likes of you!"

Two other men follow him out. I'm teaching two sections of the course, and senior men of considerable reputation are teaching the other three. The students' desire to switch professors stems not only from my sex, but also from their perceptions of my young age and relative inexperience.

"Anybody else?" I ask gamely.

No one else leaves.

But my troubles are not over. Although I don't ever face quite that degree of rudeness again, I get many hostile and anti-intellectual comments. One day, while I'm teaching several different theories of interest rate determination, one student calls out:

"I don't want to hear all these theories. I'm here for the answers. Which of these theories is right?"

"They all have different kinds of empirical evidence on their side. At the moment, there is no one right answer."

"Is it that there's no one right answer, or is it that you just don't *know* the right answer?"

"Look, why don't you go to the library and read up on these theories? You'll see for yourself there's no one right answer."

"The whole point of being in this class is so I don't have to go to the library. I'm paying all this tuition so I can get the answers from you."

"Well then, pipe down so I can continue."

My teaching ratings for this course are abysmal. When I confide this to one of my colleagues, a social psychologist, he suggests that the problem lies in how I handle students' comments.

"You're too nice. You need to be nasty with them."

"But I don't know how to be nasty. That's not my style."

"I know. And that's the problem. They'll like you much better and give you much higher ratings if you're nasty. If you want, I'll give you lessons on how to be nasty. We've got nine months before you have to teach that course again. Plenty of time for tutoring you on nastiness."

So I "enroll" in private sessions on becoming meaner, and next time I teach the class, anytime a student asks a question, I put him down. For example: "That's just a stupid question. I think you can figure the answer out for yourself if you put your small mind to it."

My teaching ratings go way up, but I hate behaving that way. Grandpa's philosophy that there is a piece of God inside every human being is a core value for me. Seeking to hurt people by disparaging their ideas is simply against my nature.

When I teach the class the third time in my old way, taking each question seriously and doing my best to answer it, down go my ratings. But by then I'm beyond caring, and the fourth time I teach the course, I simply ignore hostile comments and move on, calling on other students or continuing my lecture. My ratings that year are higher than they were my first year, but never again as high as in my quarter of purposeful spite.

The end of my first year at the GSB is hectic. I'm grading 120 macroeconomics exams, trying to move CROW forward, starting new research projects, and traveling to meetings of CSWEP. And the movie on my home-front screen is also in fast-forward. In June 1973, as soon as spring quarter is finished, Sam and I move.

The house in Ladera that we've lived in for three years has become too small as the kids have grown, and we've bought a larger house on the Stanford campus. Unfortunately, both of us seriously underestimate the time it will take to fix up and decorate our new home, and neither of us wants to spend the summer doing it. Sam wants to concentrate on his lab experiments and write grant proposals so he can enlarge the scope of his work, and I want to finish several research projects and write up the results. My three-year review in the coming year will be looking at completed work.

The summer's strains come on top of an enormous amount of already existing stress. Not only have I been struggling with rude and dissatisfied students and hostile colleagues, but Sam has also been working extremely hard, seeing patients at his clinic, setting up his research projects, and continually applying for grants. One month a year, he's also the attending physician on the general medical service.

The stress pot boils over when our move coincides with my parents' move from New York to Palo Alto. Mom has been retired for three years, and now that Dad is retiring they want to be near their grandchildren. I'm relieved that they won't face another New York winter, and that Dad will finally leave the job and the subway commute he has disliked for so many years, but the added responsibilities of helping them get resettled prove difficult.

Eventually, Mom and Dad's living ten minutes away makes my life much easier. They stay with the children when we travel, and Dad is always ready to babysit during the week, even on very short notice, which is particularly helpful if Margie is sick and can't come, or needs to leave early to take care of something for her own family. But in that summer of prodigious pressure, my parents' arrival in California adds an unwelcome burden. Sam and I are two young adults trying to jump-start extremely demanding careers, run a complicated household, and raise two children. We have no friends doing what we're trying to do, and no models of older couples that have succeeded.

My closest colleague at the GSB is Francine Gordon, and she is having even more trouble with teaching than I. This is her first year at the front of a classroom. She is seven years my junior and a year younger than the average MBA student. The deck is truly stacked against her.

Our conversations about our difficulties lead us to read the emerging sociological literature on women in management. There's not much there, but we're particularly impressed with Cynthia Fuchs Epstein's new book, *Women's Place: Options and Limits in Professional Careers*, which explains the power dynamics in organizations when women are in the minority and play roles different from those men expect women to play based on their usual cross-sex interactions. The more we read and talk, the more we think we'd like to organize a conference on women in management for male executives to be held at the GSB. As far as we know, this is the first such conference. Our thinking is that rather than viewing men as the enemy—common rhetoric among feminists—we will enlist men in our efforts to change the system. When we present our idea to Arjay, he is encouraging.

"You plan a first-rate conference, and I'll guarantee the audience. I'll get all my business buddies to come. They're all under pressure now to hire more women managers, and they don't know how to do it."

In May 1974, GSB hosts a highly successful conference on women in management. Arjay delivers on his promise, and the audience is packed with middle-aged men in suits. He's so enthusiastic about the conference that he provides corsages for all the women speakers. Cynthia is taken aback by this gesture, but Francine and I assure her that he means the flowers as tokens of esteem and would be insulted if we didn't wear them. She assents, but I realize that by working at the GSB, I make frequent compromises between my new feminist consciousness and the patriarchal habits of my male students and colleagues. I've opted for a style of gradual modification, not radical transformation. Years later, social psychologist Debra Meyerson will write a book about people like me, calling us tempered radicals: people who gain the trust of those in power in a work organization and are able to make change from within the system.

In addition to presentations by Cynthia Fuchs Epstein and David Bradford, Francine and I each give talks—she on the critical role of the senior executive in bringing women into management, and I on basic strategies for organizations interested in hiring and retaining women in management positions. After the conference, we contact several publishers about turning the proceedings into a book and wind up signing a contract with McGraw-Hill. Arjay writes the introduction, and my friend Ruth Franklin, who was instrumental in getting my résumé to Arjay in the first place, edits the contributors' chapters. Unfortunately, so little progress has taken place in bringing women into management that the book we published almost forty years ago, *Bringing Women into Management*, is still cutting-edge.

8

Forging New Doors, 1974–1981

When Mariam Chamberlain, the program officer at the Ford Foundation in charge of grants on women's issues, writes to Jim March and Eleanor Maccoby approving their request for a planning grant for CROW, and saying that she will be pleased to entertain a proposal for more substantial funding, Stanford's president and provost approve the center on an interim basis. We put together a nine-member Policy Board with Eleanor and Jim as cochairs and Elizabeth Cohen, Tom Ehrlich (dean of the law school), and me as additional faculty members. Leah Kaplan represents staff, and Susan Heck is one of three student members. Beth and Cindy are not on the board. Both are about to graduate, and Beth will go to law school at the University of Michigan in the fall. However, when Cindy decides to remain on campus after graduation and continue working with CROW, we offer her a job as our (paid!) office coordinator.

At the beginning of fall quarter, we formally launch CROW at a well-publicized reception. Eventually, there will be more than one hundred centers for research on women in the United States, but in 1974 Stanford and Wellesley College are the first two. After the reception, full of excitement, we hold our first official Policy Board meeting. But a few weeks later, when the board meets for the second time, Eleanor and Jim report that they have done nothing to move a new grant proposal along and say they wish to resign as cochairs.

"Myra, you should chair the Policy Board," Eleanor says. "You're the one with the enthusiasm for this."

It's a tough moment for me. Part of me wants to say to Eleanor what I said to the students when they first asked me to start a center: "Junior faculty don't start research centers." But part of me is so alienated at the

GSB that the thought of spending my time starting a center for research on women is really attractive.

Jim intervenes. "We can't ask Myra to head up this center unless we figure out how to get released time for her. She can't have a full teaching load, get her publications ready for a tenure review, and also start this center."

Much nodding around the table.

"Here's what I think we have to do," Jim continues. "We have to propose Myra for the Faculty Fellows Program. That will give her some course relief and starting the center can be her project for that program."

"What's the Faculty Fellows Program?" I ask, starting to get excited.

"The president and provost choose a few faculty every year that they think have the potential to be university leaders and give them course relief to get to know the university better. They meet once a month with administrators, and they also do some university-wide projects."

"That sounds amazing," I say.

"OK, Eleanor," Jim says, smiling, as we adjourn. "Let's see if we can make this happen."

They can. And they do.

When I receive President Lyman's letter asking me to become a university fellow, I reconvene the Policy Board and agree to chair it. Then we talk about how to use the $25,000 from the Ford Foundation to prepare a major grant proposal.

My first step is a trip to New York to meet with Mariam Chamberlain. I've never been to the Ford Foundation and am hugely impressed by its soaring glass building and inner courtyard. But the most remarkable part of my visit is getting to know Mariam. Already in her fifties, she is a seasoned program officer. She's an economist with a PhD from Yale, and she wants to be not only my financial benefactor but also my mentor. She suggests that I ask Ford for $100,000 and tells me exactly what I need to do at Stanford to get permanent status for the center.

My two most important tasks, she says, are to get to know Stanford's provost and to start raising money from other sources. If Stanford wants money from Ford for a center for research on women, its provost is going to have to promise Mariam that Stanford will also put money into the center. In addition, I'm going to have to show that we can get funding from foundations besides Ford. Fortunately, Mariam has a list of those other likely foundations and is happy to share it with me.

What a challenge I've taken on! I spend the six-hour cross-country flight making a gigantic to-do list—all the people I need to talk to, all the ideas I need to gather. It feels overwhelming but exhilarating.

Sam is less than enthusiastic about my new role. He (rightly) doesn't see that a reduction in my course load is going to make up for the time I'll be spending starting the center, and he's not all that excited by my feminism. He much prefers the woman he married to the one he lives with now. He comes to hear me lecture and is appalled by the applause and "right on" comments in the audience when I talk about the need for women to take their careers as seriously as men do, the need for women to be admitted to men's careers, and the need for women to have paychecks equal to those of men. Although I see myself as struggling to attain power and influence, he sees me as radical and powerful, and he's not happy with that view of me.

I'm not sure what to do about Sam's concerns. I'm on a roll. I can't turn back. I redouble my efforts to keep the house clean, cook food that he enjoys, be as sexy as I can in the evenings (hard when you're dog-tired), and be a supermom. But I'm definitely no longer a woman who jimmies locked doors with screwdrivers. I'm a woman learning to construct new doors, wide open from the start.

And, of course, Sam is no longer the man he was when he first took my breath away at the Windsor Hotel. Years of seeing very sick patients have taken their toll. He was always serious, but now he's often somber, the world's distresses directly on his shoulders.

Shortly after my visit to the Ford Foundation, I receive a message from Jing Lyman, the wife of Stanford's president. Both her husband and Leah Kaplan have filled her in on what I'm trying to do, and she wants to help. Her secretary and I make an appointment for me to visit her at the president's residence, Lou Henry Hoover House.

Hoover House reminds me a bit of Risley Hall, my freshman dorm at Cornell. Built at about the same time, both have large richly furnished rooms that invoke an Edwardian society long passed. But Jing herself, lively, enthusiastic, and exceedingly friendly, softens the house considerably. She's tall, with a warm smile, a firm handshake, and a deep voice. *A fellow alto*, I think to myself. Her four children are now grown, and she has taken the energy that used to go into raising her family and transferred it to her role as Stanford's first lady. She is passionate about the university and its intellectual, political, and administrative goings-on. She also works in the community to increase the supply of housing for low-income families.

I don't know this yet, but Jing will turn out to be one of CROW's staunchest supporters, attending almost all our events while she knits intricately patterned sweaters in striking colors. She will turn out to be a knitter of people as well, continually introducing me to one or another woman in her gigantic network.

We settle into tea with delicious little cakes as I tell her about my recent meeting with Mariam Chamberlain.

"If you need to show Ford that you can raise money, I can help you," Jing says. "Not by writing grants to foundations—I leave that to you— but by helping you get contributions from women of means who live in this community. I know a lot of them. I can introduce you and help you solicit them."

"That sounds terrific. How do we do this?"

"I'll put together a small luncheon, and we'll go from there. By the way, not only Ford will be impressed if you can raise money from private individuals—my husband and the provost will as well. They like entre-preneurial efforts, and they're already excited about what you're doing, but they'll be even more excited if they see that you can bring in private money."

I tell Arjay about my meeting with Jing.

"Ah," he says. "I need to introduce you to my wife, Frances. She'll want to contribute to this, too. And I need to give you some fundraising advice."

Wow, fundraising advice from Arjay! He's renowned at Stanford for his fundraising.

"You have to have a certain mindset to do fundraising," he says. "Problem is, most people don't understand what it's like to be wealthy, to have money that you know ahead of time you're going to give away. So they make the mistake of thinking that when you solicit a wealthy person, you're asking for a favor. In fact, when you ask a wealthy man for a donation, you're doing *him* a favor. He needs to put his money somewhere, and you're helping him find a good place to put it."

This is indeed a new way for me to think about financial support. I'm stunned. I'm also amused that Arjay is telling me how to raise money for a feminist cause but still using the pronoun "he."

When I meet with the provost, Bill Miller, for the first time and tell him about my meeting with Jing, he says he already knows about it. Jing has contacted Bill's wife, Pat, and told her all about her fundraising ideas. But Bill says he has a fundraising idea of his own. He wants to encourage me to solicit men to make donations in honor of their mothers! I want to ask if he would be the first to donate in honor of his mother, but I don't dare. I do tell him, though, that Mariam said that Ford will not give money to Stanford for the center unless Stanford itself does so. He says he thinks that's fair enough, and that I should submit a budget to him for Stanford support.

The gathering that Jing sets up is small. She's invited Rosemary Young, whose husband is high up at Hewlett Packard; Margie Robertson, the wife of a banker; and a few others. She asks me to speak about the center and where we are in our negotiations with Ford, then she presents her idea: those assembled should form the core of an associates group that would contribute to the center and also ask their friends to contribute. In return, contributors would be invited to an annual or semiannual meeting with faculty members affiliated with the center to discuss their research. Jing says she'd like to sign up as the first associate.

The women ask numerous questions—about me, the other faculty involved, and my ideas for the future. I'm nervous. I explain that we are just beginning the process of writing a grant to Ford, and that I welcome their ideas. Much to my surprise, they see the lack of a fixed plan as a plus, and by the end of our get-together, Rosemary has agreed to chair an associates group.

As a result of my meeting with Provost Miller, he assigns a staff member from the Development Office to work with me for a few hours a month to help solicit gifts from private donors and corporations. Unfortunately, I find the Development Office less than helpful. Their primary goal, it seems to me, is to make sure that I don't solicit funds from donors they have determined should give gifts elsewhere.

For example, when representatives from IBM's "giving arm" come to campus, the Development Office sets up a meeting for me, which goes exceedingly well. IBM is concerned with the dearth of women in engineering and management, and their representatives tell me they are very interested in giving a gift to support CROW's research. However, after the meeting, the Development Office informs me that it has authorized the School of Engineering to request a large grant from IBM and that it doesn't want CROW to "muck up" that process. The maximum gift I can request from IBM is $5,000. Development simply won't process any request larger than that.

There are similar problems with individual donors. If a potential donor is a female Stanford graduate married to a man with a graduate degree from Stanford's business school, law school, or medical school, I can't solicit her. According to Development Office "rules," that couple "belongs" to whichever school the husband graduated from.

I discuss all this with the Policy Board and get some advice from Jim March. "Transgress!" he tells me. "You'll know you're doing a good job when they slap your hand for violating their rules."

What I ultimately learn is that if I establish a relationship with a potential donor outside the Development Office's aegis, and that person or company wants to contribute to the center, the Development Office may "slap my hand" but won't return the gift. In other words, I'm far better off without their "help" than with it.

As my reputation at Stanford grows, so does enrollment in my course on women and work, and the class is no longer a small seminar. Many of the students are undergraduates and graduate students from other schools, but increasingly, as the number of women grows at the GSB, they are MBA students. The support and friendship of these female MBAs sustains me, and many of them become lifelong friends.

Today's class is on occupational segregation, probably one of the most complex topics in the course.

"Why do you think women and men are in such different occupations?" I ask.

"Men's occupations are dirty, and women want clean occupations."

"Women are more patient than men, so they want to be teachers and nurses; and they're more dexterous, so they want to do fine work on an assembly line."

"Women don't want jobs that require them to travel."

"OK, let's take a hard look at this." I say. "Notice that all of your explanations have to do with women's preferences. This is not unusual. Most people think women's preferences explain why men and women do different jobs. But these explanations just don't hold up. Some of women's occupations are clean, but plenty of them, like nursing and childcare work, are not, and plenty of men's occupations require patience and dexterity. And if women are so dexterous, why aren't they brain surgeons? If they're so patient, why aren't they scientists? If they hate to travel, why are they airline stewardesses? And if they're traveling for work, why are they stewardesses but not pilots?

"I see your point," one of the students counters, "but women are socialized to be in certain jobs. Women don't *want* to be surgeons or pilots. Those are men's jobs."

"You're right. Once jobs are labeled male or female, there are powerful forces keeping them that way, including the fact that many women are afraid they'll be seen as too masculine if they take a traditionally male job. But there's nothing inherently male or female about jobs, except perhaps wet nurse. And jobs do change their sex designation. Before the typewriter was invented, clerical workers were men. Look at what's happening right here at the B-School: a few years ago, there were virtually no women MBA students here. Then the school let it be known that they wanted women applicants, and suddenly women began applying in droves. Jobs for MBAs haven't changed, and women's job preferences haven't changed. A door opened, and women walked in."

"So what does determine which jobs are men's and which are women's?" a student asks.

"I'm studying that right now. The one characteristic that traditionally male jobs have is that they pay better and have better promotion opportunities than traditionally female jobs that require the same level of education."

"Then why do jobs change from being male to being female?"

"Again, I'm still studying this, but what it looks like is that when an occupation becomes less desirable in terms of pay and promotion, men switch to some other occupation. I think it's men's preferences that are the drivers of occupation changes, not women's."

I seem to have hit a nerve with this topic. At the end of class, students are lined up at my lectern to ask questions. Another class is coming in, and I have to move the whole group into the hall. Katherine Poss, a doctoral student from the School of Education, is waiting patiently at the end of the queue.

"You really ought to meet Dave Tyack," she says when it's finally her turn. "The stuff you were talking about today? What happens when occupations switch from being male to female? That's just what Dave cares about. I'm his research assistant. I could introduce you."

Katherine's matchmaking changes my life. Dave is a professor of education, and his specialization is American education history. He's a gentle man who ponders interesting questions at every turn and invites everyone in his presence to ponder along with him. Right now he's puzzling over how and why teaching became a woman's occupation. He knows all the ins and outs of the education system in the period when women came to dominate teaching (1850–1920), but he's searching for a theory to explain what happened. We're a good team, because I know almost nothing about the history of teaching in the United States, but based on my reading about secretarial work and some of my own research on bank tellers, I'm beginning to develop a theory about how occupations switch from male to female.

"Lots of historians say that teaching became a woman's occupation because women were cheaper to hire than men," Dave says.

"I don't think that's the reason. Women are cheaper than men for *every* occupation, but you don't see employers hiring them. Something has to *happen* for employers to start hiring women instead of men."

"Let's work together," he suggests. "Let's put together a grant proposal and send it to the NIE. And let's set up a discussion group with Martin Carnoy and Hank Levin. I know you'll like them, and I know they'll be interested in your ideas."

Both of Dave's suggestions work well. The NIE awards us a nice pot of money, and our small faculty discussion group is fun as well as productive. What a relief to be involved again with progressive economists!

We use most of the NIE grant to hire graduate students in history and the social sciences, and after several months, they present their work at a team meeting. The history students are excited. They've found several diaries, and they're using them to understand teachers' reasons for entering the profession. They bring the diaries to the meeting and handle them lovingly. But the students working with me are dismissive. Trained as quantitative researchers, they feel the diaries are unreliable and biased sources, representative only of those teachers who happened to write diaries.

Later in the meeting, the tables turn. My students have large piles of computer output, complex statistical regressions on economic and educational data from several states. But the history students argue that the quality of these nineteenth-century data is poor and say they don't trust them. Besides, the regressions explain only 50 percent of the variance. Can you really think you've explained something when half the explanation is still unknown? Dave and I remind the students that by using both quantitative and qualitative methods, we're developing a richer understanding of the feminization process; although we agree that both methodologies have flaws, each contributes something of value to solving the puzzle. It's a hard sell.

In the end, Dave and I come to understand that the explanations for the feminization of teaching are different for rural and urban areas. In urban areas, women were sought after as teachers from the beginning, and men were hired as principals to supervise them and handle their disciplinary problems. But in rural areas, where male teachers were basically farmers who taught in the off-season, teaching became feminized because men left the occupation. As state laws demanded more days of teaching per year and more summer institutes to keep up skills, teaching became less attractive to men than it had been in earlier years, and women moved in to take the newly available jobs.

This idea that occupations become female because men are no longer interested in them is new. I call it the relative attractiveness theory: when men find an occupation less attractive than some competing occupation that requires the same level of education, they move out and women begin applying to fill the new vacancies. That's the supply side of the theory.

But what about the demand side, the employers? In a capitalist economy, *why* do employers give men the power to determine which occupations they'll occupy? Why don't employers hire whichever worker will do the best job for the lowest wage? The answer lies outside of economics, in the social structure. Employers may be profit maximizers (or cost minimizers in the public sector), but they are still members of society; and because society assigns men the job of supporting their families, employers give men first choice of occupations, even if they have to pay more than they would to have women in the same job.

We find that women did indeed teach for less money than men. When men still accounted for about half the teachers in rural schools, they earned about 25 percent more than women. In urban areas, the difference between women's and men's earnings was even greater.

One day, one of my undergraduate students, Laura Best, comes to my office excited by a book she's found in the Education School library, a report from almost a hundred years ago by the California superintendent of schools. Incredibly, it lists every San Francisco teacher who taught in 1879 by name and home address, along with his or her position, salary, age, and years of teaching experience. We marvel at this treasure trove of data, and decide to investigate the differences in salary between women and men.

We find that although only 8 percent of the professional employees in the school district were men, they earned 1.6 times what women earned, even after holding age or experience constant. Why? Because, as Elizabeth Cady Stanton suggested, men monopolized the lucrative positions: most men, but almost no women, were school principals or high school teachers, and both those jobs paid a salary premium.

By 1974, the number of women in the Stanford MBA class is sufficient to make a meaningful comparison between the starting salaries of women and men, and Francine Gordon and I survey the graduates to ascertain their salary, occupation, and years of pre-MBA experience. Interestingly, we find no sex difference in starting salaries. But four years later, when I resurvey the class, women's earnings are only 80 percent of their male classmates.

Two factors account for the disparity. Once again, occupational segregation is critical: although 13 percent of the men are employed in the two most lucrative occupations, investment banking and real estate development, not a single woman is employed in either. But becoming a mother is also important: holding all else constant, the 30 percent of women who took time out to care for a baby for a month or more (12 percent were out for a year or more) paid an earnings penalty of slightly more than a quarter of the average annual total compensation earned by those who had not taken time out!

Women were now allowed into the MBA club, but they were not allowed to take time out to raise a young child without enormous financial penalty. Part of the reason for this penalty may have been that the women who came back sought a more family-friendly and therefore less lucrative position, but it was also due to employers' perception that women who took time out could not be relied on for total job commitment, including willingness to travel and to be promoted into more stressful and time-consuming positions.

As I'm doing research and publishing, I'm also directing CROW, and in December 1975, I submit a grant proposal to Mariam Chamberlain at the Ford Foundation for $100,000 to support the center over three years. A couple of months later, Mariam comes out for a site visit and we put on an impressive set of meetings. Soon thereafter, we get the funds we've requested.

Now we can do some serious hiring! Now we can have a *real* research center. I put together a hiring committee that includes faculty, students, and several independent scholars in the community who are doing important work on women. We hire literary scholar Marilyn Yalom to head up a research project on mothers and daughters and psychologist Laraine Zappert to lead a project comparing career development and stress among recent female and male MBA graduates.

After a year or so, I realize that Marilyn would make a fabulous associate director of CROW. She's off-the-charts smart and entrepreneurial, and she has a million ideas about how to incorporate scholarship in the humanities into the center's program. Moving Marilyn into this position is the best administrative decision I make. When Cindy Davis, who has been our chief administrator, leaves to take another position, we hire Estela Estrada to be our CFO and Margo Davis to coordinate our lecture series.

CROW makes substantial progress in its first two years, carrying out several small projects at the center itself and seeding additional faculty projects in departments. We also continue our signature lunchtime lecture series, which attracts larger and larger audiences each quarter, and we keep raising small amounts of funds from private donors.

In the spring of 1976, the Center for Interdisciplinary Research, to which CROW reports, carries out a review to decide whether or not to recommend to the provost that we be given "regular" status. The result of their review is a long letter that spells out their dissatisfactions with what they see as our lack of progress. What their executive committee has in mind is that we become a social science center on the model of the science centers they oversee, with large federal grants, numerous faculty associates, and multiple publications in leading journals. They want us to raise a great deal of money, and then dole it out to faculty.

I tell them as politely as I can that their view of CROW's future is not mine, that there is no way at this stage in my career that I can attract large-scale, virtually untied research funds—and that nobody can, because large sums of money are not currently available to fund research on women. They say they understand. But then they tell me they have another issue that makes them uncomfortable.

"Do you agree," one of them asks me, "that when the problems CROW deals with no longer exist, the university will be justified in closing down the center?"

The question seems funny to me, almost ludicrous. Do they really think sexism is going to end anytime soon? But I answer with utmost seriousness.

"Yes, sir, as soon as these problems are solved, CROW should be shut down."

They seem to breathe a collective sigh of relief at my "reasonable" stance and ultimately recommend to the provost that CROW be put on "permanent" status—subject, of course, to review in three years.

After this decision, I decide to return to full-time teaching at the GSB. I'll still be the principal investigator on the Ford grant, but I need time to publish several more papers before my upcoming review for tenure and promotion, and I need to put in more face time with my GSB colleagues. But I can't just quit as director. I need to find someone to replace me, and no senior faculty member on the Policy Board is willing.

There are two other women besides me who are Faculty Fellows: Diane Middlebrook, who by 1976 has been promoted to associate professor with tenure in the English Department, and Anne Miner, Stanford's affirmative action officer for staff, who reports directly to President Lyman.

One evening, at a Fellows dinner meeting at the Faculty Club, when we three adjourn to the ladies' room, I explain my dilemma.

"Diane, you need to be the next director of CROW," Anne says.

"I'd be a lousy director," Diane replies. "I have no administrative skills."

"Fair enough," Anne says. "Let's be codirectors. You work on research and programs, and I'll handle the administration and show you the administrative ropes. They're not that hard. You'll be a pro in less than a year."

After a bit more arm-twisting, Diane agrees, and we laugh. For years, we've heard about deals being struck in the men's room. When we present our accession plan to the Policy Board and CIR, everyone agrees it's a win-win, and in the fall of '76 Diane and Anne take over. Although I'm no longer director of CROW, I continue to spend a good deal of time at the center, partly because of the Ford grant and party because CROW gives me the intellectual sustenance I find sorely lacking at the GSB.

Diane and Anne's two years as co-directors are fruitful and exciting. First, Diane creates the CROW Group—a group of faculty from all over the university interested in scholarship and research on women, who meet on a regular basis to teach each other disciplinary knowledge about women's issues. In addition to Diane and me, the participants are Carol Jacklin and Eleanor Maccoby from psychology, Estelle Freedman from history, and Shelly Rosaldo and Jane Collier from anthropology.

There is so little scholarly literature on women at the time that each of us can tell the others about the work in our fields in just a few sessions. It seems impossible all these years later, with the veritable flood of scholarship that has ensued since, but in those days, each of us is familiar with the totality of literature in the fields we represent by the end of the first year.

Diane also forms a faculty committee to investigate the possibility of starting a women's studies teaching program at Stanford. By now, more women who are interested in women's issues have joined the faculty, and we believe we have enough intellectual power to offer a cogent series of courses. In our proposal to the dean of Arts and Sciences, we name our new program Feminist Studies. This is highly controversial, since most teaching programs in feminist scholarship nationally and internationally are called women's studies. But thanks to persuasive arguments from

Diane, as well as Shelly Rosaldo, Nannerl Keohane, and Estelle Freedman, Stanford approves the name and the program.

Each time the Feminist Studies program is reviewed in subsequent years, one dean or another objects to the name and asks us to consider changing it. But the governing committee steadfastly resists, and because of the intellectual strength of the program, its name endures.

One of the courses I'm asked to teach at the GSB when I return full-time is an introductory economics class for Sloan Fellows: midcareer managers (almost all of them men) in the school's one-year advanced management program. The class takes place over the three weeks before fall quarter begins and provides a crash course in basic economics concepts and methods of analysis.

Just as I'm getting ready to teach the class, a doctoral student in English with the unusual name of Gary Sue Goodman comes to see me about how she might best learn introductory economics. She is writing a dissertation about a nineteenth-century woman economist and would like to better understand her economic ideas. I suggest she audit my Sloan class. She likes the idea and begins to attend regularly.

After a few sessions, she comes up after class to talk privately.

"I don't know how you stand the hostility," she says.

"What hostility?"

"Ah, that's what I thought. You don't even see it. If you like, I'll sit in the back row, and every time one of these guys makes a hostile comment, I'll raise my pinky."

"Sure, why not? That'll be interesting."

But once she gets started, I'm sorry I've agreed to the experiment. Her finger shoots up multiple times a session, and as I get a clearer picture of the class dynamics, I find it harder and harder to teach. After my experience learning to be nasty and rejecting that behavior, I've learned to handle hostility by ignoring it—and denial, I decide, is not a bad coping strategy. I ask Gary Sue to stop raising her pinky, and though it takes a while to get back to disregarding the underlying antagonism in the class, I eventually succeed.

As I struggle with hostility at the GSB, new women hires on the General Motors (GM) assembly line are struggling with a different and far less subtle kind of enmity. In 1978, GM invites a team of women from academia—including Cynthia Fuchs Epstein, Carol Jacklin, Rosabeth Kanter, Brigid O'Farrell, and me—to come to a Cadillac plant in Detroit to consult with them about improving the situation.

On our first day, we tour the plant; talk to the women, who have only recently been hired (GM had never had women on the line before); and meet with various union and management representatives. The term "sexual harassment" hasn't been invented yet, but several men who are dead set against having women work with them on the line are engaging in what will later be called "hostile environment sexual harassment." Because the women have no seniority, they get the least desirable shifts; and when they leave the plant to return to their cars in the middle of the night, they find they cannot drive away. Their tires have been slashed, and their male coworkers are in the shadows laughing. The women are scared and intimidated.

On the morning of our second day, we meet with management, try to help them make sense of what is happening, and offer some recommendations. After that, our hosts invite us to the executive dining room for lunch. One of the execs asks me about my research.

"I'm looking at the differences in spending patterns in single-earner as compared to two-earner families when they both earn the same total amount of money."

"Do the two kinds of families spend differently?"

"Yes. And one of the ways they spend differently is on cars. Even when they have the same total income, two-earner families are much more likely to have two cars so the wife can get to work."

Suddenly, I see an opportunity in this conversation and warm to the challenge.

"You know," I continue, "wives who work and need a second car are very much involved in the decision about which one to buy—because, after all, they're the ones who will be driving it. So, for example, when my family needed a second car, I carefully watched your ads on TV and looked at them in magazines and newspapers. And you know what? I was not impressed. A seminude woman lying on her back draped over the hood? That didn't particularly make me want to buy a Chevy or a Caddy or any other GM car."

My listener is thunderstruck.

"Wait," he says, rising from his chair. "Don't go away. I need to call the VP of advertising. He needs to talk to you."

Shortly thereafter, another middle-aged white man arrives, and I tell him the same story. He's flabbergasted as well, and I realize that GM is in deep trouble. I'm the first person to tell them women are significant car buyers, and that their ads likely don't appeal to women? What an insulated bubble these guys are in. Years later, when GM files for bankruptcy—in part because they've never made cars for people who want small, gas-efficient models—I'm not surprised.

Throughout my years at the GSB, Mom and Dad are worried about me.

"You're working way too hard. You're a good mom, you do everything around the house, you work like a dog, and you don't sleep enough."

What can I say? It's all true.

They have two suggestions. One, I should hire more help, particularly with cooking. Two, Sam and I should go on a long vacation, just the two of us, and they'll take care of the kids.

When I tell Sam their thoughts, he rejects the one about hiring someone to cook, but is enthusiastic about their vacation idea. So in the summer of 1976, he and I spend three weeks in Israel, and the following summer, in celebration of his positive tenure decision at the medical school, we spend three weeks in India and Nepal.

These trips feel like honeymoons. Grant deadlines and seriously ill patients don't weigh on Sam, and I'm not busy returning phone calls and reading dissertations. I'm also not diverted by the kids or angry that he's *not* diverted by them. There's no housework to do, and I'm not trying to get him to handle his "fair share." We don't fight about how often to see my parents. We have time for uninterrupted conversations and feel connected again. But as soon as we're home, we're back on the old roller-coaster, and the salutary effects of the vacation quickly dissipate.

Shortly after our trip to India, Dad falls ill. He has a blood disease that turns into leukemia, and he needs frequent transfusions. He still loves to spend time with Jason and Liz, but he often feels weak and not able to keep up with them.

To make matters worse, Sam seems distant. We still go out together to the opera and theater, we entertain frequently and have an active social life, and we still talk endlessly about politics. But he no longer seems particularly interested in *me,* and sometimes the way he looks at other women at parties scares me. He's still an extremely handsome man, and I worry that maybe I should pay more attention to my hair or my clothes.

I had thought that after he got tenure, he would be more amenable to sharing housework, but he isn't. I'd also thought the pressure on him to get grants would be reduced. But that's not happening either. We still take the whole family to Yosemite in the summer and skiing at Lake Tahoe in the winter, but he doesn't seem particularly engaged with Jason or Liz.

The situation at the GSB also feels foreboding. At the beginning of the summer, Francine leaves Stanford to work with her husband, and I miss her sorely. From our first days together, we were each other's escape valves. Whenever the pressure became dangerously high, we could simply walk across the hall to the other's office, knowing that a sympathetic heart was just steps away. All summer long, I'm the only woman faculty member at the GSB. Then, in the fall, Joanne Martin arrives. Like Francine, she will teach organizational behavior, and I hope fervently that her experience will be positive.

I'm busy getting my papers together for my tenure review, but I'm not feeling optimistic. Candidates for tenure and promotion write a short statement defining their field and provide the names of about ten senior scholars in that field that they would like the review committee to contact. The committee sends out requests for letters to the senior scholars suggested by the candidate, as well as to scholars not on the candidate's list. The letters ask the reviewers for a candid evaluation of the candidate's research and for named comparisons to other junior people in the field. At Stanford, in order for a review committee to make a positive tenure recommendation to the faculty, the letters from senior scholars have to be virtually unanimous in viewing the candidate as one of the top junior people in the world in their field.

I'm proud of the record I've assembled, but I keep getting unsettling visits from my economist colleagues at the GSB.

"I'm worried," one of them tells me.

"*You're* worried? What should *I* say?"

"No, seriously. Whom are you going to recommend as evaluators for your review?"

I tell him that among my evaluators I will recommend Barbara Reagan, Barbara Bergmann, Cynthia Epstein, and Rosabeth Kanter.

"Too many women. That's a problem."

"Why?"

"The committee will discount what they have to say."

"Really? They think women can't review the work of other women objectively?"

"Something like that."

I point out that that such thinking is discriminatory, but my colleague dismisses that idea. He wants me to be sure to put men on my list.

"I'm putting Dave Tyack on the list."

"But he's not an economist."

"Well, you know my work extends beyond economics. I use history and sociology to better understand economics."

"Yes, and that's yet another problem. Even worse, you're in a new field, and it's hard to find people to compare you with."

Writing this memoir more than thirty years after my tenure review at the GSB, I realize how highly irregular my review process was. I called my field "women and work," but in truth it was never officially defined. That should have happened when I was hired or soon thereafter. But I never had a single conversation with Lee Bach, the head of the economics group, or with either of the associate deans about what my field was, who the senior people in that field were, or to which junior people I would be compared. I was also never told who was on my review committee.

I know I should be looking for jobs at other universities in case I'm turned down for tenure, and I bring this up with Sam. But he doesn't want me to do that. He doesn't want us to consider leaving Stanford.

"But what will I do if I'm turned down?" I ask him.

He seems weary. "Why don't we take it one day at a time? Why don't we cross that bridge if we get to it?"

I'm weary, too, not really wanting to go on the job market and certainly lacking the strength to argue with Sam about it. Then I get a call from the president of Tulane University. He tells me that his friend Richard Lyman, Stanford's president, has recommended me for the deanship of Sophie Newcomb College, the women's college at Tulane. Would I come to New Orleans and meet with him and the search committee?

I tell him about Sam. "No problem," he says. "We'll set him up for interviews with the right people at our medical school."

So Sam and I go to New Orleans. I'm not enthralled with the idea of living in the south, and I'm not at all sure I'm ready to give up research and teaching to become a full-time administrator. But Sam is even more negative than that.

"No way I'm leaving Stanford for Tulane," he says.

So it's back to waiting for the tenure decision, and in early December, it finally comes.

"Stay in your office and wait for our phone call," associate dean Jaedicke tells me on the morning of the vote. "As soon as the faculty meeting is over, I'll call you."

My office feels like a small prison cell. Despite the December chill, I open the windows wide and breathe deeply. Then I close them. Too cold. I pace back and forth. I try to read. It feels like my whole life depends on that phone call.

Finally, shortly after noon, the phone rings. At least Jaedicke doesn't prolong the suspense.

"It's a negative decision, Myra. Please come down to my office now and meet with Van Horne and me."

I stumble down the stairs and into his office. I have a strange sensation. I'm both *in* the room and an observer *of* the room.

"What happened? I ask.

"Well," Jim Van Horne says, "the faculty felt you didn't hit a home run, that your work wasn't seminal."

Wow, my observer self says, *two male metaphors in one sentence*. The baseball metaphor seems inapt. The one thing about a real home run is that it's definitive. Everybody recognizes it instantaneously. That's not true with academic work. Someday, when people read my work in a less prejudiced way, I think they'll see that I did hit a home run, that I helped to open up a new and important field.

But I don't say any of this.

What I do say is that I would like to see redacted copies of the letters that reviewers wrote to the tenure and promotion committee.

"I know I can't see the names of the people who wrote the letters," I say, "but I'd like to see what they said, what criticisms they had. That would help me as I go forward."

"Sure, sure," they say, as I stand up. They offer handshakes, but I'm not in the mood. I head for the door and leave.

Well, that was a good speech, I think to myself. *But exactly where and how am I going forward? I've done no job search, and my husband won't leave Stanford.*

As the day wears on, numerous colleagues come to my office. I learn that nobody got tenure that morning. My three male colleagues were also turned down. So many colleagues come to say they're sorry about my decision that I wonder how the vote could possibly have been negative. Did they vote against me and still come to see me?

Late in the afternoon, Arjay calls. Would I please come down and meet with him? When I get to his office, he tells me he knows I'm crushed, but he wants me to know that he's crushed, too—that he's ashamed of his colleagues and of his inability to deliver on my behalf. Not long afterward, when Arjay announces his retirement from the deanship, he tells me privately that the decision about my tenure is part of the reason why he is leaving.

Meanwhile, I eventually get a small envelope filled with tiny pieces of paper. Jaedicke and Van Horne have taken the letters evaluating my work and cut them up into sentences. This is my feedback, sentences that have been mixed together. I try to separate them out by typeface, but the task is too difficult. In the end, I have no sense at all of why the faculty voted negatively. What I have is a sense that my work has been cut to pieces, trashed and invalidated. I put the envelope into a file drawer.

When I tell my friends about the faculty's verdict, many of them ask if I'm going to sue for sex discrimination.

"I don't think I can sue. Four people were turned down—two of them white guys. I don't think I'd have a good case. Besides, I don't want my life to be about a lawsuit for the next five years. I want to move on."

Two colleagues, Dave Tyack and Artie Bienenstock (the university's affirmative action officer for faculty), are particularly supportive of my moving on. Moreover, they think they can make it happen. The key is Arthur Coladarci, dean of the School of Education. First, Dave goes to Coladarci, tells him about me and the work he and I are doing together, says he thinks the GSB has made a mistake, and suggests that SUSE hire me as a tenured faculty member. He also tells him to "check me out" with four SUSE faculty members who know my work: the economists Hank

Levin and Martin Carnoy, who have been part of the discussion group Dave set up, and my associates from CROW, Jim March and Elizabeth Cohen.

Then Artie goes to see Coladarci and offers a sweetener: the provost's office will give SUSE funding for an appointment for me as a half-time tenured associate professor at SUSE; for the other half of my appointment, I would return to being director of CROW. Coladarci likes the idea and asks me to come meet with him. I tell him I would be happy with the proposed arrangement. So he appoints another tenure review committee, and once again I'm asked to define my field and provide the names of senior scholars who can write about my work and compare me to others.

The process grinds through its procedures, the letters come in, the review committee makes a positive recommendation, and one day in late spring, the SUSE faculty votes to offer me a half-time position as associate professor with tenure. I'm ecstatic. I like the faculty I've met at SUSE, and the idea of moving there feels wonderful.

The appointment papers wend their way through the bureaucracy to the University Advisory Board, a group of six or so faculty from across the university who advise the provost on whether or not to accept the tenure and promotion decisions made by the university's schools. In the middle of summer, I get a call from Coladarci.

"The Advisory Board said no. They say they can't understand how in the space of less than six months, based on an unchanged record, one school in the university turns you down for tenure and promotion while the other makes a positive decision."

Coladarci is about to retire from the deanship, but he assures me that my half-time appointment at SUSE still stands (that is, I'll still get half a paycheck). However, I won't be an associate professor, and I won't have tenure. He urges me to move my office from GSB to SUSE and "see what happens." In other words, I'm in academic limbo.

I do move my office, and soon thereafter, when I answer my phone there, the incoming dean, Mike Atkin, is on the other end.

"Who are you?" he asks. "Your papers are all over my desk."

I ask for an appointment to explain. He sits at his desk, listens patiently, looks pained, and finally concludes: "Well, we'll just have to start from scratch. I'll appoint a new review committee and we'll go through the whole process again."

Carl Thoresen, chair of the new review committee, asks me for names of reviewers. I give him the same names I've given twice before, and soon thereafter I get calls from each of them, now asked to write about me for the third time.

"What the hell is happening out there in California? Have you all gone *completely* nuts?" they ask.

Still, they all write reviews, yet again, and the SUSE faculty once again votes positively. But this time, the stars seem to align. Last year's Advisory Board is gone, and this year's is happy to approve the SUSE faculty's vote. More than a year after the review process first started, it's finally over. I'm happy but traumatized. I'm never going through a review again, I tell myself. I'll remain at the associate professor level for the rest of my career.

When I return to CROW as director, I have a new boss. My former boss, Bill Massey, has been promoted to vice president of business and finance, and the new vice provost for research is Jerry Lieberman. From the start, it's clear that Jerry is extremely supportive of CROW and wants to serve as my mentor. Jerry and I are both from New York, and he says he needs to explain to me why he had to change his New York style to be successful at Stanford, and why I will have to change mine. In New York, he tells me, people can just argue outright, and the loudest screamer wins. Not so at Stanford, he counsels, with a smile. He had to learn to argue "like a gentleman," softly, and I have to learn that, too.

"Everything at Stanford is understated," he says. "Tough, but gentlemanly and understated."

I understand what he's saying. I've also noticed a big difference between the New York and Stanford styles. I appreciate this conversation with Jerry, and it becomes a source of humor throughout our relationship. Whenever either of us bargains hard and loudly, we admonish the other to "put away" the New York style and become more Stanford-like.

Shortly after my promotion and tenure are approved, I'm asked to give a talk to SUSE support staff. They're excited about my appointment and want to hear about my research.

"Do you and your husband share housework?" one of the staff members asks me during the Q&A following my talk.

"No, I do both the housework and childcare."

"How come?"

"Neither of us has much time, but I feel that his work is more important than mine. He's saving lives every day, and his research on transplant rejection is far more important than my research."

"The hell it is," she says. "In my book, *nothing* is more important than research on how to rid the world of sexism."

The entire audience stands and cheers. I'm astonished. But I'm finally cured of my own sexism, and I redouble my efforts to get Sam to do more housework and childcare.

In the summer of 1980, Alice and I attend the meetings of the Western Economic Association in San Diego. She is just about to publish an edited collection on the economics of women and work with Penguin Books (the only time she works on this topic), and we are taking a shift together handing out literature on CSWEP. The CSWEP desk is in the front lobby of the hotel, just before the conference registration desk, and both desks have large identifying signs. Nonetheless, man after man comes to the CSWEP desk, and I patiently point to the place where they can pick up their registration materials. After several such interactions, Alice grows impatient.

"Let me handle the next guy."

Oh, boy, I think, *here goes.*

"Are you blind?" she asks the unsuspecting male economist. "Can't you read? The sign says CSWEP, not Registration. Just because we're women behind the desk doesn't mean that we're registering people. You're just a chauvinist pig."

"Did you have to be so rude?" I ask after the guy slinks off.

"Let me ask you something. Which guy is going to remember that not all women are clerical workers? The one I told off or the ones you sweet-talked?"

"He may remember that not all women are clerical workers, but he'll also remember that women economists are rude and best avoided. I like people to still hang out with me after they've learned something about women."

"Good luck, Goody Two-Shoes. It can't be done."

Over the years, I've thought many times about the contrast between Alice's and my approaches to social change, and have grown more appreciative of her approach. I now think it takes multiple techniques to achieve major transformation—radically rude tactics as well as my more tempered-radical style. But I also think Alice was wrong about the possibility of maintaining good relationships with people I'm trying to change. If I can get away from "blame" and gently get people to see that they are engaged in stereotyped behavior, I can often get them to change that behavior without resenting me.

In August 1980, Jason celebrates his bar mitzvah at Congregation Beth Am. Our whole family gathers, with numerous relatives coming from the East Coast. Jason wears a suit and tie, reads the Torah beautifully, and gives a short sermon on false prophets. My little boy has become a young man.

We'd joined Beth Am, a Reform temple not far from our house, about five years earlier so Jason and Liz could learn Hebrew and Jewish history and prepare for their bar and bat mitzvahs. I like the congregation. Rabbi Axelrod is learned and kind, and there is no organ or choir, so congregants sing along with the cantor. But now I have a new problem: I find the prayer book sexist.

The patriarchal fathers, Abraham, Isaac, and Jacob, are praised throughout, but there is no reverence for their wives: Sarah, Rebecca, Leah, and Rachel. And God is presented as male. I've never thought about this before. To my mind, God has no gender. In Judaism, it is not permitted to mention God's name. God is called YHVH, four Hebrew letters that are neither female nor male. But in Hebrew, all verbs are gendered, and God's actions are rendered in the masculine form. In English, however, verbs are not gendered, and the fact that the English translation of God's actions is not gender-neutral interferes with my prayers. Instead of concentrating on God, my mind is busy editing.

A few days after Jason's bar mitzvah, Dad's health deteriorates. It's as though he's held himself together for the celebration but then lets go.

In December, there's more bad news: I learn that Alice and Jon are getting divorced. Alice has been teaching at Barnard while Jon remains in Los Angeles, and the strain of frequent separation has taken its toll. Alice is extremely sad and decides to take a semester's leave from Barnard and come out to Palo Alto. We talk some, but mostly she keeps her own counsel.

One of the benefits of Alice's being on leave is that she has time to spend with Dad in his last days, and as his condition becomes progressively worse, she helps Mom care for him. In May 1981, Dad passes away; we bury him in Staten Island, where all of Mom's family is buried. In my eulogy, I talk about his gentleness and his caring for others. He always listened to me and loved me unconditionally, and I miss him terribly.

Five months after his death, I go to Beth Am with Mom for Yizkor, a memorial service held on the afternoon of Yom Kippur. In the Reform tradition, everyone may attend Yizkor, but in the Orthodox tradition, only people mourning a close relative attend. As a child I was told it was bad luck for anyone else to attend a Yizkor service, so I have never been before.

Mom and I hold each other and cry together through most of the service, and I find the prayers beautiful and inspiring:

Make me to ponder the end, the measure of my days; help me to realize how fleeting is my life.

9

Reinvention, 1982–1989

In December 1981, Sam, the kids, and I are flying back to San Francisco from New York, where we've unveiled Dad's gravestone. It's been raining all day, and our boots are still spattered with cemetery mud. Sam says he wants to talk, so we tell the kids we'll be right back and find an empty corner in the back of the plane.

He says he's unhappy with our marriage and is thinking of leaving. I see that the flight attendant passing by is all ears, but I don't care. My heart is beating so fast I fear I will faint, and only a great effort of will allows me to respond.

"What's making you so unhappy?" I ask, assuming that he's tired of my pestering him to do more housework.

But no, that's not it at all.

"I missed the sexual revolution," he says. "I never got a chance to sow my wild oats. I feel confined, tied down."

I'm trembling and feel extremely nauseated.

"I need to use the facilities," I say, locking myself into one of the restrooms.

Gradually the trembling and nausea lessen, and I look at myself in the mirror. I'm forty. If Clairol weren't helping me to be blond, I'd have prominent patches of gray. My neck and forehead have wrinkles they didn't have twenty years ago, and I weigh about twenty pounds more than I did before I became pregnant with Jason. I look exhausted—a combination of Dad's unveiling and Sam's unwelcome news. I'd better get it together. I'm going to need every ounce of strength I can muster.

When I come out of the restroom, Sam's back in his seat with the kids. No opportunity to continue until we get home.

"Would you agree to see a marriage counselor?" I ask after the kids have gone to bed.

"No, I think I'd like to see a therapist on my own."

Several weeks pass, and we manage to completely avoid discussing the elephant in the room. But one night, he says the therapist he's seen suggests we have a trial separation.

"I'm in the wrong marriage," he says. "I don't want to be married to someone whose career is so demanding. I want to be married to someone who is different from me, not to someone who's trying to be the same as me."

I begin trembling again. That seems to be the physical manifestation of my psychic pain.

A few weeks later, Sam moves out. Jason is fourteen, and Liz is twelve.

❖

The ache of my impending divorce dominates the conversation as I jog around the Stanford track with my friend Leah Friedman. It's early March, and we look like California snowmen in gray sweatpants and colorful sweatshirts, our hoods tied tightly to keep our ears warm. I'm always amazed at how many people run in the early morning. Mostly they're students speeding along twice as fast as we are, but there are also plenty of older folks trying to keep their hearts ticking, their lungs pumping, and their osteoporosis at bay.

I'd met Leah five years before, at a Fourth of July party at the home of our mutual friend Mollie Rosenhan. Leah was in her mid-forties then, and she had recently enrolled in a PhD program in psychology. We talked about her decision to return to school and the dissertation she was beginning on social support. Toward the end of our chat, I mentioned that my doctor had suggested I get more exercise by jogging several times a week. She was excited. She also wanted to start jogging, and the following morning, when we tried it out, we both loved it. Ever since, week after week, year after year, we've yakked away the laps, and in the process we've become close friends.

"You're a therapist," I say as we circle around. "Tell me, how come I didn't see this coming? How come I didn't know my marriage was in trouble?"

"Maybe you did know, but you pushed it away. Maybe you denied it. Denial is a potent coping mechanism—very effective, actually."

Hmm, I think. *Denial again. I guess I've been denying at home as much as I have at work.*

Leah tells me that by denying I've postponed the pain, and now that Liz and Jason are older and I have a secure job, I'm better able to cope with it. She's right. I can't imagine what all this would be like if I didn't have a place to go every day and become totally absorbed in something other than my personal life. To say nothing of having an income. What if I had no income, and I had to figure out how to *find* a job?

Leah also suggests that I see a therapist, and I call him that very morning. He's calming, supportive, and insightful.

"You'll see," he says, "when you look back, this will just be a bump in the road."

I'm sure he's right, but right now the bump feels like a boulder, and I'm constantly on the phone with my friends.

Like Leah, my friend Suzanne Greenberg tells me to call her anytime, "even in the middle of the night." Suzanne and I met in the mid-1970s at two parties, one right after the other, and her empathy combined with her intellectual breadth drew me to her. Shortly afterward she became a doctoral student in the history of education at the School of Education, and our friendship deepened quickly. Now she calls me daily and listens patiently as I work through my sorrow.

My friends on the East Coast, Judy (now Judith) Berman Brandenburg and Helen Goldzimer Kaplan, are also loyal and compassionate, and I make a trip to the New York area to visit them. Judith is now Yale's sexual harassment officer and living in New Haven. Despite her challenging job and the demands of her own family, she spends a full day with me "just to talk." She takes me to Mory's, of Yale drinking song fame, and I pour out my woes as I drink their beer.

When I go to Larchmont to see Helen, it's the day before her son's bar mitzvah, and she's frantic. But as I drive around with her for last-minute consultations with the caterer and florist, and to the bakery for goodies, she gives me her full attention and wisdom, reaffirming both our long friendship and assuring me that I'm sturdy enough to overcome this misfortune.

Helen's brother Ed, my old flame, has also come for the bar mitzvah, and he and I take several walks together in the winter chill. He lives in San Diego now, and neither of us is used to freezing weather anymore. We keep adding sweaters under our unfamiliar heavy coats, wincing as the cold air stings our nostrils. Ed tells me his marriage is in trouble, too, and we talk about what we think went wrong for each of us.

"Do you think if we'd married each other, things would have gone better?" I ask.

We laugh heartily, remembering the difficulties we had.

❖

At the end of March, when Sam tells me he's filed for divorce, I tell him that I want to go to couples therapy to understand more fully what went wrong. He agrees to a few sessions.

What do I learn from the therapist?

We married too early. We married before either of us knew what we wanted for our own lives or what we wanted in a mate. Although Sam fully encouraged my getting a doctorate, neither of us realized how challenging it would be to be a professor, especially at a high-powered research university. Along the way, he came to understand that what he wanted in a wife was a helpmate, not someone playing "his" game. But for me, the sexism I encountered made me more determined than ever to succeed and work toward making the world a better place for women. Over the twenty years of our relationship, Sam and I both grew—but in opposite directions.

I'm grateful for this awareness, but it does little to reduce my desire to fix our marriage. Don't wedding vows mean that when things go awry, you work to repair them? Aren't there compromises we can make? Can't we commit to improved communication? Regrettably, the answers are no, no, and no.

❖

One of the unhappy consequences of our impending divorce is Liz's decision to cancel her upcoming bat mitzvah.

"No way am I going to stand on the *bima* with both of you and pretend everything is fine," she says.

I'm fully supportive of her decision. Jason's bar mitzvah was a family joy. Hers could be a family farce, with each side blaming the other for what's happened.

Liz and I go together to explain her decision to Rabbi Axelrod. He's kindly, soft-spoken, and sage, and his words spill out like warm fudge—sweet and smooth.

"You are very wise and very brave," he tells Liz. "You have had to make a sad decision, but you haven't run away from it. You've faced it squarely. And you've made the *right* decision. But don't forget, this is not your only chance to have a bat mitzvah. A person can have a bar or bat mitzvah anytime, even when they're in their nineties. I hope you'll have one someday."

Wow, I think, *I didn't know that.* I thought when I wasn't allowed to have a bat mitzvah at thirteen, I'd missed out forever. I make a mental note: put a bat mitzvah for myself on my long-term to-do list.

❖

A few months after meeting with the couples therapist, I begin going to singles events, and one evening I have the *South Pacific* experience, except the roles are reversed. It is I, a woman, who's attracted to the stranger across a crowded room.

Ted is tall and thin, with a nicely trimmed beard. His glasses, his intense look, and his utter absorption in his conversation make him look smart. Smart's still very important to me. And he looks kind. Also very important. I cross the room. There's no music playing, so I can't ask him to dance (though I'd like to), but I stand right next to him and listen to his conversation, and when he finishes speaking, I introduce myself and ask him what he does.

Then we're off to the races. He's a solar engineer, and I learn more about solar energy that evening than I ever knew I wanted to know. We also talk a bit about my work. But all this intensive listening is exhausting. I'm ready to go home.

"I have to leave now," I say, "but I'd love to talk to you again sometime. May I give you my phone number?"

I can hardly believe how forward I am. Truly, though, I would like to see this man again, and who knows whether he will or won't take the lead?

Several days go by, and he doesn't call. I'm just about ready to write the whole experience off to dating practice when I hear his voice on the phone. He'd like to make dinner for me. Well, that's a change from my old life!

Ted and I begin to see each other frequently. He's wonderful with Jason and Liz, and he becomes part of our family. His sister and brother-in-law have bought several acres of land about five hours north of Palo Alto, and all four of us visit them while Ted helps build their house. I find out how to clear land, site a septic tank, and design a house for maximum solar exposure. I follow a "water witch" around for several hours and learn how to figure out where to drill for a well. None of these things are remotely like anything I've done before.

Ted and I both love to sing, and we join the Stanford Chorus. Now that Liz and Jason are teenagers, I feel OK about going out on a weeknight and leaving them to their homework. I find I enjoy singing as much as I did in high school. Following the alto part is demanding and takes my mind off everything else, and I feel some of the pain of my divorce evaporate into the soaring reverberations that fill the room.

Ted and I also do a lot of hiking, and he teaches me a good deal about love. In the later years of my marriage, when I sensed that Sam was losing interest in me, I often felt jealous of other women. Now I see that jealousy is not necessarily the dark side of love, that if there's trust as well as love, then jealousy need not be part of the equation.

Ted encourages me to sign up for a Sierra Club backpacking trip (my first ever) and Sam's parents and my Aunt Bimi and Uncle Max agree to take care of the children while I do the trip. So while my children fly off to Florida, I head for the Eastern Sierra.

Hour after hour, day and evening, I have time for myself, and as I trudge through the rough terrain, I slowly review what has happened to me. One night toward the end of the trip, alone in the absolute silence of my tent, gently massaging my aching calves, I notice how happy and optimistic I feel. The mountains' quiet has entered my soul.

I return home feeling as though years of debris have been flushed away, and the spirituality of the Sierra is reinforced by High Holiday services at Stanford Hillel with Jason, Liz, and Mom. The prayers transport me to another plane, and especially during the memorial service at Yom Kippur, I can practically feel Dad, Grandpa, Baba, and Tante Annie in the room.

Ted comes with us to services. He asks Mom and me numerous questions about the holidays and the prayers, and we try our best to explain. He's not particularly excited about Judaism, or indeed any religion, but he's respectful and enjoys learning. He's extremely kind to Mom, and she likes him a lot. She says it doesn't matter to her at all that he's not Jewish. He's helping me get over Sam, and that's enough for her.

Although having Ted in my life is a big plus, I still frequently feel as though an axe has severed my life, and once my teaching starts up again, the peace I felt in the Sierra is gone. What will my relationship be like with Sam, the man that I lived with and loved for almost twenty years? I have no brothers, so I can't think of him as a brother. Will he be like my male cousins? No, he will be like nobody else. He will be my ex-husband, the father of my children. I have to figure out what that feels like.

Strangely, what bothers me most is the idea that he won't be at my funeral. Of course, I realize that statistically, I'm likely to outlive him. But his not being at my funeral is symbolic, emblematic of the end of our linkage. Then one day I have a breakthrough, a moment in which I come to terms with existential aloneness. For sure, *I'll* be at my funeral, I think. And somehow that gives me great comfort.

At Halloween, I go to the Webb Ranch, just a couple of miles from my house, and can hardly see the pumpkins through my tears. Thanksgiving is worse. Sam and I each have separate dinners with the children, and Jason complains of a stomachache.

❖

Interestingly but perhaps not surprisingly, as a result of my discomfort in participating in Ted's family's Christmas celebrations, I strengthen my commitment to Judaism. I'm no longer a member of Beth Am, and I put all my energy into Stanford Hillel. Ari Cartun, Hillel's rabbi, is a force of nature. Young, charismatic, and funny, he has built a tremendous following at Hillel since his arrival in 1976. His High Holiday services are particularly popular, in part because they are melodic and joyful, but also because they are free, unlike services at synagogues in the community. Ari's philosophy is that no one should have to pay for services, but everyone should feel duty-bound to make a donation to Stanford Hillel.

I can't believe the change that has occurred in Hillel services over the past twelve years. From a small dank room at the Old Union with fewer than thirty people in attendance, they have moved to one of Stanford's most beautiful theaters, Memorial Auditorium, which holds fifteen hundred—and that capacity is not enough for all the students, faculty, staff, and community members who want to come, so Hillel now holds *two* services on the evenings before Rosh Hashanah and Yom Kippur, and all the seats are filled.

Although I've attended High Holiday services at Hillel several times, I've never met Rabbi Cartun in person. Now my friend Mollie Rosenhan is about to remedy that. She tells me that she's working with Ari on a new project to create a gender-free English prayer book for Hillel, and I decide to join her. All my silent editing during services is about to pay off. I enjoy the project, and soon Ari asks me to become a member of the Hillel Advisory Board.

As a board member and an economist, I'm fascinated by Ari's business model. His financial philosophy works perfectly, and the vast majority of Hillel funds come from voluntary donations from those who attend High Holiday services free of charge. In 1990, I become president of the Hillel Board of Directors.

The nonsexist Hillel prayer book, as it comes to be called, is a great hit with many, including me. I find that with gendered language removed from the texts and biblical women permitted in, I can relate more to both the liturgy and to God. I become interested in feminist Jewish writing and begin to see that there are numerous women who struggle, as I do, to maintain a commitment to Judaism in the face of its inherently sexist ideas and practices.

I wish Grandpa were still around. How I would love to talk about a gender-free God with him. I think he would approve. I think his concept of God was, in fact, gender-free. Certainly mine always has been. To me, God is a force, not some anthropomorphic creation. In fact, I'm attracted to the concept of "the Force" in *Star Wars*. Whatever it is that helps Luke, Yoda, and Obi-Wan is probably closer to my conception of God than an old man with a beard, and I have little patience with feminist writings that want to re-create God as a woman.

After all the upheaval during my tenure decision, the work part of my life is now going well. When Sam first left, I threw all my energy into writing a multiyear grant proposal to the Russell Sage Foundation to work on occupational segregation. Toiling away on that proposal was marvelous therapy, exciting and absolutely engrossing. And now I reap the fruits of that work. The grant comes through.

I begin a major project with my doctoral student Carolyn Arnold on how bank telling became a women's occupation during World War II. Our jumping-off point is a study of bank employment in the United States in 1936, which found that although women were employed in numerous clerical jobs in banks, not a single woman was employed as a bank teller. When the researchers followed up with bank managers about this, they were told: "Are you crazy? Who in their right mind would walk into a bank and hand their money over to a *woman*?"

Bank telling was an excellent job for a high school graduate in the 1930s. It paid 40 percent more than the average wage for men with a high school degree, and it offered considerable upward mobility. But the war changed everything. When men were called into the armed forces, banks had no choice but to hire women as bank tellers—and much to their surprise, customers happily handed their cash over to women tellers. After the war, employers tried to rehire men into the occupation, but with the GI Bill, men who might have returned to bank telling or entered it for the first time went to college. If they became bank employees when they graduated, it was not in the teller ranks but as branch managers.

By 1970, bank telling was 90 percent female and no longer an attractive occupation. The upward mobility that used to be associated with it was dead, and it now paid *less* than the average wage for high school graduates.

Generally, when people talk of the feminization of an occupation, they concentrate on women coming *into* the occupation. But our study shows that the movers in occupational musical chairs are really men. When men find a job relatively less attractive compared with jobs that require the same level of education, they go elsewhere. Women move in because men have moved out. This is precisely what I found when I studied the feminization of elementary school teachers.

The relative attractiveness theory also goes a long way toward explaining the shift in the gender composition of factory workers in the maquiladoras in Juárez, Mexico. The maquiladora project is born when another of my doctoral students, Lisa Catanzarite, and I read an article in the *New York Times* that reports a marked increase in the employment of men in the Juárez factories. The article explains that men are now being hired because factory owners have finally acceded to the demands of the Catholic Church in Mexico to stop "destroying" families by employing only young women.

"Why should factory managers all of a sudden pay attention to what the Catholic Church has been saying for twenty years?" Lisa asks.

"And why should factory managers employed by U.S. and European companies care what the Catholic Church in Mexico is saying?" I add.

"We should go down there and see what's really going on," Lisa suggests.

I agree, and Lisa arranges our interviews. We fly to El Paso and easily cross the border into Juárez, a beautiful city with flowers blooming everywhere. Even the large industrial parks are attractive.

Although Lisa uses her Spanish to conduct interviews with workers, all the factory managers we interview speak perfect English. In our first interviews with managers, when we ask them directly why they're employing men in formerly all-female jobs, we spark lots of interesting discussions about irrelevant matters but no straight answers. So we alter our strategy and ask instead about the education level required for workers in the factory. This indirection works, and before too long, the managers are telling *us* about the change in the gender composition of their workforce.

What we learn is that up until recently, men had not applied for jobs in the foreign factories because they were able to earn better salaries working for Mexican companies. But once a major recession hit and men were unable to find work in Mexican factories, they began applying for maquiladora jobs. And they were hired. This sequence of events provides valuable corroboration of my theory that employers give men first choice of occupations, and that occupations become female only when men are no longer interested in them.

❖

I very much enjoy being at SUSE with colleagues who accept and admire my work, and smart and caring doctoral students writing fascinating dissertations. Bill Perron is working on the economics of childcare, Cecile Andrews is studying occupational segregation in community colleges, Carol Muller is examining women faculty's career paths, and Wenda O'Reilly is looking at negotiation patterns in dual-career couples.

I'm beyond busy. I have two half-time jobs (SUSE faculty member and director of CROW), each of which is really a full-time job. Except for running at the track, I have no time for me! No time to just think and "be." Between my kids, Ted, my students, and my research, every moment is filled. My calendar looks like a kindergartener scribbled all over it, and I'm still getting only five or six hours of sleep a night, even though my kids are older now.

Of course, I have only myself to blame, since it is I who keep taking on new tasks. In 1982, I'm asked to become the first chair of the new National Council for Research on Women, a consortium of all the centers for research on women in the United States. The creator of the council is my old mentor, Mariam Chamberlain, formerly at the Ford Foundation. I surely can't say no when she asks me to chair the council's board. Besides, I want to be involved—shape its agenda, learn firsthand about the research taking place at other centers across the country, and keep my fingers on the pulse of the lively East Coast women's movement. Traveling to New York several times a year also means I get to see Helen and Judith.

A second big new task is becoming an associate editor of *Signs*, the premier women's studies journal. Catharine Stimpson, Barnard College professor of English, started *Signs* in 1975; in late 1979, both Stimpson and the journal's publisher, the University of Chicago Press, decide that for maximum innovation, the editor and associate editors of the journal should rotate every five years, and they put out a request for proposals to house the journal.

I think that having *Signs* at CROW would be a great boon, giving us first crack at new ideas in feminist scholarship all over the world. The CROW Policy Board agrees and authorizes me to talk with Barbara Gelpi, associate professor of English at Stanford, to gauge her interest in becoming *Signs'* next editor and in writing a proposal with me to bring the journal to Stanford. Barbara loves the idea, and together we brainstorm our interdisciplinary team of associate editors—Estelle Freedman in history, Carol Jacklin in psychology, Nannerl Keohane in political theory, Shelly Rosaldo in anthropology, and me in economics.

Next we speak to Stanford's new provost, Donald Kennedy, who is enthusiastic.

"This will be very competitive," he prophesies. "You have a terrific editorial team, but Chicago Press will also be looking for university support. You need to let me know what Stanford has to do to get this journal here."

Kennedy is correct. In the end, Stanford and Wellesley are the only two institutions that receive site visits from Chicago, and our visitors tell us that the keen interest and financial support from Stanford's two top administrators, Provost Kennedy and President Lyman, are key factors in their decision to bring the journal to CROW.

Working with Barbara, Estelle, Carol, Nan, and Shelly is every bit as intellectually exciting as I had imagined, as we try to wrap our minds around a field growing geometrically in numerous countries. Our most valiant efforts lie in trying to understand French feminist literary theory.

We bond personally as well as academically, and CROW becomes a place we call home. In 1981, when Shelly dies in an accident in the Philippines while doing fieldwork, each of us comes immediately to CROW when we hear the tragic news. We sit together for hours, taking solace in our common grief.

We also lose Nan Keohane and Carol Jacklin from our team, but for much more positive reasons. Nan leaves to become president of Wellesley College, and Carol moves from senior research associate at Stanford to full professor of psychology and director of women's studies at the University of Southern California.

In 1984, Mike Atkin, dean of the School of Education, asks me to give up my position as director of CROW and take over as director of the school's Institute for Finance and Governance. In return, he agrees to change my appointment at SUSE from half-time to full-time. As part of our negotiations, I ask him for a salary increase. Because Stanford doesn't publish its salaries, I don't know by how much I'm underpaid, but I know from conversations with other faculty that I'm not being paid fairly.

"If you want a salary increase," Mike says, "you have to come up for promotion to full professor."

"I don't want to come up for review," I tell him. "I was traumatized by the last review, and I don't want to be reviewed for promotion again. I want you to increase my *associate* professor salary. This is not about being promoted."

"No can do. Either you come up for review or you keep your current salary."

"No review," I tell him. But I do accept the full-time position and agree to direct the institute. Deborah Rhode, a feminist law professor, takes over as the next director of CROW.

Alice is also making a shift in her career. When she comes up for a tenure and promotion review at Barnard, the college's review is positive. But when Barnard's decision is reviewed by Columbia University (of which Barnard is part), they turn her down. My heart goes out to her. I know all too well what it's like to be turned down for tenure. For the first time in a long while, she accepts my empathy and we talk frequently. I listen to her anger and help her strategize about finding a new job.

Her story has a happy ending, for she soon discovers not one but two silver linings. A professor at Harvard Business School hears her give a talk at a conference and asks her to come and speak there. Shortly thereafter, Harvard offers her a faculty position, which she accepts. Then, not long after she arrives at Harvard, she meets Takashi Hikino at a seminar, and they begin a long and loving relationship. I'm delighted for her but sad for me. Now that she's settled into her new life, our talks once again become brief and infrequent.

During my job transition, Jason is applying to colleges.

"It's going to be really lonely in this house next year with Jason gone," Liz says.

I get an idea. "What would you think about moving into the Stanford dorm?" I explain that I could apply to be a faculty resident fellow, and we could rent out our house and live in the dorm.

She loves the idea, so I apply and am selected. The Residence Office says it would be happy to have Ted be a resident fellow with me. It doesn't matter to them that we're not married. They think his interest in solar energy would be a wonderful addition to dorm life. They also offer to give Liz her own dorm room because they think the apartment they're proposing is too small for three people.

"This sounds better and better," Liz says.

So Liz, Ted, and I spend the next two years at Schiff House. The students treat Liz like a younger sister, and she has a very positive experience. But in our second year there, Ted's and my relationship begins to unravel. Now that Liz will be off to college the next year, I want to move out of the dorm and return home, but Ted wants us to continue to be resident fellows. I'm excited about his solar energy ideas and admire his tenacity, but I don't want to continue to be the sole breadwinner in our partnership. I want him to find a paid job and try to fund his solar energy ideas on the side, but he wants to continue to work full-time seeking funding for his project.

❖

Meanwhile, back in my professional life: two other anthropologists, Jane Collier and Margery Wolf, take Shelly Rosaldo's place as associate editors at *Signs*. We also get new associate editors to replace Nan and Carol. One of the decisions of the reconstituted editorial board is that *Signs* should look more closely at women's communities, and we resolve to have a conference on that topic at Stanford, and then a special issue of the journal with papers from the conference.

The conference takes place in February 1983, and its undisputed star is Sister Joan Chittister, the abbess of a Benedictine nunnery in Erie, Pennsylvania. Sister Joan joined her order when she was sixteen and has spent her entire adult life in the same convent. She is well known for her rabble-rousing, as well as for her inspiring stories about the political and personal goals that women can accomplish through Catholic sisterhood. We ask her to give the closing address to conference participants, and she receives a standing ovation.

Before she leaves, she extends an invitation to our editorial team to visit her convent "next time we're in Erie."

"Right," I say to Carol Jacklin. "Any plans to be in Erie?"

But a couple of years later, Carol and I are invited to give a joint presentation at the Winchester-Thurston School, a private girls' high school in Pittsburgh.

"That's the closest we're getting to Erie," Carol says. "Why don't we call Sister Joan and see if we can visit?"

We rent a car, and after our Saturday talk, we drive up to Erie. The highlight of the visit is the early Sunday morning mass that Sister Joan leads for her sisters. In her sermon, she acknowledges Carol and me and says that in my honor, she will speak about Rabbi Hillel and how much her own philosophy derives from his teachings.

My mind opens further and further. An abbess who is inspired by Hillel! I'm so glad I've come.

❖

On our drive back to Pittsburgh, I talk with Carol about Ted's and my disagreements.

"Well, Myra," she says with great wisdom, "I've come to the conclusion that men are like blue plate specials. Ya gotta take the mashed potatoes with the roast beef. No substitutions allowed. If you don't want the mashed potatoes, find some other dinner."

So in June 1987, I break up with Ted and move back to my house. My friends and Mom agree that this is the right decision for me, but Jason is not so sure.

"I don't know what you should do," he tells me, "but one thing I can tell you is that Ted loves you. It's not so easy to find love, it seems to me. Maybe you should stay with him."

I disagree, but I'm touched by Jason's love and concern, and I'm very sorry to leave my relationship with Ted. He's taught me a great deal about love and generosity, and I know I will miss him greatly.

I spend New Year's Eve with my friend Diane Pincus in Nashville, where she takes me to my first country and western concert with Naomi and Wynonna Judd, whom I find inspirational. On New Year's Day, we have a leisurely breakfast and talk about the characteristics we want in our next husbands. Our conversation is lengthy because although we agree on smart and kind, we have trouble delineating the rest. Smart and kind by themselves seem boring. We want excitement, too, but no more drama. I find it comforting that although we're both in our forties, she is also still searching for Mr. Right.

It takes a year after I leave Ted before I meet another man, and during that time what I miss most is physical closeness. I'm constantly asking my children and women friends for hugs. Eventually I meet Larry at a singles party, and we begin building a relationship. A computer programmer, he's tall, easygoing, and fun. But after several months, my excitement about our relationship diminishes. More singles parties? All over again? I don't think I have the energy for yet another round.

I want so much to be in a permanent loving relationship. But as a scholar of the family, I know the statistics all too well. The remarriage rate for divorced women over forty is low. Twenty years after separation from their husbands, only about one-third are remarried.

10

Flow, 1989–2000

My former student Wenda O'Reilly and I both have birthdays at the end of March, and in 1989, she proposes we celebrate by paying a visit to a psychic she knows in the East Bay.

"Can you put your rationality on hold for an afternoon and try a new way of knowing?" she asks.

"Let's go," I say.

I'm expecting an old woman with a turban silently gazing into a crystal ball. But this psychic is youthful, jeans-clad, and garrulous. The first thing she tells us is that Wenda and I knew each other in a past life: we were Vikings together. We laugh, and I think this is probably going to be more entertainment than a new way of knowing. But then she invites me in for a private session, and the tenor of her prognostications changes.

"In about six months," she says, "you are going to meet your soul mate, the man you're going to be with for the rest of your life. He's someone you already know."

"It's certainly better than hearing that I'm going to shrivel up and die in six months," I tell Wenda. But I pay the prediction little mind. Relying on fortune-tellers is not my style.

❖

In late July, I'm measuring out dried food and checking my cookstove in preparation for a backpacking trip when I get a call from my old friend Jay Jackman, who's visiting his daughter in San Francisco. He says he's coming back in a month or so and would like to get together.

"Great," I say. "I'll be back from Yosemite by then, and if you come down to Stanford, we can have lunch."

On the appointed day, I wait for his airport shuttle at the top of the Oval on Palm Drive. He climbs into my ancient Dodge Dart, and we drive up to Portola Valley to enjoy the scenery. I wish I had a convertible. It's a spectacular day, pure Palo Alto summer—bright sunlight and perfect mid-70s temperature.

I've known Jay for almost thirty years. He was Sam's friend and fraternity brother at Columbia, his classmate at Harvard Medical School, and an usher in Sam's and my wedding. Jay became a psychiatrist and eventually married Judith Meisels. (I sure have a lot of Judiths in my life!) When Sam and I moved to Palo Alto, Jay and Judith were living in Berkeley with their young daughter, Tenaya. But they were hippies and Sam and I were quite straight, so we saw them only occasionally.

In 1976, Jay and Judith moved to Hawaii with their two kids, and for many years we saw them only when they visited the Bay Area. But after his and Judith's separation in 1983, Jay began coming to the mainland more regularly. He and Tenaya stayed at my house when she was looking at colleges in 1984, and he and his son Rashi stayed when they came through on a similar college search a few years later. On that occasion, Jay and Ted and I stayed up into the early morning hours philosophizing about life, love, and politics. Most recently, Jay came to Stanford on his way back from some work he was doing in Colorado, and we spent a day together. He sat in on some of my classes, and in the evening we went out for dinner and dancing.

"If you lived in Hawaii, I'd like to date you," he'd said then.

"That's nice," I'd said, ever practical, "but I don't live in Hawaii."

Now Jay and I head for a lovely outdoor restaurant in Portola Valley, and somewhere between the salad and the entrée, he leans over the table and brushes my hair from my eyes.

"You know," he says, "you're the sort of girl I should marry."

How life changes in an instant. I smile and think to myself, *yes, I really could marry this man*. Then, suddenly, I recall the psychic's forecast.

The rest of lunch is a blur, but afterward we go to my house to sit out in the garden. Pretty soon Liz comes home and strolls out to say hello. She knows Jay because a few years earlier, when she went to Camp

Tawonga, near Yosemite, he was the camp doctor. She ambles down the stairs toward where we're sitting, and then does a double take.

"Something is going on here," she says, and turns back to the house.

I've asked Liz many times what she saw when she walked toward us that afternoon, but she says she doesn't know. She could just see that something was brewing.

In the late afternoon, Tenaya comes to take her dad to dinner and the airport.

"We'll talk tomorrow," Jay says as he leaves, and thus begins a wonderful romance that enriches both AT&T and United Airlines.

At Rosh Hashanah, when Jay comes to Palo Alto to go with Jason and me and Mom to Hillel services, he schedules a lunch with Sam. Uh-oh. What if Sam convinces him that I'm a horrible person, and Jay decides not to continue our relationship? But when Jay returns, he says Sam gave him "a good report." Whew!

Soon Jay breaks up with the woman he's been seeing in Hawaii, and I end my relationship with Larry. At Christmas and New Year's, I spend time with Jay at his place in Lanikai and see that he's an incredibly loving man—to his colleagues, his friends, and his family. And now he turns all that love toward me. Not since my childhood have I been enfolded by such love. For so many years, I wondered if I would ever find a smart and successful man who would love me as I am and not be afraid of *my* being smart and successful.

During the two weeks in Lanikai, I also spend some time with Rashi and Tenaya and very much enjoy their company. Each is accepting of me, and we begin to develop new relationships.

Even so, Jay and I begin planning our future with considerable trepidation. Samuel Johnson once said that second marriages are the triumph of hope over experience, and that feels exactly right. We are optimistic but want to avoid the mistakes we made the first time around.

In January, when I go to Germany for a conference, Jay and I try to continue to talk every day, but the eleven-hour time difference makes it challenging. We miss our daily tête-à-têtes, and when I'm finally back in the States, he proposes over the phone.

"I can close down my practice by the end of the summer and move to Palo Alto," he says.

I accept.

One of the issues we discuss before our wedding is whether I'm going to change my name. Jay's brother and sister-in-law lobby hard for me to take this step, but I don't really want to.

This issue first came up for me after my divorce, when some friends suggested I stop being Myra Strober and go back to being Myra Hoffenberg. I told them I didn't see what was so feminist about having my father's last name instead of my ex-husband's.

"So take your mother's maiden name, Scharer, or your maternal grandmother's maiden name, Greenberg," they said.

"But those are men's names, too. They're my grandfather's name and my great-grandfather's name. There's no winning here."

My decision to stick with Strober after my divorce was a practical one. That was the name by which I was known professionally, that was my children's name, and that was the name I could keep without having to do anything further. The same line of argument seems persuasive now, although there is a lot more pressure this time. Not only do Jay's brother and sister-in-law think I should become a Jackman but so do my aunts, Bimi and Sibi.

"A married woman should have her husband's name," they say.

Well, of course *that* reasoning makes me want to stick with Strober all the more.

I ask Mom what she thinks.

"It doesn't matter one bit. Think about important things."

Jay has the same view.

"I'm marrying *you*. I don't care in the least what your last name is."

So I keep my name, but for years, when Bimi sends me a birthday check, it's made out to Myra Jackman.

*

In late October, the evening before our wedding, Suzanne and Peter Greenberg host a party in our honor, complete with a sumptuous banquet courtesy of Suzanne's culinary genius. Helen Kaplan accompanies our singing on the piano for a good part of the evening, and when we get to "Ride the Chariot," Alice treats us to her soprano highs. Like Alice, Helen can play any song you suggest without a single piece of sheet music, but unlike Alice, she plays the correct left-hand chords. I'm never sure why Alice has not taken the time to learn the correct left-hand piano chords, or why she enjoys searching for singing notes she cannot quite reach, but that is most definitely part of Alice.

As our wedding day unfolds, Jay's friends from Hawaii arrive with leis for us and our families. Although we're in California, the flowers make us feel like we've escaped back to the islands.

I wear a simple, short white dress borrowed from my friend Dania's daughter (twenty-five years after my first wedding, I still don't see the point of spending money for a dress I'll wear only once). I have a tube-rose lei around my neck and a flower lei woven into my hair. Jay wears a bright purple shirt with a long tea-leaf lei and a crown lei. In our wedding pictures, I look like a dryad from a Grecian woodland and he like Titian's Bacchus. Our kids and mothers also wear leis, and the overall scene is one of great beauty.

Rabbi Ari Cartun officiates, and Tenaya, Liz, Rashi, and Jason each clasp one of the four poles holding up the *chuppah,* which we have fashioned from Dad's *tallit,* so that even though Dad is absent, his spirit is with us. Tenaya has come to the wedding from Ghana, where she has been working at a maternal and child health center in a rural area outside Accra, and Liz has flown in from Seattle, where she is getting an MA in social work at the University of Washington. Rashi and Jason don't have nearly as far to travel. Jason is working as a consultant in the East Bay, and Rashi is finishing his BA at Santa Cruz. Sadly, Jay's youngest child, Jason Scott, is not present.

During a ceremony bathed in golden autumn light, Rabbi Cartun gives us advice.

"You've both had love, and you've both lost love. Now you've both found love again, and you want to keep it. Just remember, it's always better to nurture your love than to be right."

We pay close attention.

Jay and I take a short honeymoon in Sedona, Arizona, and then return to business. Jay has the difficult job of creating a new career. He doesn't want to do private patient therapy anymore and, as he puts it, "The last thing Palo Alto needs is another therapist in private practice." Instead, he begins to network so he can continue some of the expert witness work in criminal cases that he began doing in Hawaii. It takes several years to build this practice, but he's ultimately successful, and over the next twenty years, he will be called as an expert witness in more than two hundred murder cases.

For me, business means facing a review for promotion to full professor. The year before, a new dean, Mike Smith, took over at SUSE, and he insists that I come up for review.

"You absolutely can't stay at the associate professor level anymore," he says. "Your record warrants promotion, and I'm going to appoint a review committee."

So I get all my papers together and give the committee a list of names, just as I did eleven years before. It's lucky I'm married to a psychiatrist. He assures me every day that this time won't be like the last.

It isn't. The review is positive, as is the faculty vote, and I'm finally a full professor. But I'm quite disappointed in the miniscule salary increase the dean proposes.

"I am seriously underpaid," I tell him, "and you know it as well as I do. I would like a substantial salary increase in connection with this promotion."

"Can't do it. You know how the game is played. If you want anything more than a token increase, you need to get an outside offer."

"That's impossible. My colleagues all over the country know that I just got married, that my husband moved from Hawaii to be with me, and that he's settling into his career here. Nobody's going to believe I'm seriously on the job market."

"I'd like to help you, but my hands are tied. Unless you get an outside offer, I can't get funds to increase your salary."

Even though my pay is not what it should be, the combination of being married to Jay and being a full professor puts me into nirvana. The fusion of personal fulfillment and professional recognition creates a perpetual high, and I walk around with a permanent grin.

The psychologist Mihaly Csikszentmihalyi applied the term "flow" to explain a state of happiness where people are so in harmony with work and life that they experience great joy. The tasks they face are exactly right, challenging but not frustrating. That's where I am, in a persistent state of flow. What will I do next? How will I use my success to help others unlock their doors?

The universe seems to have its own answers to these questions—without my making any conscious plans, new projects come to the fore. First, several companies call to ask me to consult with them on bringing women into management positions, and when I tell Jay about these, he suggests we collaborate. In Hawaii, he did several consultations for companies on human resource issues.

When I was married to Sam, work and home were always colliding, and I did my best to keep my professional self out of our personal lives. But Jay and I have the opposite experience. Although some colleagues tell us that working with their spouses is detrimental to their marriage, we find working together is great fun, and we get a particularly big kick out of reversing companies' gender expectations: he turns out to be the touchy-feely consultant, and I'm the number cruncher.

We also enjoy writing together, and we publish two articles for the *Harvard Business Review (HBR)* based on our consulting: the first about why women in management should forge alliances, especially with men, when they seek to make changes at their workplace. The second, "Fear of Feedback," is about why workers and managers are afraid to ask for and give honest feedback. A decade later, *HBR* will republish "Fear of Feedback" in a special issue highlighting its fifteen most outstanding articles on emotional intelligence in business.

My second new challenge is also thrown into my lap. Jerry Lieberman, my former boss at CROW and now the university's provost, asks me to chair a new ad hoc committee he is forming on the recruitment and retention of women faculty. Women now make up 16 percent of the Stanford faculty, slightly more than three times the percentage they were when I first arrived, but still low compared with our peer institutions. Jerry wants me to lead the committee in figuring out what Stanford can do to raise that percentage and keep it growing.

The committee's charge is broad, and its male and female members, prominent faculty from all over the university, have quite varied opinions. After several meetings, we decide to focus our efforts on junior faculty. We break up into groups of two or three, with at least one woman and one man in each, and conduct focus groups with both men and women assistant professors.

What we hear is disturbing. Junior faculty tell us that they feel the absence of what committee members begin to term a "culture of support."

Although Stanford departments make heroic efforts to recruit the very best junior faculty, including young scholars from other countries, once those faculty arrive and take up their posts, senior faculty in their departments often pay them little mind, perhaps not even reading their work. Both junior women and junior men tell this tale. On the other hand, there are several problems unique to women: encountering the extra scrutiny given to people in the minority, fending off sexual harassment, and being underpaid.

The committee feels that the charges of underpayment are serious, and I bring up the matter in a meeting with Jerry, remembering his counsel years earlier that I negotiate "like a gentleman," not like a former New Yorker.

"In our focus groups, a lot of the women faculty we talked to said they feel they're underpaid, but we can't verify that the university pays women less than men at the same stage of their career unless we have salary data by gender for each school."

"No way," he says. "Salary information is confidential."

"Well, that may be," I say in my most gentle way, "but you appointed this committee to make suggestions about improving the hiring and retention of women faculty, and it looks like one reason women may be leaving Stanford is that they feel underpaid."

"OK, I'll take a look at the data and see."

"Jerry, you can look at the data anytime. But you appointed a committee to help you with this. *We* need to look at the data."

Silence.

"We don't need names, you know, just numbers."

I smile my most "gentlemanly" smile.

After several go-rounds, we compromise. Jerry agrees to provide a series of scatter plots of full professors' salaries, by years of experience, in five fields: humanities, social sciences and education, science, clinical medicine, and nonclinical medicine. In each scatter plot, any dot that represents a woman is circled in black. That way, we can see the overall distribution of salaries in a particular field as well as the distribution of women's salaries. No such plots have ever been prepared, but Jerry asks members of his staff to create them.

He allows only three members of our committee to look at the data with him, and he won't permit any of us to take the plots out of his office.

What we see is crystal clear, and we don't need much time or analysis to understand the pattern. At all levels of experience, women are over-represented in the lowest quintile of the salary distribution and under-represented in the highest. I'm not at all surprised, but Jerry is, and so are many of the deans to whom he shows the plots. Indeed, the creation of those simple quintile plots becomes the first step in Stanford's emerging efforts to redress salary discrimination. Jerry creates a fund that deans can draw on for salary equity raises, and over the next few years, many women faculty, including me, find that our paychecks are substantially increased.

The report of our committee, which has come to be known as the Strober Report, has sixteen recommendations, including that the pro-vost require deans to monitor women's salaries on an ongoing basis, ask departments with few women to draw up hiring plans for increasing their female faculty, and create ongoing programs designed to educate and sen-sitize faculty members about sexual harassment. But perhaps our most important recommendation is to create a culture of support, a culture in which human beings with outstanding brainpower are actually told by their colleagues that they are valued and appreciated—a foreign notion at most research universities.

No sooner is my work with the provost's committee complete than I'm elected the SUSE representative to Stanford's Faculty Senate, where I become chair of the Committee on Committees. Despite the name, this is more than bureaucratic nonsense—through its recommendations for various university committees and task forces, the Committee on Com-mittees plays a key role in university governance. Because I am able to put procedures in place to ensure that women and minority faculty are fairly considered for important positions, I significantly increase the power of women and minority faculty.

I'm also asked by Nel Noddings, the School of Education's new acting dean, to serve as the school's associate dean for academic affairs. In that position, I'm privy to data on faculty salaries, and for the first time I see how seriously underpaid I am, despite my recent salary adjustment. Nel is sympathetic (she's been underpaid for years as well), and now that there is a fund for rectifying women faculty's salaries, she is able to successfully ask the provost for a substantial increase in my salary.

❖

In addition to my administrative work, I begin a whole new line of research, a project on how highly educated women and men combine work and family. My data come from the Stanford class of 1980, whose members were surveyed by the university ten years after their graduation. I contributed several questions on work and family to the survey, and now I'm busily analyzing the results to see how the work and family lives of the women graduates compare to those of their male classmates.

Working with me is a large group of doctoral students. One of them is a new student, Agnes Chan. Agnes doesn't know much about statistics when she arrives from Tokyo, but she takes some classes and begins working on my project. The best way to learn statistics is to work with real data. Other students on the project—particularly Lisa Petrides, Chris Golde, and Cassie Guarino—have much more statistical experience than Agnes, and they help her learn. Agnes becomes extremely interested in the research and decides that for her doctoral dissertation, she will translate the Stanford survey into Japanese and send it to the graduates of Tokyo University (Todai), class of 1980. When she completes her thesis, we begin writing a book together comparing the results for the graduates of Stanford and Todai, and in 1999, the MIT Press publishes our work in *The Road Winds Uphill All the Way: Gender, Work, and Family in the United States and Japan*.

As expected, we find that both the Todai and Stanford women were leaders in the gender revolution in their countries, more likely to major in subjects not traditional for women, and more likely to be employed. Also, the married Stanford graduates were much more likely to share housework than other U.S. married couples. Almost 45 percent of the Stanford couples shared housework, but in surveys of all married U.S. couples done at about the same time as the Stanford survey, fewer than 20 percent shared cooking and cleaning equally, and fewer than 30 percent shared shopping equally.

On the other hand, Todai graduates were no more likely to share household tasks than other Japanese. Ninety percent of Todai men and 87 percent of Todai women said the women in their family were responsible for household tasks, virtually the same percentage found in a 1982 national survey of all Japanese families.

In other ways, though, our findings were surprising. Despite the substantial investment they made in their education by attending two of the most selective universities in the world, only about two-thirds of the Stanford women and only about one-half of the Todai women were employed full-time, compared with 90 percent of the Stanford and Todai men. And one-third of the Stanford mothers and one-quarter of the Todai mothers were not employed at all.

Also surprising was the similarity in the female/male earnings ratio in the two countries. Although the female/male earnings ratio for *all* full-time workers in 1989–1990 was much higher (more equal) in the United States than in Japan (69 percent versus 55 percent), among the women and men from Todai and Stanford who worked full-time, the female/male earnings ratio was the same, 80 percent in both samples.

I am also involved in two research projects on an earlier interest, the economics of childcare. In the first, my doctoral student Ken Yeager and I study an election held in Fremont, California, in June 1989 to determine whether the city should levy a $12 annual property tax to pay for before- and after-school childcare services. This is the nation's first city election ever held on this issue, and it is being watched carefully. On the day of the election, Ken does an exit poll asking voters why they voted as they did.

The city council and public opinion pundits are shocked when the tax is defeated by a margin of 3.5 to 1. The exit poll data explain why. Those who voted no did not see childcare as a public good. They felt that helping to raise other people's children was simply not their responsibility. As a result of the Fremont election, many cities that had hoped to put a childcare tax on their own ballots change their mind. Ken and I are dejected by these results and wonder what the outcome would be if voters were asked to reratify their financial commitment to public education. Would they also feel that *educating* other people's kids was not their responsibility?

In a second study with Ken, along with Suzanne Gerlach-Downey, I look at childcare centers as workplaces. We visit four types of centers, interview twenty childcare teachers and aides, and write a paper that gives voice to childcare workers' concerns. It is well known that childcare is a very low-paying occupation that provides little reward for training and experience, and our interviewees emphasize these facts. But less understood is the stress stemming from inadequate staffing, debilitation from the frequent colds caught from their charges, and frustration in being managed by inexperienced directors. Many say they would appreciate more training in both child development and in dealing with parents. The workers' voices make it clear why the turnover rate among childcare workers is one of the highest in the labor force (to the detriment of children who need continuity of care), and the kind of information we have collected is important for those seeking to improve the quality of childcare centers.

❖

As these research projects begin to wind down, a new challenge rises to the fore: feminist economics. For several years now, I've attended interdisciplinary faculty seminars in feminist theory sponsored by Stanford's Feminist Studies program. In many ways, these seminars are a continuation of the original CROW group of the late 1970s, where a small group of feminist scholars learned about new scholarship and research in the social sciences, history, and literature. Participating in these feminist theory seminars, I have thought a great deal about how feminist thought might change economic theory, but I have not been able to conceptualize the possible transformations.

In economics, there have been no feminist methodological or theoretical breakthroughs similar to those in other disciplines. For example, in psychology and medicine, feminist scholars have emphasized the differences in findings when researchers employ both female and male subjects rather than having solely male subjects, and in anthropology and literature, feminist scholars have shown how different subject matter and style can be when women are the researchers or writers. In history, scholars have shown how focusing on women's experiences and those of common people fundamentally changes historical understanding.

Then one afternoon, as I'm sorting the day's mail, I begin reading a manuscript sent to me by Julie Nelson, a young economist whose work I don't know, in which she argues that economics has lost its way, that it has concentrated on choice and exchange and in the process has forgotten Adam Smith's dictum that economics must be concerned first and foremost with the process of "provisioning," the fulfillment of human beings' material needs. How extraordinary! A feminist economist arguing that Adam Smith, the so-called father of economics and certainly not an avowed feminist, got it right to begin with—but that those who followed have lost their way.

Julie's paper opens a door deep in my brain, and I suddenly see how feminist analysis can be applied to economics. Julie is an assistant professor at the University of California at Davis, about a two-hour car ride away, and when I call her to congratulate her on her paper, we arrange for me to drive up to Davis to talk with her. When we meet, I ask her what she thinks enabled her to have this theoretical breakthrough.

She explains that while she was an economics doctoral student at the University of Wisconsin, she also took classes in women's studies. In other words, she was exposed to economic theory and feminist theory at the same time, and her mind learned to think simultaneously in both disciplines. This contrasts greatly with my own experience, in which economic analysis was tightly wired into my brain *before* I learned feminist theory, so that I had difficulty merging the two sets of ideas.

I think a great deal about Julie's experience versus mine, and also about the intolerance that the doctoral students in history and quantitative social science who worked with Dave Tyack and me on the feminization of teaching showed to methodologies other than their own. For them, too, exposure to a second discipline seemed to come too late in their training for them to be able to meld the two sets of ideas. On a back burner of my mind, ideas begin to simmer about doing a research project on interdisciplinarity.

My front burner, however, concentrates on feminist economics. In 1990, Diana Strassmann organizes a session on feminist economics at the annual AEA meetings, and in the same way that the 1971 meetings resulted in the formation of CSWEP, the 1990 session results in the creation of the International Association for Feminist Economics (IAFFE). The creation of CSWEP was the first gender revolution in economics; the birth of IAFFE is the second. But while CSWEP is a committee of the AEA whose mission is to increase the number of women economists and ensure they are hired and paid fairly, IAFFE is an independent nonprofit entity seeking to revolutionize the discipline of economics. Within three years, it has more than five hundred members all across the globe.

In 1993, Diana puts together another session at the AEA's annual meetings, and I present a paper titled "Rethinking Economics through a Feminist Lens." In it, I note that feminist economics is a radical endeavor. In a discipline that believes strongly in objectivity of analysis, feminist economics argues that what one chooses to work on and how one formulates theory and policy recommendations are *not* objective but dependent on one's culture, position in society, and life experiences. I also discuss the ways in which women are disadvantaged by several of mainstream economics' central constructs, such as the existence of scarcity, the value of efficiency, and the omnipresence of selfishness.

Diana has asked my former MIT professor and recent Nobel Prize winner Bob Solow to be a discussant at the session, and many AEA members are interested in what Bob thinks about feminist economics (he says he's unsure), so the session is packed to overflowing. One of the attendees is from Melbourne University, and a month or so after the meetings, he invites me to come there to deliver the prestigious Downing Lecture. I accept the invitation, and Jay and I spend a wonderful month in Australia while I bring Australian economists up to speed on feminist economics.

Later in 1993, the University of Chicago Press publishes a book edited by Julie Nelson and Marianne Ferber, *Beyond Economic Man: Feminist Theory and Economics*, the first ever on feminist economics. In it, Paula England argues that economic theorists' idea of a separative self that makes decisions without a family or social context is ludicrous; Nancy Folbre contends that unpaid caring labor for one's children, spouse, or elderly parents is a significant part of economic activity, even though it is not "counted" as part of GNP or other economic measures of output and productivity; and Diana Strassmann maintains that mainstream economists focus far too much on choice and far too little on the constraints that operate to lessen choice.

That same year, the University of Amsterdam sponsors the first-ever conference on feminist economic theory, and in 1994 Routledge publishes the first issue of IAFFE's new journal, *Feminist Economics*, with Diana Strassmann as editor. I serve as one of the associate editors and also agree to be a member of IAFFE's executive board. From 1996 to 1998, I serve as IAFFE's president.

Feminist economics creates a stir in the academic and popular press, and in June 1993, the *Chronicle of Higher Education* publishes an article explaining how feminist economics is attempting to open the marketplace of ideas in the "dismal science," and I'm frequently asked to explain what feminist economics is all about.

I always begin by talking about what it is *not*. It is not essentialist; that is, it does not hold that there are fundamental (essential) differences between women and men. It is also not about fundamental differences between women and men economists, that is, it doesn't say that women economists do economics differently from men or even that women economists have a special pipeline to understanding women's economic oppression, although some of the insights women economists have may come from experiences that most men economists do not have.

The central tenets of feminist economics are its concern with human well-being and material provisioning rather than with market processes or income and its insistence that the gender division of labor be a fundamental part of economic analysis. It argues that vital economic contributions are made by unpaid labor, especially the care of children, the sick, and the elderly, and it gives voice to the frustration that women's jobs are frequently paid far less than their contribution to society would suggest.

Although most mainstream economists completely ignore feminist economics (it's just a fad, most of them say), *Feminist Economics* becomes a prestigious journal, wins an award as the best new academic journal, and is accepted as a journal that should be indexed. In other words, feminist economics' reception is far better outside the economics profession than within.

Also in 1993, I begin to put feminist economics into action. I agree to join the board of the NOW Legal Defense and Education Fund (NOWLDEF). Based in New York City, NOWLDEF provides legal assistance to women who bring cases involving sex discrimination and sexual harassment, and the organization also trains lawyers and judges in these matters. Once again, I travel to New York several times a year, and whenever I'm there, I stay one night with Judith Brandenburg and one with Helen Kaplan. These short visits bring my friendships with these two women up to date, and I enjoy watching them take on new challenges as their children grow. Judith becomes the first woman dean of Columbia's Teachers College, and Helen starts a business helping people organize their homes and offices.

❖

As a result of my involvement with NOWLDEF, I'm asked to be an expert witness in a Connecticut divorce case involving Lorna and Gary Wendt. I've done some expert witness work before on cases of earnings discrimination and sexual harassment, but none as complicated as this. My assignment is to value Mrs. Wendt's unpaid labor caring for her family and her home over a thirty-year marriage that is now ending in divorce.

Unpaid labor has tremendous value to a family. My first understanding of this was as a teenager, when I saw how much both Mom and Dad had to increase the amount of work they did around the house to fill in for what Tante Annie was no longer doing. My perspective has also been affected by my own experience of housework and childcare. Even though I have always had paid childcare and recently have been able to afford more help with housecleaning, I still do an enormous amount of work raising my children, managing the household, and providing my family with a social life, including entertaining, buying tickets, planning travel, and so on.

Mr. Wendt is the CEO of GE Capital, and he has asked his wife for a divorce. At the end of most long-term marriages, the couple or the court splits the couple's joint assets 50–50, even in non-community-property states such as Connecticut. But sometimes in non-community-property states where the couple's joint assets are greater than $15 million or so, as they are in the Wendt case, the court balks at a 50–50 split, particularly if the wife has been a homemaker throughout the marriage.

The Wendts' assets are about $100 million, and Mr. Wendt has offered his wife $10 million, saying that she surely doesn't "need" any more than this. But Mrs. Wendt believes she is entitled to half the couple's assets and hires me as her expert to testify as to why the property split should be based not on need but rather on the value of her labor as a wife and mother over thirty years.

The Wendts were high school sweethearts who married in 1963, right after Lorna graduated from college. At that time, they had no assets. Shortly after their marriage, they moved to Cambridge, where Mr. Wendt attended Harvard Business School and his wife supported them by working as a public-school music teacher. At Harvard's graduation, she got an honorary "degree" commonly known at the time: a PHT—Putting Hubby Through.

After their marriage, they moved several times as he developed his career. She stopped working for pay and cared for her husband, their children, and their home, and each time they moved, she took care of buying and selling their house and getting them settled in their new community.

Coming from California, I'm used to community-property reasoning: except for assets that the partners bring into the marriage or those obtained during the marriage from inheritance, all property is community property and is to be split equally at divorce. Even if one party does nothing during the marriage but sit in a rocking chair for decades, he or she is entitled to half the community property. But in non-community-property states (equitable-distribution states), when making a property determination at divorce, the courts are interested in what each party contributed to the marriage. My role in the case is to determine Mrs. Wendt's economic contribution to the marriage, then put a price on it.

Just before the trial begins, Mrs. Wendt calls in the *Wall Street Journal*. Of course, once the *Journal* is involved, so are all the other major media. Mrs. Wendt says she wants publicity because she wants it to be established in Connecticut law—and indeed in the law of all equitable-distribution states—that in a long-term breadwinner-homemaker marriage, the wife is entitled to half the couple's assets.

I fly to the East Coast to testify in December 1996, and in the taxi that takes me from Kennedy Airport to Grand Central Station for my train to Greenwich, Connecticut, a talk radio station is blaring away. The caller is incensed about the Wendt case.

"What does her husband mean that all she *needs* is $10 million? Does that mean he *needs* $90 million?"

When I take the stand, I testify that there are two methods that economists generally use to value the labor of a homemaker/wife/mother: the *market replacement method*, which asks how much it would cost to replace all her activities by hiring other people to do them, and the *opportunity cost method*, which asks how much income the homemaker/wife/mother is forgoing in the workforce by working at home instead. I then explain why both of these methods are seriously flawed and describe the method I have derived instead.

My method is based on human capital theory and a partnership theory of marriage. The two spouses made very different economic investments in their marriage. She did nonmarket labor while he earned income. But throughout their marriage, they shared the fruits of the two types of economic contributions equally. At the time of separation, the couple had fully used up all of her contributions—but they had not used up his, for a substantial part of his contribution remained in the form of assets. She is entitled to half of those assets because the couple have been in a partnership, and, barring any legal document to the contrary, the rebuttable presumption is that it was a 50–50 partnership.

I use a business analogy. If two people form a business partnership, and one has expertise in production while the other has expertise in marketing, at the time the business breaks up, they don't ask how much of the remaining assets came from production expertise and how much from marketing expertise. Unless they have a contract to the contrary, the presumption is that they were in a 50–50 partnership, and the remaining assets are divided equally.

The judge takes a year to reach his decision, and when he does, he issues a 519-page opinion. (Most of it is about valuing unvested stock options, not unpaid labor.) He says he doesn't think marriage is a partnership, but nonetheless awards Lorna half the couple's hard assets.

Because of all the media attention surrounding the case, I'm asked to be an expert in five additional high-asset divorce cases. I'm deposed in all of them, but none goes to trial. In all the cases, the attorneys tell me that after my deposition, the couple settled for "close" to a 50–50 distribution of assets.

The astonishing publicity at the time of the Wendt case considerably raises my stock on the cocktail and dinner party circuits. Colleagues, friends, and neighbors all want to tell me how much they disagree with me, and what better place than in their living or dining room? Most men are incredulous that I believe that by "merely being a housewife for thirty years, a woman is entitled to $50 million." Liberal feminists think I'm "selling out" because I'm promoting the idea that it's "OK" to be a housewife. Radical feminists don't like the idea that I'm treating marriage like a commodity by putting a price on it, and Marxist feminists wonder why I'm spending time defending rich women when poor women need my services far more.

Despite the ubiquitous criticism, I feel good about my role in these cases. I think our tax system should make it far more difficult to accumulate $100 million than it is now, but given our current tax system, each spouse should participate fully in the other's gains. If a particular couple doesn't like that idea, they should write a prenuptial or postnuptial agreement, legally codifying any other arrangement they like. I think rich women deserve their day in court as much as poor women do, and that women and men whose husbands or wives have "killer jobs" deserve our full support if they must give up their careers to be full-time parents. I wish there were no "killer jobs," but that's not the case today, and the 24/7 demands of new technologies such as mobile phones make things more difficult, not less.

Shortly after the Wendt decision is handed down, my attention turns to my own family. When Jay and I married, he said he wanted us to include his ex-wife, Judith, as well as Sam in our family celebrations and in our lives. I couldn't bring myself to do that and suggested he bring up the topic again in five years.

So he does. He's a patient man.

"OK," I say, "let's try it. But if they don't behave, that's it. One try, that's all they get."

Jay laughs. "You sound like a kindergarten teacher. How exactly do you think they might misbehave?

"You know, if they're not nice, if they say mean things."

"Now you sound like one of the kindergarten kids. Don't worry, it'll all be fine."

We invite them both for Thanksgiving dinner, and it turns out even better than fine. By then Sam is married to Linda and they have a young son, Will. Linda is lovely, one of those rare people from whom you never hear a harsh word, and at the dinner, both Sam and Judith make toasts to Jay and me, thanking us for reaching out. Then Jason and Tenaya toast, thanking us for "combining forces" and not making them participate in two separate Thanksgiving dinners.

Not long after, I ask Sam to lunch.

"Remember when you told me that someday I would thank you for leaving?" I ask him. "Well, today's the day."

Since that initial Thanksgiving dinner we have spent numerous holidays with Sam and his family (he and Linda now have two sons), and when Judith is in town, we see her and her husband Mark as well.

In the mid-1990s, our family begins to expand. Jason meets Joanna Aptekar, and they quickly fall in love. Joanna is brilliant, lovely, super-efficient, and fun. She and Jason make a wonderful couple, and I'm proud when a few years later she becomes my daughter-in-law.

But unhappily, at about the same time, Mom, now ninety-one, becomes severely demented, and her neighbors tell me she leaves the oven and burners on in her kitchen long after she's finished using them. They're afraid she'll burn down the building.

Alice, now a professor at MIT, frequently comes to Palo Alto to visit with Mom, and together we talk to her about moving. But Mom is adamantly opposed. She loves her apartment and is afraid of any kind of change. Eventually, though, we have no choice, and on one of Alice's visits, we move her forcibly into an assisted-care facility. It is one of the most difficult days of our lives.

Mom still recognizes us, but she's a shadow of her former high-powered self. Until her dementia, she played bridge several times a week, read the *Wall Street Journal* daily, and regularly took her forty-five-minute constitutional. I visit Mom often, but not much transpires. She mostly sits and stares into space, rarely interested even in food. After five months in assisted living, she dies of pneumonia.

As a widow for fifteen years, and with seriously impaired hearing, she has often been lonely. But Mom has been a survivor, a master at coping with challenges.

When Dad died, I asked Mom what she thought the purpose of life was.

"Survival," she said fiercely.

When she was in her late eighties, and I asked her what she enjoyed most about living a long life, she said, her eyes shining, "I love to see what's on the next page."

No more pages for Mom.

Mom's funeral is in Staten Island, at the same cemetery I went to as a teenager when my family buried Grandpa, Tante Annie, and Baba, the same cemetery where we unveiled Dad's gravestone in the pouring rain fifteen years earlier. Baba's brothers, their families, and several of Mom's sisters are buried there, too. So many memories. So many tears.

❖

A few years after Mom's death, Jay's mother also passes away, at the age of ninety-four, and we bury her ashes in a cemetery in Colma, just south of San Francisco. Our family is changing drastically. All four of our parents have now died, and we keenly feel the absence of a buffer generation.

Now we are the seniors, and as if to emphasize our new role, our first grandchild, Sarah, is born to Jason and Joanna in 1998.

Just a year later, Liz marries Bryan Cohen. He is handsome, loving, creative, and entertaining, and his and Liz's energies are an excellent match. I am thrilled that he is my son-in-law. Alice and Takashi marry around the same time as Liz and Bryan. They have been together for fourteen years, and Jay and I have come to like Takashi a great deal.

When Jason Scott, Jay's youngest child, turns eighteen, he writes to Jay saying he would like to visit us. We're nervous. What will he be like? What will our relationship with him be like? We needn't have worried. We find him easygoing, smart, and remarkably mature, and we have numerous long talks to try to catch up on the years we missed. Jay has his son back, and I have another stepchild.

I'm almost sixty. I've had a life I never dreamed possible, and a new chapter is starting. I stop coloring my hair. It's completely white now—a symbol of a new me, and hopefully a sign of increased wisdom.

11

Transformation, 2000–2012

In spring 2002, as I'm walking to campus, one of my former colleagues at the business school rides past me on his bike. Suddenly he slams on his brakes, gets off his seat, and waits for me to catch up.

"Do you remember when we turned you down for tenure twenty-five years ago?" he asks.

I'm stunned. And silent.

"Do you remember?" he persists.

"Uh, yes, something like that is pretty hard to forget."

"Do you remember *why* we turned you down?"

"You're asking *me* why you turned me down? What's this all about?"

"At yesterday's faculty meeting, we had to vote on whether to give you a courtesy appointment so you can direct the joint degree program between the B-School and the Ed School."

"Yes, I knew this was in the works."

"Well, after the meeting, a few of us who were there when you got turned down asked each other if anybody remembered *why* you'd been turned down. None of us could remember."

"Uh-huh."

Long silence.

"Do you think it was because we were male chauvinist pigs?"

I have to laugh. I haven't heard that term in so long.

"Yes," I tell him. "I'm sure that was a big part of it."

I take his comment as an olive branch. Not exactly an apology, but perhaps a gesture of truce? With maybe even a tinge of repentance? Whatever the precise sentiment, it's been a long time coming, and it feels wonderful. I soon receive word that the GSB faculty has approved my courtesy appointment, and the following fall I begin a five-year term as director of the joint degree program.

When I received a PhD in economics from MIT, I was given a key that, along with hard work, should have unlocked the door to a tenured position at the GSB. But sexism prevented my key from working. No matter how I tried twisting it in the lock, I could not get the door to open. Now the situation is different. The old guys have died. The locks have been changed.

I teach a seminar for about twenty-five students enrolled for the joint degree, and also have numerous MBA students in my SUSE course on the economics of higher education. None of them ever questions my authority or knowledge, and I find their considerable intellect a pleasure. I particularly enjoy showing them that mainstream microeconomic theory doesn't even begin to explain the economics of American higher education.

My teaching at the GSB increases when, a few years later, GSB professor Joanne Martin goes on sabbatical and suggests to the dean that I teach a course on women and work to replace her course on women in organizations. My course goes exceedingly well, and when she returns, she tells the dean she thinks I should continue to teach it, even though she will also teach hers.

"I'm a social psychologist, and Myra is an economist," she says. "We teach very different courses. Nothing would be harmed by having *two* courses dealing with women's issues." He agrees.

Some time later, one of the men in the class recommends that I change the title of the class to Work and Family.

"You'll get more guys if you change the name," he says.

I take his counsel and find his prediction accurate. Every year since the name change, the percentage of men in the class has increased; in the spring of 2012, 40 percent of the students are men. They write papers with titles like "How Can I Be the Best Father I'm Capable of Being?" and "What Are the Effects of Childcare on Children?" What a different group of men from the ones who rudely interrupted my macroeconomics class when I first taught at the GSB!

Elizabeth Cady Stanton insisted that men must be part of the fight for women's rights, and Francine and I took her advice seriously when we collaborated with Arjay to hold a conference on women in management for male managers. Now my class works on the same principle.

One of the joys of teaching the class is having my daughter-in-law, Joanna Strober, as a guest speaker. Joanna is co-author of the book *Getting to 50–50*, on how to have an egalitarian marriage. She is honest in class, telling students that she and Jason don't yet have a 50–50 marriage but are working on getting there. The students love her sessions.

"Jason got the theory from you," she tells me. "But he gets the practice from me."

The class is a combination of economics, sociology, and social psychology, and it gives me an opportunity to use my own experience, as well as the social science literature, to teach students from all over the world about combining family life with the exceedingly demanding careers they are about to enter. To supplement my own knowledge and experience, I bring in successful women and men from the business world, who also share stories and advice.

I teach in a beautiful new building with wood paneling and comfortably padded chairs, and the afternoon sun streams in from large shaded windows. I begin each class with a short lecture, but the Q&A that follows is far more stimulating, and even though there are sixty students in the class, women and men share their apprehensions frankly. Most have not had working mothers, and while some have older siblings who are combining work and family, many have older sisters or sisters-in-law who have failed at their efforts.

The all-time favorite student question, the one that comes up every year, is "Can I have it all?"

"The idea that anybody can have it all is a fiction," I say, "and it's a fiction that's particularly unpalatable to economists, who think in terms of opportunity costs and trade-offs. You *can't* have it all. Nobody can."

"But is it possible to have both a demanding career and a family?"

"Most definitely. Two people can be in a sustained and nourishing personal relationship with satisfying careers for both, but *only* if both are fully committed to going that route. If both you and your partner *are* committed, you will find a way to make it work."

I stress the fact that whom you marry or partner with is the most important career decision you will ever make, that if the person you live with doesn't support your career, you will have a long and difficult road.

The course also deals with relationships at work. We talk about how people can obtain more control over their work environments, and guest speakers address this issue as well. I tell them that as managers, they will play a critical role in the lives of their subordinates who are trying to balance work and family, and we have class discussions about how to offer subordinates work flexibility while operating in a competitive environment.

The twenty-first century brings further growth in my family. In May 2001, Jay and I have great joy at the birth of Jason and Joanna's second child, Jared. Then, a few months later, we celebrate Rashi's marriage to Maike Ahrends, a tall, blond, beautiful woman with a PhD in German from the University of Michigan, where she and Rashi met. She teaches German at Ohio University.

About a year after Rashi and Maike's marriage, they have a son, Jasper, and a year after that, Liz and Bryan's son, Leo, is born. At this point, our grandchild count includes one girl, Sarah, and three boys, Jared, Jasper, and Leo. We love our new role and try to see these amazing new lights in our life as often as possible. That's easy with Sarah and Jared, who live about ten minutes away, but a good deal harder with Jasper and Leo.

We love to take the kids without their parents so that we can play by our (rather lenient) rules and not deal with the kids' complex interactions with their parents. Mostly, we laugh at their active antics and enjoy their unusual takes on the world. We love to participate in Sarah's make-believe games and help the boys build with Lego, although they soon outperform us in figuring out how to put the tiny pieces in the right spots.

When they get a bit older, we swim with them and they help us cook (pancakes with chocolate chips are an all-time favorite). On rainy days, we play an endless variety of board games (Sorry!, Clue, Qwirkle, Scrabble Junior, and a bit of Monopoly). When we get tired, we take them home. Or, if they're sleeping over, we declare "quiet time" and read to them. We do little of the hard work of childrearing but reap all the pleasures of their parents' labors. What a deal!

In 2006, Jason and Joanna have a third child, Ari, and in the summer of 2011, our family grows again when Jason Scott marries Lena Chu. Ever since Jason Scott's visit to Jay and me when he became eighteen, our relationship with him has grown, and he has become an integral part of our family. Our grandchildren adore him. Lena is a stunning woman, gentle and loving, who is getting a doctorate at Stanford in clinical psychology—a perfect field for her because, like Jay, she has an extraordinary capacity to listen and understand.

Two years after their marriage, Jason and Lena have a son, Leander. He's our sixth grandchild, and the count is now one girl and five boys! Leander is thirteen weeks premature and weighs only slightly over two pounds. He spends three months in neonatal intensive care, and we are grateful for his miraculous growth.

Just before Sarah's birth in 1998, Joanna and Jason asked me what I would like to be called by my granddaughter-to-be, and I knew the answer in an instant.

"Baba—that's what I called my grandmother, and that's what I'd like my grandchildren to call me."

And so they do.

When I hear them calling, I get double pleasure. Not only do I adore being needed by these incredibly loving and interesting toddlers, but hearing the word "Baba" reminds me of *my* Baba. Nobody gets lessons on being a grandma, but whenever I'm in doubt about what to do, I ask myself what *my* Baba would have done. She may have had zero book learning, but after seven children and twelve grandchildren, she figured it out.

It seems to me that she operated by three rules: love your grandchildren unconditionally at every possible moment. Listen! Make sure they know that you hear and care about their every word, and teach by example. Live your life the way you'd like them to live theirs.

In 2000, I begin a new research project on interdisciplinarity. Throughout the 1990s, interdisciplinary conversations and collaboration were widely acclaimed as strategies for solving complex problems that do not obey traditional disciplinary boundaries. But interdisciplinarity is difficult to achieve, and there is little research about why that is so. My own work has always been interdisciplinary, and for a long time I have been interested in better understanding how collaboration with scholars from other fields can be achieved more smoothly.

With a grant from the Ford Foundation, I interview a sample of faculty who have participated in interdisciplinary seminars at three universities to try to discern the factors that make such seminars successful or unsuccessful. It takes me ten years to digest my interviewees' experiences and write up the lessons I learn.

What I find is that for many faculty, decades of considering issues solely through their own disciplinary lens leads them to develop mental blinders; they simply become unable to listen to ideas from "foreign" frameworks. This was my own experience in trying to combine economics and feminist theory, and now I find the same is true for many others. Even when faculty say they would like to understand ideas and frameworks from other disciplines, fruitful cross-disciplinary conversations occur only if a seminar leader is able to make faculty aware of their disciplinary blinders and specifically structure the seminar to overcome them.

In 2010, Stanford University Press publishes my book, *Interdisciplinary Conversations: Challenging Habits of Thought*. When I show the book to my twelve-year-old granddaughter, Sarah, she asks some interesting questions.

"Will the book make you rich, Baba?"

I laugh. "Absolutely not."

"Will it make you famous?"

"Not in the way you're thinking about it. Not like Lady Gaga."

"Will millions of people read it?

I laugh again, this time even more heartily.

"No, definitely not millions."

"So let me get this straight. You spent ten years writing a book that won't make you rich or famous and that very few people will read? Why did you do it?"

"Because I had an important puzzle that took me a long time to solve. But I enjoyed solving it, and I enjoyed writing about my solution."

Answering Sarah's questions is clarifying. How fortunate I am to have a career that has allowed me to solve meaningful puzzles.

❖

After 2000, not only does my teaching at the GSB come full circle, but other aspects of my life do as well. At a symposium dinner in his honor, I have an opportunity to publicly thank my old mentor at Berkeley, Lloyd Ulman. When it's my turn to raise my glass and toast, I remind him of the conversation he and I had in 1971, when he jokingly agreed to let me teach a course on women and work the following year *if* I gave him the Susan B. Anthony award.

"I never presented you with that award, Lloyd, but I want to present it to you now. And I want to say a long overdue thank-you. That course launched my career."

Later I give him a Susan B. Anthony dollar on a small plaque: "To Lloyd Ulman, in recognition of his early feminism."

My connection with CROW also comes full circle. In 2009, CROW celebrates its thirty-fifth anniversary. It's now called the Clayman Institute for Gender Research because it has been endowed in perpetuity by Michelle Clayman, who received her MBA from the GSB in the mid-1970s, when I was on the faculty, and who has become extremely successful as the founder, partner, and investment officer of a money management firm in New York. When I started CROW, we had great difficulty raising money, in large part because there were few women of independent means—and those who did have substantial assets were generally not free to manage them as they wished. Today there *are* women with the ability and desire to put their money into research on women.

In the panel discussions for the institute's birthday, faculty and others make it clear that the problems CROW and now Clayman address are still very much with us. The gender revolution has stalled. Women's earnings are not rising relative to men's. Women who are mothers face a mommy pay penalty. Women who head families are more likely to be in poverty than ever before. The representation of women in science and engineering is still very low, and women are still embarrassingly scant as leaders in large corporations and as members of corporate boards.

In 2010, Clayman gets a new director, Shelley Correll, who invites me to serve as a life member of Clayman's National Advisory Board. In May 2011, I attend my first meeting of that board, along with the three former students who helped me start CROW back in 1972. I am stunned and elated by the progress Clayman has made since its first days. The budget is solidly in the black, and we have a close and cooperative relationship with Stanford's development office. We have a board of women and men who are managerially wise and generous in their gifts, and an associate director who is super-savvy about public relations and social media and frequently gets the institute's research into the public eye. We also have Shelley, an energetic, brilliant sociologist whose vision for Clayman's future is exciting and far-reaching.

Beginning in 2000, I am profoundly saddened and transformed by an epidemic of deaths. Mollie Rosenhan, who introduced me to Rabbi Ari Cartun and his project developing a nonsexist prayerbook at Stanford's Hillel, dies of lung cancer; Judith Brandenburg and Susan Heck of colon cancer; Helen Kaplan of pancreatic cancer; and Carol Jacklin of mediastinal cancer. In addition, my sister-in-law, Marlene Strober, is killed in an automobile accident.

In a forest fire, the ashes of burned-out trees provide nutrients for new seedlings, and so it is with people. Grieving for my friends, I vow to live more fully than ever, not only for myself, but also for them.

In the summer of 2011, Aunt Bimi dies. Like Mom, she became demented in the last months of her life and was ready to go. At Grandpa's funeral more than fifty years earlier, Bimi told me his death was the end of an era. Now, at her funeral, Max's sister, Rosie, tells me the same thing.

"She's the last of the Scharer sisters. You're the eldest in your family now, Myra. Starting today, you're the matriarch."

I know Rosie means that I'm the matriarch of Mom's family, but I hear her words differently. I take them to mean that now I'm the matriarch of the family Jay and I have created. Now *I'm* the baba and the mom, and I feel the weight of my years.

❖

Shortly after Bimi's death Alice is hospitalized because she is unable to swallow and needs surgery. Jay and I go to Boston to help her, and her words help ease our long history of conflict.

"Myra," she says from her hospital bed, "I want to say thank you for all you are doing for me. And I want to say I'm sorry for all the terrible things I've said to you over the years."

Eight months later, Alice passes away. Her autopsy provides no clues to either her underlying illness or the cause of her death, and I spend many months trying to make peace with the suffering she endured. At Alice's funeral, I think of the inspiring words of Sister Joan Chittister, the Benedictine abbess whom Carol Jacklin and I visited so many years ago at her convent in Pennsylvania:

Grief is that slice of life that takes us beyond the boundaries of our mind and makes us see life anew … death is a very vibrant thing. It makes us all begin together again, more grateful for one another than ever before.

About six months after Alice's death, MIT holds a two-day symposium in her honor, and her colleagues and former students come from all over the world to celebrate her life and the legacy of her work.

The most moving testimonial comes from a colleague from Korea. Alice's 1992 book, *Asia's Next Giant*, predicted the growth of the Korean economy some years before Korea became an economic powerhouse.

"Not only did Alice change the way academics looked at Korea," her colleague says, "the book was translated into Korean and was read by many nonacademics. Alice changed the way Korean people looked at their own country."

A year after Alice's death, we have an unveiling of her gravestone. The cantor at Beth Am officiates, and she and I sing "Ride the Chariot," the song Alice and I learned in Midwood High School's mixed chorus and sang together in our high school years, the song we sang the night before Jay's and my wedding. As our harmonies float upward, I imagine Alice's spirit. I hope it is at peace. I hope it can feel my love.

Time becomes exceedingly precious to me as I mourn these many deaths, and I decide to retire from Stanford. At about the same time, Jay retires from his expert-witness work. Neither of us sees retirement as perpetual vacation. Jay increases his work in the Democratic Party and I'm still involved in teaching, speaking, and academic writing. But without a full-time job, I hope to have more time for family, travel, and creative writing.

The School of Education and the Clayman Institute sponsor a joint retirement dinner in my honor and a symposium on my work, titled "Looking Back/Moving Forward: Forty Years of Women's Education, Work, and Families." Eight of my former doctoral students and my colleagues Cynthia Epstein, Deborah Rhode, and Diana Strassmann talk about the work they've done with me over the years. In the final session, it's my turn to talk about what it's been like to be a pioneer, a fighter for women's rights, and a feminist economist.

I say that I count myself a lucky woman, that while my sojourn at Stanford has often been rocky—and my retirement fund a lot smaller than it would have been had I been paid fairly all along—I've had the opportunity to change institutions of higher education and expand the field of economics. I say that even though some of my women students tell me they would never want to do what I have done, that they think it is just too hard to raise a family and succeed at a demanding research university, I'd do it all again in a flash.

I say that there is still much for the next generation to do. I remind my audience that although Stanford went from 7 percent women on the faculty in 1974 to almost 25 percent some thirty years later, that's a rate of change of only about one-half a percentage point a year, and that if we continue at that pace, it will be another fifty years before women are half of Stanford's faculty.

A few weeks after my retirement symposium, the women's student organization at the GSB, Women in Management (WIM), organizes a large and loving banquet to celebrate both my retirement and Joanne Martin's. Although Joanne is younger than I, we both retire in the same year, and WIM honors both of us for our pioneering work for women in business. One of the most gratifying parts of our joint acclaim is witnessing the large number of male students who rise enthusiastically and applaud us along with their female colleagues.

In my talk at the banquet, I tell students that Stanford today is a much better place for women than when I came. Not only has the percentage of women faculty increased, but the university is far more aware of the potential for gender discrimination in salaries, and the provost regularly checks salary allocations for possible problems. There is also a strong anti–sexual harassment program in place, childcare is far more plentiful, and the university has made important changes with regard to parental leave and stopping the tenure clock for both new moms and new dads. But I tell them that even though the business school is now a very different place, it has a long way to go to attain gender parity. More than 80 percent of the GSB faculty is still male, and more than 60 percent of MBA students are men.

❖

My friends' deaths also lead me to become bat mitzvah, something I have wanted to do for over fifty years. On the Friday night after Helen's funeral, when Jay and I attend services at Beth Am, I notice a blue flyer announcing a new adult b'nai mitzvah class. I sign up that same week.

Beth Am has become my spiritual home. After years of searching, I have found a synagogue where the service is sacred, understandable, and egalitarian all at the same time. There is a new rabbi, Janet Marder, who is an intellectual powerhouse as well as a spiritual inspiration, and I feel fortunate beyond measure that I will have the honor of becoming bat mitzvah at Beth Am.

Every Tuesday evening for eighteen months, nine tired women, all of whom missed out on a bat mitzvah at age thirteen, meet for three hours. We learn (or relearn) Hebrew, and study Jewish history and philosophy. But it's not just Tuesday night that takes our time: becoming proficient in Hebrew requires many hours of additional study and practice throughout the week.

On May 6, 2006, we are rewarded. We lead the prayers for the Saturday morning service, and each of us reads from the Torah. Fortunately, we have a dress rehearsal the previous Thursday evening, because I burst into tears that night when I realize I can read the words I am pointing to with the *yad* (a beautifully carved silver rod in the form of a hand used to point to the Torah text). I can't believe I'm being permitted to read the Torah publicly, to recite the words written on parchment some three thousand years ago, to orate words that Jews have read all over the world every year for untold generations. I feel I have entered an awesome spiritual community that transcends time, space, and, finally, gender. I feel that if Grandpa could hear me, he'd be shocked—plenty shocked—but I think he'd be proud, too.

On Saturday morning, when I read to a synagogue filled with family and friends, I have no tears at all, just joy. Before we read, we march around the synagogue holding the Torah. Sarah and Jared march with me, and I hold Leo in my arms. It doesn't get better than this. Ari is not born until a few weeks after my bat mitzvah, but he's there in utero, and when I recall the day, I always think of him as present.

After our procession up and down the aisles of the synagogue, we take the Torah up to the *bima*. Cantor Kay unrolls it and finds our place amid the long lines of text. I'm the first to read. Our portion is Leviticus, chapter 19, verses 1 through 37. It's called *Kedoshim* in Hebrew and is often referred to in English as the Holiness Code. Both its message and its physical placement are at the center of the Torah.

The chapter begins with God instructing Moses:

Speak to the whole Israelite community and say to them, "You shall be holy, for I, the Lord your God, am holy."

The text then specifies exactly what being holy means. All of the Ten Commandments are listed, and there are some additional instructions.

I find it inspiring that the Torah teaches that *all* people are meant to be holy—not just clergy, but every single human being.

Each of us celebrating our bat mitzvah gives a short speech during the service. I have struggled for many months to put the teachings of the Torah together with feminist economics, and my talk tries to explain the synthesis. I begin by quoting from Rabbi Hillel.

"'If I am not for myself, who will be for me? But if I am *only* for myself, who am I?' Hillel asked more than two thousand years ago."

I contrast Hillel's philosophy with mainstream economics' emphasis on individualism and greed, and its absence of concern for others. Then I suggest that in many ways, feminist economics' stress on the importance of provisioning *everyone* to meet basic material needs is akin to a spiritual injection into mainstream thinking. Afterward, many in the congregation tell me that although they have never heard of feminist economics, they agree with my ideas.

After the service, we have a communal lunch. In addition to family and friends, I've invited all my students, including a Muslim student from Pakistan, a Hindu student from India, and several Israelis who have never been to a Reform service (they all like it a lot and say they might be much more inclined to go to services in Israel if they were Reform services).

In the evening, I invite about seventy-five people to a party. My bat mitzvah takes place about six weeks after my sixty-fifth birthday, and I decide to celebrate them together with one big bash at the Stanford Faculty Club. One of the young rabbis at Beth Am has a band that I like, and he agrees to play. It's an unforgettable night, but dancing with my granddaughter, Sarah, in the center of a hora circle is most memorable of all.

12

Lessons Learned about Sharing the Work

Students and others often ask me to give them the recipe for my "secret sauce." What does one have to do, they ask, to create a life that includes both a successful career and a loving family? It's a daunting question because I have had exceptionally good fortune—good health (including access to good doctors and health insurance when I need them), intellectual resources, an abundance of energy, devoted parents of adequate economic means, and grandparents who imparted lifelong spiritual and practical values. I never take any of these for granted, and I can't ensure that my questioners will have similar luck. Still, I try to answer their queries.

The success of Sheryl Sandburg's book, *Lean In,* is testimony to women's fervent wish to succeed at demanding jobs. But hard work, perseverance and effectiveness cannot by themselves generate occupational equity. Context matters greatly. For a woman to achieve power, she must also rely on a favorable legal environment, a societal ideology that promotes gender equality, institutions that actively support her aspirations, and allies, both male and female, who lend a hand along the way. Not every woman wants to put up with what pioneers of my generation endured. Widespread success requires a world where society and employers meet women halfway, providing support, flexibility, and a culture that honors women's contributions.

In my personal life, my ex-husband's support was a key factor in my deciding to obtain a Ph.D., and since our marriage in 1990, my husband, Jay, has been an untiring and enthusiastic ally, as well as a co-consultant, and a co-author. In my career, I triumphed over gender bias in part because of my own efforts, but also because I came along at a favorable time, a time when society was beginning to change. The women's movement was also crucial for my success, not only for the support it gave me but also for its unceasing efforts to transform our entire culture, including the law, educational institutions, work organizations, families, the media, and thought.

My career was significantly enabled by two executive orders signed by President Lyndon Johnson, Executive Order 11246 in 1965 and 11375 in 1967, which outlawed discrimination, including sex discrimination, and mandated affirmative action by federal contractors. I also benefited from the complaint filed by Bernice Sandler and the Women's Equity Action League, which asked the secretary of labor to ensure that universities comply with those executive orders. As I see it, Johnson and Sandler played indirect but critical roles in my receiving assistant professor offers from both Berkeley and Stanford.

My career was also positively affected by a series of allies, including men. While some men inhibited my success, others provided vital assistance. And I could never have succeeded without women colleagues and friends who bestowed support, humor, and camaraderie.

Several years ago, my husband and I were asked by the *Harvard Business Review* to comment on a case study by Kathleen Reardon, "The Letter Every Woman Keeps in Her Desk." The fictitious letter in question was to a CEO from a woman executive about sexism in her organization, and the question Jay and I (and others) were asked was whether the woman should send the letter. Jay and I argued that she should definitely bring up the issue of sexism with the CEO, but not in a memo, not alone, and not without considerable preparation. We likened trying to change the CEO's views to ascending Mount Everest and maintained that just as such an ascent requires a team, so does trying to make transformative change in work organizations. We suggested that the woman executive enlist the most powerful allies she could find, both male and female. In our view, the value of powerful allies is inestimable.

Young women and men also ask my opinion on the optimum time to have a child. Another daunting question. There is no optimum time. From a career perspective, it's never the right time, because having a baby may well slow a mother's career progress for a while, and if the baby's father is actively engaged in childcare, it may also slow his. On the other hand, from a personal perspective, if a child is wanted, *any* time is the right time.

Having a wanted child is truly wondrous, the closest thing I can think of to a miracle.

There are arguments for having children early and equally powerful ones for having them later. In favor of relatively early parenthood: you're more likely to conceive and less likely to have a child with a birth defect, you're more energetic when your children are young, and you're likely to be younger and more energetic when you have grandchildren. In favor of having babies later: you're more mature, more likely to have greater economic resources, more likely to be further established in your career, and more likely to be successful in bargaining with your employer for flexibility.

But often, this question of early versus late is moot. If you haven't found the right partner yet, unless you want to have a child without a partner, it may not really matter that you might prefer to have children early. Far more important than when you have a child is whom you marry or partner with, and whether you are sufficiently mature to make this decision at a relatively early age. My husband Jay and I have remarkably few conflicts, and greatly enjoy one another and our large family. But when we ask ourselves how we think we would have fared had we married each other when we married our first spouses at ages twenty-four and twenty-two respectively, we're not at all sure our marriage would have succeeded. We think we were simply too young and unpracticed to have created a loving long-term relationship.

Finding the right partner is key to both career and family success, and when students tell me that they have just ended a relationship with a partner because they don't think that individual will support their career aspirations, I cheer them on.

"It's painful at first," I say, "but in the long-term you've done yourself a big favor. The most important career decision you make is deciding who will be your spouse or partner."

People err in thinking that having a spouse or a partner and then having children is the only way to create loving relationships. Hardly. Some people who have a partner or spouse do not achieve loving relationships, while others without such a person in their life create loving relationships nonetheless, some with family members and others with friends.

When love relationships crumble, forgiveness is critical to moving on. My life is richer because I have a friendly relationship with my ex-husband. Sometimes people are surprised when I tell them that I am about to celebrate Thanksgiving with him and his family as well as with my own family. But all of us in both families are thankful for our friendly relationship. What enabled us to make peace? Mutual recognition that each of us had responsibility for our divorce. The law talks about no-fault divorce, but dual-fault divorce is closer to the actuality. It's not true that nobody has fault; both members of the couple are responsible for the failure of a marriage, and while it is important to forgive your ex-spouse's behaviors, it is also important to forgive your own counterproductive behaviors. Sometimes, that is hardest.

Achieving peace in a post-divorce relationship is easier if the divorce process is nonbelligerent. Psychological pain and profound disagreements are generally unavoidable accompaniments to divorce, but aggressive actions are not. If you have to forgive a former spouse not only for the divorce but also for hiding assets, nonpayment of child support, or seeking to turn children against you, forgiveness may be unattainable. In the heat of divorce, couples might benefit from looking beyond the immediate quarrels, and, especially if they have children, concentrating instead on what they would like their future relationship to look like.

Having both a demanding career and a family with children is difficult because both require massive inputs of time. Yet, although nobody can "have it all," two people committed to two demanding careers and a family can succeed at both. They may have to give up most leisure activities in the short run, and they may have to hire a "third parent," if both their work schedules require substantial travel, but they can succeed. The key is mutual commitment. Each must agree that the other's career is of central importance, and each must commit substantial time and energy to the family.

When people first realize how pressed for time they are when they seek to balance two challenging careers plus a family, they often think that learning to "save time" is the magic bullet. But while timesaving strategies, including outsourcing, are indispensable, constantly trying to be efficient interferes with life satisfaction. The way we spend our time is the way we live our lives, and if we continually focus on saving time, we lose sight of simple pleasures. In the midst of pressures both personal and professional, it's often hard to focus on life's joys. But it's always worth the effort.

Having a family with two exacting careers requires that each partner prioritize carefully. The metaphor of stuffing the jar of life is helpful. If there are rocks (the most important activities in your life), pebbles (somewhat less important activities), and sand (definitely secondary activities) that must go into the jar, put the rocks in first, the pebbles second, and the sand last. Otherwise, the jar is filled with sand, and the pebbles and rocks don't fit.

I myself don't like the juggling metaphor for combining work and family because envisioning multiple balls in the air feels stressful in and of itself. But people who like this metaphor say they find prioritizing easier if they visualize two different kinds of balls—rubber balls and crystal balls. If they drop a rubber ball, it bounces back, but if they drop a crystal ball, the damage is irrevocable.

I find it more useful to conceptualize work/family balance dynamically by visualizing a rocket trajectory. A rocket is exactly on target only at take-off and landing. Between those two points, it constantly moves away from its trajectory and has to be "straightened out." So, too, with work and family. The two are rarely in balance, and each member of the couple needs to keep an eye out to discern when the imbalance requires correction.

Students and others ask me to reflect not only about personal and professional life, but also about priorities for public policy. Public policies may seem more remote than one's personal and professional goals, but in fact they are inextricably linked, as my memoir clearly shows. There is much that still needs to change in our legal, educational and work institutions to empower women in the public sphere and to provide sufficient time for men and women to nurture their families.

After fifty years of feminist activism, a plethora of executive orders and legislation at the federal and state levels, and numerous successful lawsuits, gender inequality persists. Indeed, the gender revolution has stalled, and women are making few further inroads into jobs traditionally closed to them or obtaining salaries in line with those of similarly educated men. Despite the accomplishments of a few women who have made it to the highest ranks of corporations, women's representation in the C-suite and on corporate boards remains low.

In academia, difficulties continue as well. The old problem of sexual harassment has become the new tragedy of sexual assault, and in the most lucrative and prestigious fields, the playing field is far from leveled. In September 2013, a lead article in the *New York Times Magazine* highlighted gender bias at the Harvard Business School and examined the efforts of Harvard's president to "remake gender relations at the business school." In June 2014, the *Wall Street Journal* reported that an internal study at the Anderson Business School at the University of California, Los Angeles, judged the school "inhospitable to its women faculty."

In the United States, new legislation providing for paid parental leave is high on the list of policies that need change. Shamefully, the United States is one of only a very few countries that do not provide paid maternity leave; the others are Papua New Guinea, Lesotho, and Swaziland. Although the Family and Medical Leave Act (FMLA) protects a woman's job for twelve weeks if she takes leave, that leave is unpaid, and to be covered under the law, she has to have worked for at least a year at a government agency or a private employer that has at least fifty employees. Some women have paid maternity leave through their employer, and in certain states, some women have paid maternity leave through a state system, but the vast majority of American women have no paid leave, and few can afford to take much unpaid leave.

Men can also take unpaid leave under the FMLA, but paid parental leave is even rarer for men than it is for women. Although several Silicon Valley companies have made headlines with newly instituted paid paternity leave programs, the vast majority of men are ineligible for such leave.

In 2013, Senator Kirsten Gillibrand proposed a bill that would require employers to offer new parents three months of paid leave at two-thirds of their salary, but the bill has languished. Only when constituents organize to pressure their representatives about parental leave will we change the situation.

Not only do most American parents have no paid parental leave, they also have unreliable childcare. I began investigating the economics of childcare more than forty years ago, and the situation remains problematic. The number of slots is insufficient, much of the available care is unaffordable, and it is often of poor quality. As I argued in my first talk to faculty at Stanford's Graduate School of Business (the GSB), childcare, like education, has numerous external benefits, and there are sound economic reasons for subsidizing it for those whose incomes are low. There are also sound economic reasons for subsidizing community colleges to embark on massive programs to train childcare workers. We talk a lot about the importance of preschool education but do very little to promote the training of those who work with our youngest children.

I have concentrated my policy recommendations on the United States because that is where my expertise lies, but changes are necessary in other countries as well, particularly in less developed countries, where women and men, but especially women, continue to be disempowered by illiteracy and cultural norms.

❖

As I think about my own future, I recall the words of Rabbi Tarfon, written two thousand years ago in *Pirkei Avot* (Ethics of the Fathers):

It is not incumbent upon you to complete the work, but neither are you at liberty to desist from it.

I'm positive that Rabbi Tarfon was not thinking about gender equality or reform of economic theory when he offered his insight, but his words remind me that since my encounters with Elizabeth Cady Stanton and feminist economics, I am truly not at liberty to desist. I understand now, even more than when I started, that the changes I seek are deep and difficult, and that I won't see the desired outcomes in my own lifetime. But I also know that for as long as I'm able, as both player and coach, I'll continue to work toward a world in which every person's basic economic needs are met, and each of us has the opportunity to fulfill our potential in the public sphere as well as in private life. And I know that not only my former students but also my children and grandchildren will carry on this work—probably not as economists, possibly not as professors, but as women and men profoundly committed to a world where *everyone* has the opportunity to achieve both power and intimacy.

I hope you, the reader, will join us in this work.

Acknowledgments

After decades of writing academic articles and books, I needed help learning to write a memoir. For their classes and tutorials, I thank Ryan Hardy, Robin Hemley, and especially Michelle Herman and Ellen Sussman. I also thank the members of my writing group, Jerry Burger, Heather Haven, and Carter Schwonke, who generously shared their time and expertise.

I am grateful to colleagues, friends, and former students who read early drafts of the manuscript and offered critique as well as validation: Cecile Andrews, Morgan Beller, Clair Brown, Helen Chang, Marianne Cooper, Joelle Emerson, Leah Friedman, Velia Frost, Suzanne Greenberg, Caryn Huberman, Edward Lee, Joanne Martin, Carol Muller, Burt Neuborne, Helen Neuborne, Wenda O'Reilly, Joel Orr, Lisa Petrides, Diane Pincus, Cynthia Russell, Eva Sage-Gavin, Frank Sortino, and Marilyn Yalom. I also thank my editor, John Covell, and five anonymous reviewers.

For assistance at various critical points in the process, I thank Nan Gefen, Edie Gellis, Mary Felstiner, Mary Hughes, Michael Larson, Janet Marder, Sylvia Paull, Elizabeth Pomada, and Victoria Zackheim.

My children, Elizabeth Strober and Jason Strober, read drafts and provided thoughtful and loving feedback, as did my granddaughter, Sarah Strober. Thank you!

My husband, Jay Jackman, has been an extraordinary partner in this endeavor—believing in the project from the outset, cheering me whenever I flagged, commenting on multiple drafts, and helping to make the whole process exciting and pleasurable.

Memoir is an unusual genre. Everything I relate here is exactly as I remember it, but others may recall different events, or none at all. People often ask how I can remember incidents from so long ago. The answer is that once I begin writing, they all rush back. But of course, while the dialogue I use conveys the content I remember, I rarely recall the precise words that people used.

All the names in the memoir are real, except for Ted, who asked me to use a fictitious name.

A few of the stories in this book are also in my chapter, "Sailing into the Wind," in *Eminent Economists II: Their Life and Work Philosophies,* edited by Michael Szenberg and Lall B. Ramrattan and published by Cambridge University Press in 2014, and parts of chapter 1 are in my article "Kicking Down the Door: Berkeley 1970," published in the Summer 2012 issue of *Noyo River Review* by the 23rd Annual Mendocino Coast Writers' Conference, where the piece won first place for nonfiction.

Index

African Americans, 13, 17, 70, 94, 96, 103
Aggression, 110–111, 216
Ahrends, Jasper, 204
Ahrends, Maike, 204
Alcoa, 7
Alfred Knopf (publisher), 15
American Economic Association (AEA), 101, 115–117, 132, 191–192
American Economic Review, 12, 132
American University, 89
Amsden, Alice Hoffenberg (sister)
  Barnard College and, 128, 174,
  childhood of, 27, 30–31, 37, 42–44, 48, 51
  Cornell and, 62–63
  CSWEP and, 159–160
  death of, 208–209
  divorce of, 160–161
  different worldview of, 55, 63, 76–77, 84, 128
  Harvard Business School and, 175
  London School of Economics and, 84, 128
  marriages of, 83, 199
  MIT and, 198, 209
  motorcycle accident of, 128
  PhD of, 84
  publications of, 159, 209
  singing with, 44, 182–183
  social life of, 127
Amsden, Jon, 76–77, 83–84, 128, 160
Andrews, Cecile, 172

Anthony, Susan B., 6, 22, 206–207
Anthropology, 9, 107, 129, 132, 149, 170, 173, 176, 190
Antiwar movement, 90, 102, 108
Arnold, Carolyn, 170–171
Asia's Next Giant (Amsden), 209
Assertiveness, 111
Atkin, Mike, 157, 174
Axelrod, Rabbi, 160, 166

Babcock, Barbara, 123, 131
Babysitter, 3, 15, 94, 99, 102, 135
Bach, Lee, 119, 120, 124–125, 154
Bain Consulting, ix
Bar mitzvah, 33–34, 160, 165–166
Barnard College, 128, 173, 175
Baruch College, 37, 40
Bat mitzvah, 33–35, 45, 75, 160, 166–167, 210–212
Becker, Gary, 20
Bedford-Stuyvesant, 70
Bell, Carolyn Shaw, 116–118
Benedictine nunnery, 176, 208
Bergmann, Barbara, 95–96, 100, 116, 154
Beyond Economic Man: Feminist Theory and Economics (Nelson and Ferber), 192
Bienenstock, Artie, 156
Big Blue, 3, 22, 110
Bima, 34, 166, 211
Bimi (aunt), 33, 45, 50, 168, 182, 208
Birth control, 124
Blau, Francine, 116, 118

B'nai B'rith Girls (BBG), 39
Bohemian Club, 128
Boulding, Kenneth, 118
Bradford, David, 136
Bradshaw, Margaret, 48–51, 62
Brandenburg, Judith Berman, 58–59,
    66, 72, 165, 173, 193, 208
Break, George
  description of, 3
  follow-up appointment with, 7, 10,
    12–13
  lecturer position and, 103, 113
  male culture and, 3–5, 7, 10, 12–13,
    21, 35, 103, 113, 115, 120, 125
Bringing Women into Management
    (Gordon and Strober), 136
Bris, 93–94
Brooklyn, New York, 6, 25, 38, 48,
    50, 57, 62–63, 68, 70, 80, 101, 123
Brooklyn College, 46–48, 50, 62
Bunting, Mary, 129
Bus Riding 101, 57–58

Cain, Glen, 16
Cambodia, 90, 101
Campbell, Glen, 120
Campbell, Rita Ricardo, 119–120
Canarsie, 25, 37–38, 73
Career. *See also* Publications
  assistant professor positions, 10,
    89, 95–96, 100–103, 112, 115,
    120–121, 123, 128, 130, 133, 185,
    191, 214
  deciding to obtain a doctorate, 67–
    68, 75, 78
  demands of, 20, 22, 41–42, 59, 66,
    100, 120, 124, 126–127, 135, 139,
    147–150, 158, 164, 172, 174, 184,
    186, 190, 212
  family and, 197, 203, 214–218
  gender equality and, 76, 95–96 (*see
    also* Gender equality)
  lecturer position, 4, 8–11, 13, 17, 95,
    102–103, 115, 128
  maternity and, 97–98, 218
  mentors and, 8, 48, 118, 138, 158,
    173, 206–207

occupational segregation and, 21,
    108, 110–111, 142–147, 170–172
  pregnancy and, 88–92, 96–99
  salary and, 90, 174, 186, 187 (*see
    also* Salaries)
  sexism and, 3–5, 120, 148, 159, 166,
    202, 214
  stress and, 84–85
  tenure and, 3–4, 9–12, 19–20, 117,
    123, 126–127, 138, 148, 152–158,
    170, 174–175, 201–202, 210
Carnoy, Martin, 144, 157
Carroll, Lewis, 83
Cartun, Ari, 169–170, 183, 208
Catanzarite, Lisa, 171–172
Catholic Church, 171–172, 176
Center for Interdisciplinary Research,
    148–149
Center for Research on Women
    (CROW)
  Center for Interdisciplinary Research
    and, 148–149
  as Clayman Institute for Gender Re-
    search, 207, 209
  Clayman, Michelle, and, 207
  Correll, Shelley, and, 207
  Feminist Studies program and, 190
  Ford Foundation and, 131, 138–141,
    147–149
  founding of, 134, 137–139,
    141–142
  Lieberman, Jerry and, 158, 185
  Lyman, Jing, and, 139–141
  Middlebrook, Diane, and, 148–150
  Miner, Anne, and, 148–149
  Policy Board and, 137–138, 149,
    173
  Rhode, Deborah, and, 174
  second term as director and,
    157–158
  Signs journal and, 173–174
  Yalom, Marilyn, and, 147
  Young, Rosemary and, 141
  Zappert, Laraine, and, 147
Chamberlain, Mariam, 137–139, 140,
    147, 173
Chan, Agnes, 188

Changing surname after marriage, 182

Chauvinist pigs, 159, 201

Childcare, 31, 132, 194, 214
American Economic Association (AEA) and, 117
babysitting and, 3, 15, 94, 99, 102, 135
Comprehensive Child Development Act and, 121, 125
economics of, 103, 121, 124–126, 132, 172, 189, 218
external benefits of, 125
Friedan on, 15
gender equality and, 18–20
government subsidization and, 125
group care and, 15, 103, 121
housework and, 15–20 (*see also* Housework)
improvements in, 210
opposition to funding for, 125–126, 130
National Organization for Women and, 108
Nixon and, 125
playgroup and, 112–114
public policy and, 218–219
salaries of providers, 114
skills needed for, 143
subsidized, 15, 125, 218–219
taxes and, 189–190
unreliable, 218–219
working mothers and, 14–15

Chittister, Joan, 176, 208

Chronicle of Higher Education, 192

Chu, Lena, 204–205

Civil Rights Act, 108

Clark, M. Gardner, 67

Clayman, Michelle, 207

Clayman Institute for Gender Research, 207, 209. *See also* Center for Research on Women (CROW)

Cohen, Bryan, 199, 204

Cohen, Elizabeth, 130, 137, 157

Coladarci, Arthur, 156–157

Cold War, 74–75

Collier, Jane, 129, 149, 176

Columbia University, 17, 85, 175

Committee on the Status of Women in the Economics Profession (CSWEP), 117–119, 134, 159, 191

Communist Manifesto, 15

Comprehensive Child Development Act, 121

Conable, Charlotte, 56

Congregation Beth Am, 160–161, 169, 209, 210–212

Cook, Alice, 66

Cornell, Ezra, 56

Cornell University, 6, 68, 76, 81
application and acceptance to, 49–51
Alice and, 62–63
beauty of, 55, 57–58
Bus Riding 101 and, 57–58
Conable on, 56
education classes of, 71
elementary economics education and, 73
founding of, 56
Greek life and, 58–61, 63
Hillel services and, 59, 115
orientation and, 55–56
parietal rules of, 56–57
religion and, 59
resident assistants (RAs) and, 58
Risley Hall and, 55, 139
School of Industrial and Labor Relations (ILR), 49–51, 60, 62–64, 67, 73, 75
Women's Self-Government Association (WSGA) and, 56–57

Cornwall, John, 71, 73–74

Correll, Shelley, 207

Crever, Patrice, 112

Cross-Cultural Perspectives, 129

Crossovers, 59, 127

CROW Group, 149

Csikszentmihalyi, Mihaly, 184

Cuban missile crisis, 74

"Current Struggle for Sex-Role Equality, The" (Babcock), 131

Custer, Vicki (now Slater), 75

Davis, Cynthia (now Russell) 129–
    131, 137, 147
Davis, Margo, 147
De Beauvoir, Simone, 15–16, 109
Declaration of Sentiments, 7–8, 15
Denial, 150, 164–165
Depression, 93–94, 99
Dewey Library (MIT), 14
Dietrich, Donald, 64, 67, 77
Dinner parties, 112, 121, 126–127,
    196
Discrimination
    Bohemian Club and, 128
    Civil Rights Act and, 108
    Executive Order 11246 and, 214
    Executive Order 11375 and, 214
    Family Club and, 128
    informal, 124
    peer review and, 154
    salary, 10–11, 146, 172, 174, 184–
        187, 210, 217–218
    sex, 9–11, 13, 17–18, 117, 120, 127–
        128, 156, 193–194, 214
Discrimination Against Women
    (House Committee on Education
    and Labor), 17
Dissertations, 14, 86–87, 97, 100, 115,
    120, 150, 152, 164, 172, 188
Divorce
    Alice and, 160
    dual-fault, 216
    Myra and, 164, 166, 168, 182
    remarriage rate and, 177
    Wendt case and, 193–197
Domar, Evsey, 83, 86–87
Donahoe, John, ix-x
Downing Lecture, 192
Dowry, 132
Dress codes, 123
Dunkelberg, Bill, 133

Earnings. *See* Salaries
eBay, x
Economics
    American Economics Association
    (AEA) and, 101, 115–118, 132,
    191–192

Break, George, and, 3–5, 7, 10, 12–
    13, 21, 35, 103, 113, 115, 120,
    125
childcare and, 103, 121, 124–126,
    132, 172, 189, 218
Committee on the Status of Women
    (CSWEP) and, 117–119, 134, 159,
    191
consumer demand and, 74
Cornwall, John, and, 71, 73, 74
cost-benefit analysis and, 90
demand side of labor market and,
    145–146
Domar, Evsey, and, 83, 86–87
elementary classes, Cornell, 73
Evans, Robert, 84
feminist, 190–193, 212
growth theory and, 77, 83
Harrod, Sir Roy, and, 77
Harvard and, 71, 75
Hicks, Sir John, and, 77
Holzman, Frank, and, 67, 71, 73–74,
    85
inflation and, 13, 82
International Association for
    Feminist Economics (IAFFE) and,
    191–192
input/output analysis and, 74
interest rate determination and,
    133
investment and, 83, 146, 195
Keynesianism and, 69–70, 73, 82
linear programming and, 74
London School of Economics and,
    84, 128
macroeconomic theory and, 13, 73–
    74, 82, 95, 133–134, 202
male dominance of, 79–80
microeconomic theory and, 73–74,
    81–82, 202
Ounjian, Daniel, and, 71, 73–74
PhD in, 7, 20, 65–67, 71, 75, 78–79,
    84, 91, 120–121, 202
productivity and, 82, 86–87, 192
profit maximization and, 145–146
rate of growth and, 83
recessions and, 82–83, 172

Samuelson, Paul, and, 81–82, 107
social factors and, 84–85, 145–146
social welfare and, 82, 113
Solow, Robert, and, 82, 89–90, 192
supply side, 145
Woodrow Wilson oral exam and, 68–70, 71
Ehrlich, Tom, 137
England, Paula, 192
Epstein, Cynthia Fuchs, 135–136, 151, 154, 209
Equal Employment Opportunity Commission, 108
Estrada, Estela, 147
Evans, Robert, 84
Executive Order 11246, 214
Executive Order 11375, 214

Faculty Fellows Program (Stanford), 138, 148
Faculty retreats, 128
Family and Medical Leave Act (FMLA), 218
Family Club, 128
Family Farm, 128–129
"Fear of Feedback" (Strober and Jackman), 185
Feminine Mystique, The (Friedan), 14–15
Feminism
  Anthony, and, 6, 22, 206–207
  Bay Bridge experience and, 5
  Bergmann and, 100, 116
  de Beauvoir and, 15–16, 109
  Declaration of Sentiments and, 7–8, 15
  economics and, 116–119, 190–193, 209, 212, 219
  emerging consciousness of, 5, 7–9, 18, 35, 108–109
  feminist theory and, 21, 190–192, 206
  Friedan and, 14–15, 108
  funding and, 141
  gender equality and, ix, 16, 20 (*see also* Gender equality)

gender revolution and, ix, 191, 207, 217
  inequality and, 16–18, 217
  Jewish culture and, 170 (*see also* Jewish culture)
  Kreps, and, 16
  liberals and, 84, 107–108, 125, 196
  literary theory and, 174
  maiden names and, 182
  Mainardi and, 16
  men as enemy and, 136
  Morgan and, 16, 108–109
  Oppenheimer and, 16
  radical, 107–109, 116, 127, 136, 139, 160, 191–192, 196
  salary issues and, 17 (*see also* Salaries)
  scholarship on, 14–18, 115, 173–174, 190–193
  Stanton, and, 7–8, 10, 13–16, 117, 146, 202, 219
  suffrage and, 6, 41
Feminist economics, 190–193, 209, 212
Feminist Economics journal, 193
Feminist Studies program, 149–150, 190
Feminization of teaching, 142–146
Ferber, Marianne, 192
Filene's Basement, 79–80, 97
Flatbush, 38, 40
Ford Foundation, 131, 137–141, 147–149, 173, 205
Ford Motor Company, 120
Forest Hills (NY), 38
Foundations of Economic Analysis (Samuelson), 81
Fovitz (Jewish Daily Forward), 29
Franklin, Ruth, 119, 136
Fraternities, 58–61, 63, 87, 129, 180
Freedman, Estelle, 149–150, 173–174
Free-speech movement, 108
Friedan, Betty, 14–15, 108
Friedman, Leah, 164–165
Friedman, Milton, 82
Fromm, Gary, 75

Fundraising
  Ford Foundation and, 131, 137–141,
    147–149, 173, 205
  grants and, 11, 18, 112, 131, 134–
    135, 137–142, 144, 147–149, 152,
    170, 205
  Lyman, Jing, and, 130–141
  Miller, Arjay, and, 140–141
  NIE and, 144
  Russell Sage Foundation and, 170
  Stanford Development Office and,
    141–142, 207

Galbraith, John Kenneth, 116–118
Garfield, Beth, 130, 137
Gelpi, Barbara, 173–174
Gender equality, ix, 6–8, 14–18, 107–
  109, 111,133, 153–156
  advice about, 213, 217, 219
  characteristics and, 110–111, 143
  Department of Defense and, 89–90
  earnings and, 17, 38 (*see also*
    Salaries)
  economics and, 79
  Equal Employment Opportunity
    Commission and, 108
  feminist economics and, 190–193
  Harvard Business School and, 218
  housework and childcare and, 18–
    21, 31, 85, 95, 108, 115–116, 118,
    152, 158–159, 163, 188, 194
  illiteracy and, 28–30, 219
  labor force participation rates and,
    16–17
  medical field and, 87
  MIT and, 80
  occupational segregation and, 21,
    108, 110–111, 142–146, 170–172
  Torah and, 33–35
  University of California, Anderson
    Business School and, 218
  women's studies and, 131, 149–150
Gender-neutral office furnishings, 14
Gender revolution, ix, 183, 207, 217
General Motors (GM), 150–152
George Washington University, 89
Gerlach-Downey, Suzanne, 189

Getting to 50–50 (Joanna Strober),
  203
Gilinsky, Linda (now Klineman), 59
Gillibrand, Kirsten, 218
Golde, Chris, 188
Goldzimer, Eddie, 52–53, 58, 61–62,
  165–166
Gone with the Wind (film), 39
Goodman, Gary Sue, 150
Goodman, Nancy, 71
Gordon, Aaron, 10
Gordon, Bob, 10
Gordon, David, 10
Gordon, Francine, 123–124, 126–128,
  135–136, 146, 153
Gordon, Margaret, 10–13, 116
Gould, Joanne (now Brody), 76
Gowans, James, 76
Graduate Record Exam (GRE), 68
Great Depression, 37, 69
Greek life, 63
Green, Billy, 33–34
Green, Edith, 17–18, 108
Greenberg, Malka, 27–28
Greenberg, Peter, 182
Greenberg, Suzanne, 165, 182
Growth theory, 77, 83
Guarino, Cassie, 188

Hacker, Andrew, 59
Harrod, Sir Roy, 77
Harvard Business Review (HBR), 185,
  214
Harvard University, 6, 10, 17, 116
  Bradshaw system and, 49
  Business School, 70, 175, 194, 214
  Fromm interview and, 75
  gender equality and, 218
  Medical School, 63, 67, 72, 180
  reapplication to, 75
  Russian Research Center, 72
  Samuelson and, 81
Hawaii, 180–181, 183–185
Hebrew, 26, 32–35, 42, 59, 75, 93, 99,
  160, 211
Heck, Susan, 130, 137, 208
Hewlett Packard, 141

Hicks, Sir John, 77
High Holidays, 31–33, 59, 72–73, 114, 127, 161,168–170, 181
Hikino, Takashi, 175, 199
Hill, Marianne, 116
Hillel, 59, 114–115, 127, 168–170, 176, 181, 208, 212
Hinduism, 212
Hirschmann, Albert, 34
Hoffenberg, Julius (father), 168, 183
    Alice and, 77, 83, 128
    childcare and, 101, 135, 152
    college choices and, 45–51, 62, 66
    Cornell and, 55, 57
    curfews and, 70
    death of, 161, 163, 198
    gender separation at *shul* and, 32–33, 45
    housework and, 40, 85, 194
    illness of, 152, 160–161
    on marriage, 53
    marriage proposal of, 40–41
    mortgage concerns of, 38
    retirement of, 135
    as salesman, 43, 46
    unemployment concerns of, 38, 51
    unions and, 43
    on working wives, 31
Hoffenberg, Regina (mother)
    Alice and, 31, 62–63, 77, 83, 128, 161
    ambitions of, 37–38, 41–42, 51, 62, 64, 66, 68
    bar mitzvah and, 34
    Baruch College graduation, 37
    bat mitzvah and, 45
    Brooklyn College and, 46
    childcare and, 95, 101, 135, 152, 161
    college choices and, 50–51
    Cornell and, 49, 55, 57
    dating advice of, 41, 52–53
    dementia of, 198, 208
    on economic independence, 41
    gender separation at *shul* and, 32–33, 45
    hearing difficulties of, 41
    housework and, 39–40, 194

    literacy and, 30
    maiden names and, 182
    marriage advice of, 41
    marriage proposals to, 40–41
    pregnancy advice and, 90–91
    retirement of, 135
    Ted and, 168, 177
    tuition and, 47
    unions and, 43
    Vassar and, 50–51
    working mother, 14, 31, 42–43, 112
Holzman, Frank, 67, 71, 73–74, 85
Honorary man, 79–80, 129
Hook, Sidney, 131–132
Hoover Institution, 120, 132
House Committee on Education and Labor, 17
Housework
    careers and, 15–20
    gender equality and, 18–21, 31, 39, 85, 95, 108, 111, 115, 118, 152–153, 158–159, 163, 188, 194
    Sam and, 18–21, 85, 116, 119, 158–159, 163
    Study of Stanford graduates and, 188
    Study of Todai graduates and, 188
    SUSE talk and, 158–159
Howard, Peggy, 116
H.R. 16098, 17
Hudde Junior High School, 38–39, 123
Human capital theory, 195–196
Huntington, Emily, 11

IBM, 57, 142
Ilchman, Alice Stone, 9
Illiteracy, 27, 29–30, 219
Imperfect information, 66
India, 152
Industrial Relations journal, 132
Inflation, 13, 82
Institute for Finance and Governance, 174
Institute for Research on Labor and Employment, 21
Institute for Women's Studies, 131

Interdisciplinarity, 16, 145, 191, 206
Interdisciplinary Conversations:
  Challenging Habits of Thought
  (Strober), 206
International Association for Feminist
  Economics (IAFFE), 191–192
International Labor Organization
  (ILO), 86
Islam, 212
Ivy Room (Cornell), 59

Jacklin, Carol, 109–111, 149, 151,
  173–177, 208
Jackman, Jay, 208, 210, 213, 215
  background of, 180
  collaboration with, 185, 214
  courtship of, 179–182
  encouragement from, 213
  encouraging good relations with for-
    mer spouses, 197
  listening ability of, 205
  mother's death and, 198–199
  networking of, 183–184
  retirement of, 209
  wedding and, 182–183
Jackman, Rashi, 180–181, 183, 204
Jackman, Tenaya, 180–181, 183,
  197
Jackson Library (Stanford), 14, 121
Jaedicke, Robert 155–156
Jamaica (NY), 38
Japan, 188–189
Jarvis, Tu, 12
Jean (babysitter), 94, 99, 103
Jewish culture
  bar mitzvah and, 33–34, 160,
    165–166
  bat mitzvah and, 33–35, 45, 75, 160,
    166–167, 210–212
  charities and, 27
  chuppah and, 183
  closet Jews and, 127
  crossovers and, 59
  feminist writings and, 170
  Fovitz and, 29
  Hebrew and, 26, 32–35, 42, 59, 75,
    93, 99, 160, 211

High Holidays and, 31–33, 59, 72–
  73, 114, 127, 161, 168–170, 181
Hillel and, 59, 114–115, 127, 168–
  170, 176, 181, 208, 212
Kedoshim and, 211
kosher food and, 25, 27
mezuzah and, 25
Passover and, 71, 87
patriarchy and, 42, 136, 160
physicians and, 21
pregnancy and cemeteries and, 45
rabbis and, 34–35, 44–45, 73, 99,
  114, 160, 166, 169–170, 176, 208,
  210, 212, 219
Rosenberg trial and, 29
Rosh Hashanah and, 31–33, 59,
  72–73, 114, 127, 169, 181
Shacharit and, 26, 32
Shema and, 26
shul and, 25, 31–33, 44–45, 59, 73,
  75
Stanford University and, 115, 127,
  168–169, 208
synagogues and, 44–45, 59, 73, 169,
  210–211
tallis and, 31
tallit and, 183
tefillin and, 25–26
Ten Commandments and, 211
Torah and, 25–26, 28, 34–35, 114,
  160, 211–212
V'ahavta and, 26
yarmulke and, 31
YHVH and, 160
Yiddish and, 26, 29, 32, 59
Yizkor and, 161
Yom Kippur and, 33, 59, 114, 127,
  161, 168–169
Johnson, Lyndon B., 9, 108, 214
Johnson, Samuel, 181
Judaism, 35, 44, 61, 160, 168–170
Judd, Naomi, 177
Judd, Wynonna, 177

Kanter, Rosabeth Moss, 80, 151, 154
Kaplan, Helen Goldzimer, 52, 165,
  173, 182, 193, 208

Kaplan, Judith, 34–35
Kaplan, Leah, 130, 137, 139
Kaplan, Mordecai, 35
Kaplan, Stanley H., 48
Kedoshim, 211
Kennedy, Donald, 173
Kent State University, 102
Keohane, Nannerl, 150, 173–174
Kerr, Clark, 11
Keynesianism, 69–70, 73, 82
King, Martin Luther, Jr., 96
Kings Highway, 38
Kiptchenitz, 27
Knight, Bob, 98
Korea, 209
Kosher food, 25, 27
Kreps, Juanita, 16

Labor Department, 9, 13, 120
Labor relations, 21, 49, 62, 67, 79,
    100, 120
Labor unions, 7, 21, 43–44, 63, 69–
    70, 74–75, 77, 115–116, 151
Lamaze classes, 92–93, 98
Larry, 177, 181
Lean In (Sandburg), 213
Lebergott, Stanley, 86
Lecturers, 4, 8–11, 13, 17, 95, 102–
    103, 115, 128
Lefkowitz, Betty, 60
Lenin, Vladimir, 74, 77
Lesbianism, 108
"Letter Every Woman Keeps in Her
    Desk, The" (Reardon), 214
Levin, Hank, 144, 156–157
Leviticus, 211
Liberals, 62, 84, 107–108, 125, 196
Libraries
    authentic smell of, 6
    Dewey Library, 14
    employment in, 60, 63
    Green Library, 6, 14, 17
    Jackson Library, 14, 17, 121
    Nuffield, 77–78
    research in, 6, 8, 14, 16–17, 21, 50,
        77–78, 80, 88, 94, 133, 146
Lieberman, Jerry, 158, 185–187

Lipman-Blumen, Jean, 132
Loft, Jacob, 48–49
London School of Economics, 84,
    128
"Looking Back/Moving Forward:
    Forty Years of Women's Education,
    Work and Families" symposium,
    209
Lou Henry Hoover House, 139–140
Lyman, Jing, 139–141
Lyman, Richard, 138–139, 148, 154,
    173

Maccoby, Eleanor, 109, 130–131, 137,
    149
Macroeconomic theory, 13, 73–74, 82,
    95, 133–134
Mainardi, Pat, 16
Maquiladoras, 171–172
March, Jim, 130–131, 137–138, 142,
    157
Marder, Janet, 210–211
Margie (babysitter), 3, 15, 20, 103,
    112–114, 135
Market replacement method of valu-
    ing unpaid labor, 195
Marriage
    Alice and, 83, 199
    careers and, 185, 203–204, 215
    choosing partner and, 40–41, 215
    as commodity, 196
    changing surname after, 182
    community property and, 194–195
    divorce and, 66, 160, 164, 166, 168,
        177, 182, 193–196, 216
    gender equality and, 203
    Getting to 50-50 (Joanna Strober),
        203
    going steady and, 53
    human capital theory and, 195–196
    Jason Scott and, 204
    Jason Strober and, 198, 203
    Jay and, 182–183, 213, 215
    Liz and, 199
    median age for women and, 53
    mother's advice on, 41
    partnership theory and, 195–196

Marriage (cont.)
  Rashi and, 204
  remarriage rates and, 177, 181
  Sam and, 64, 76–77, 163–164, 166,
    168
  therapists and, 165, 166
  unpaid labor and, 193–197
  women professors and, 65–66
Martin, Joanne, 128–129, 153, 202,
  210
Marx, Karl, 15, 74, 81
Massachusetts General Hospital, 86,
  92
Massey, Bill, 158
Maternity, 31, 71, 87–88, 90–94, 97–
  100, 214–215, 218
Math achievement, 110
Matriarchal mothers, 160
Max (teacher), 43–44
Max (uncle), 168, 208
MBA students, 123–124, 133–135,
  142–144, 146–147, 202–204, 207,
  210
McGraw-Hill, 136
Meisels, Judith (then Jackman, now
  Jenya), 180
Melbourne University, 192
Mentors, 8, 48, 118, 138, 158, 173,
  206–207
Mexico, 171–172
Meyers, Charles, 79, 86, 97, 101
Meyerson, Debra, 136
Mezuzah, 25
Microeconomic theory, 73–74, 81–82,
  202
Middlebrook, Diane, 148–150
Midwood High School, 44, 48–49, 51,
  123, 209
Mill, John Stuart, 20, 65
Miller, Arjay, 119–120, 124, 128–129,
  136, 140–141, 156
Miller, Bill, 141
Miller, Frances, 140
Mills College, 51
Miner, Anne, 131–132, 148–149
MIT, 6, 14, 17, 74, 129, 188
  acceptance by, 75

Alice and, 198, 209
deferments and, 76
doctoral orals and, 97
health service and, 84
job matching at, 89
Meyers and, 79, 86, 97, 101
pregnancy and, 91, 96
reacceptance to, 78
reapplication to, 75
rejection by, 71
Samuelson and, 81–82, 107
Solow and, 82, 89–90, 192
thesis topic for, 85–87
Mommy wars, 112
Monopolies, 7–8, 15, 21, 127, 146
Monopsonies, 7
Morgan, Robin, 16, 108–109
Morning sickness, 88
Mott, Lucretia, 6, 8, 117
Mount Holyoke, 62
Muller, Carol, 172

National Council for Research on
  Women, 173
National Guard, 102
National Institute of Education (NIE),
  144
National Institutes of Health (NIH),
  86, 92, 94, 100
National Organization for Women,
  108
New York City Board of Education,
  37, 64, 68
Nelson, Julie, 190–191, 192
Nepal, 152
Nepotism, 11, 120
New Orleans, 115–118, 154–155
New York Times, 171
New York Times Magazine, 218
Nisonoff, Laurie, 116
Nixon, Richard, 101, 119, 125
Nobel Prize, 77, 82, 192
Noddings, Nel, 187
NOWLDEF (NOW Legal Defense and
  Education Fund), 193
Nuffield College Library (Oxford),
  77–78

Obstetricians, 91–93, 98–99
Occupational segregation, 21, 108, 110–111, 142–144
    bank tellers and, 170–171
    maquiladoras and, 171–172
    MBAs and, 146–147
    teachers and, 144–146
Office of Economic Opportunity, 89
Office of Federal Contract Compliance, 9, 13
Ohio University, 204
O'Laughlin, Bridget, 132
Old Union, 114, 169
Oppenheimer, Valerie, 16
Opportunity cost method of valuing unpaid labor, 195
Oral exams, 37, 42, 68–70, 87
O'Reilly, Wenda, 172, 179
Orgasm, 108–109
Ounjian, Dan, 71, 73–74
Oxford University, 60–61, 76–78, 85

Palo Alto Radcliffe Club, 119
Palo Alto Times, 129
Partnership theory of marriage, 195–196
Passover, 71, 87
Patriarchal system, 42, 136, 160
Peekskill, 38
Petrides, Lisa, 188
PhD
    Brandenburg and, 66
    Chamberlain and, 138
    economics and, 7, 20, 65–67, 71, 75, 78–79, 84, 91, 120–121, 202
    Friedman and, 164
    Gordon and, 123
    Maike and, 204
PHT (Putting Hubby Through), 194
Pincus, Diane Eder, 87, 94, 177
Pincus, Ted, 87
Pine Lake, 38–39, 52, 76
Pirkei Avot (Ethics of the Fathers), 219
Playgroup for Liz, 112–114
"Politics of Housework, The" (Mainardi), 16

Poss, Katherine, 144
Power, Marilyn, 115
Pregnancy
    career and, 88–92, 96–99
    Jewish law and, 45
    Lamaze classes and, 92–93, 98
    maternity leave and, 31, 71, 98, 218
    morning sickness and, 88
    mother-in-law and, 80–81, 88
    optimum time for, 214–215
Provost's Committee on Recruitment and Retention of Women Faculty, 185–187
Public policy, 217–219
Publications
    bank tellers (Strober and Arnold), 171–172
    Bringing Women into Management (Gordon and Strober), 136
    "Childcare Centers as Workplaces" (Strober, Gerlach-Downey, and Yeager), 189
    comment on Reardon, "The Letter Every Woman Keeps in Her Desk" (Jackman and Strober), 214
    on family expenditure patterns (Strober, Strober, and Weinberg), 132–133
    "Fear of Feedback" (Jackman and Strober), 185
    "Financing Childcare through Local Taxes" (Yeager and Strober), 189
    "Formal Extrafamily Childcare," in book published by Columbia University Press, 132
    on hierarchy of manufacturing wages, 132
    Interdisciplinary Conversations: Challenging Habits of Thought, 206
    on MBAs (Gordon and Strober, and Strober), 146–147
    on occupational segregation in the maquiladoras (Catanzarite and Strober), 171–172
    "Rethinking Economics through a Feminist Lens," 191

Publications (cont.)
  *Road Winds Uphill All the Way, The:
    Gender, Work and Family in the
    United States and Japan* (Strober
    and Chan), 188
  on salaries of men and women teach-
    ers in San Francisco, 1879 (Strober
    and Best), 146
  on women and teaching (Tyack and
    Strober), 190

Quakers, 8
Queens (NY), 38
Quick, Paddy, 116

Radcliffe College, 49, 129
Radcliffe Institute, 129
Raz, Maxine, 108–109
Reagan, Barbara, 116, 118, 154
Reardon, Kathleen, 214
Recession, 82–83, 172
Reconstructionist Judaism, 35
Reder, Mel, 101
Redstockings Manifesto, 108
Relative attractiveness theory. *See* Oc-
  cupational segregation
Religion, 8, 25, 28, 59, 61, 168. *See
  also* Jewish culture
Resident assistants (RAs), 58,
"Rethinking Economics through a
  Feminist Lens," 191–192
Rhode, Deborah, 174, 209
Ricardo, David, 81
Risley Hall, 55, 139
*Road Winds Uphill All the Way, The:
  Gender, Work and Family in the
  United States and Japan* (Strober
  and Chan), 188
Robertson, Margie, 141
Robinson, Joan, 74
Rosaldo, Shelly, 129, 149–150, 173–
  174, 176
Rosenberg trial, 29
Rosenhan, Mollie, 164, 208
Rosh Hashanah, 31–33, 59, 72–73,
  114, 127, 169, 181
ROTC, 61–62, 102
Routledge, 192

Rudoff, Carol, 112
Rundback (teacher), 42–43
Russell Sage Foundation, 170

Salaries, 17, 25, 31, 38
  childcare workers and, 114
  confidentiality and, 186–187
  discrimination and, 10–11, 146,
    172, 174, 184, 185–187, 210,
    217–218
  Lieberman and, 185–187
  Sam and, 96, 98
  Solow advice and, 90
Samuelson, Paul, 81–82, 107
Sandburg, Sheryl, 213
Sandler, Bernice, 17–18, 214
Sarah Lawrence College, 9
SAT test, 68
Scharer, Bessie (Baba), 27–30, 56,
  73, 168, 198, 205
  Aunt Bimi and, 33
  death of, 45
  description of, 28–29
  listening abilities of, 28
  literacy and, 28–30, 32
  Liz's Hebrew name and, 99
  lock jimmying of, 27, 35
  Malka and, 27
  restaurant of, 28
  Tante Annie and, 28–32, 40, 45, 73
  Yiddish and, 26, 29
Scharer, Morris, 25–27, 31–32,
  34, 168, 170, 211
  on bar mitzvahs, 34
  core values of, 134
  death of, 44–45, 198, 208
  description of, 25
  housework and, 85
  Jason's Hebrew name and, 93
  Jewish identity from, 31–32
  as *macher*, 27
  prayers of, 25–27, 32–33, 59, 75
  restaurant of, 28
  Yiddish and, 26, 29
Schell, Karl, 81
Schiff House, 175
Scott, Jason, 183, 199, 204
Scott, Leander, 205

SCREW, 131
Second Sex, The (Beauvoir), 15–16, 109
Segregation
  gender, 8, 32–35, 114, 126–127
  occupational, 21, 108, 110–111, 142–147, 170–172
  religious, 59
  sororities and, 59, 63
Seigman, Jerry, 60
Seminars, 77, 79, 91, 107–111, 124–125, 130, 142–144, 190, 205–206
Seven Sisters, 49
Sex differences in children, 109–111, 131
Sex discrimination, 3–5, 9–11, 12–13, 116–118, 120, 127, 156, 185–187, 193–197, 214
Sex in the Marketplace: American Women at Work (Kreps), 16
Sexism, 5, 120, 121, 148, 159, 166, 201, 202, 214. *See also* Discrimination; Gender equality; Gender revolution; Sex discrimination
Sexual harassment, 151, 165, 186–187, 193–194, 210, 217
Sexual revolution, 163
Shacharit, 26, 32
Shema, 26
Shul, 25, 31–33, 44–45, 59, 73, 75
Siegel, Abraham, 75, 91
Sigma Delta Tau (SDT), 59
Signs journal, 173, 176
Silverman, Judy, 59
Singing, 44, 52, 58, 114, 160, 168, 182–183, 209
Sisterhood, 8, 16, 108–109, 120, 176
Sisterhood Is Powerful (Morgan), 16, 108–109
Slavery, 8, 39
Sloan Fellows, 150
Smith, Adam, 190–191
Smith, Mike, 184
Social science, 13, 16, 144, 148, 186, 190–191, 203
Society for Cutting Up Men (SCUM), 108
Solow, Robert, 82, 89–90, 192

Sophie Newcomb College, 154
Sororities, 59, 63
Southern Methodist University, 116
Soviet Union, 73–75, 77, 86
Standard Oil, 7
Stanford Daily, 129
Stanford Graduate School of Business (GSB)
  Advisory Board of, 124
  assistant professorship offer of, 120–121
  Bach, Lee, and, 119, 120, 124–125, 154
  childcare seminar at, 124–126
  courtesy appointment and, 201–202
  CROW and, 130, 131, 134, 137, 148–149
  dinner parties and, 126–127
  emerging female faculty at, 120, 123, 129, 142, 153
  family expenditure studies and, 133
  Family Farm and, 128–129
  Gordon, Francine, and, 123–124, 126–128, 135–136, 146, 153
  hostility at, 123–124, 133–134, 150, 201
  Jackson Library, 14, 121
  lively social scene of, 126–127
  male culture of, 123–124, 128, 136, 153–154
  Martin, Joanne, and, 128–129, 153, 202, 210
  MBA students and, 123–124, 133–134, 142–144, 146–147, 202–204, 207, 210
  Miller, Arjay, 119–120, 124, 128–129, 136, 140–141, 156
  Sloan Fellows and, 150
  teaching and, 133–134, 142–144, 150, 202–204
  tenure decision and, 153–156
  Women in Management Conference, 135–136
  Women in Management (WIM) and, 210
  Work and Family class, 202–204

Stanford University, 8, 20, 100, 140, 204, 214
  Committee on Committees and, 187
  Committee on Recruitment and Retention of Women Faculty, 185–187
  culture of support for faculty, 185–186
  Development Office and, 141–142, 207
  Faculty Club and, 149, 212
  Faculty Fellow and, 138, 148
  Faculty Senate and, 187
  Feminist Studies and, 149–150, 190
  Green Library, 6, 14, 17
  Hillel at, 114, 127, 168–169, 208
  Jewish culture and, 115, 127, 168–169, 208
  junior faculty issues and, 185–187
  looking back at career at, 209–210
  Kennedy, Donald, and, 173
  Lyman, Jing, and, 139,
  Lyman, Richard, and, 138, 148, 154, 173
  Office of Public Affairs, 123
  Reder, Mel, and, 101
  Resident Fellow and, 175
  research advantage of, 131
  Sam's residency at, 3, 5,
  Signs and, 173–174, 176
  Strober Report and, 187
  study of undergraduate alumni work and family, 188–189
  unpublished salaries of, 174
Stanford University School of Education (SUSE) [now the Graduate School of Education], 130, 156–158, 172
  Atkin, and, 157, 174
  Coladarci, and, 156–157
  doctoral advisees and, 170–172, 188, 189
  Institute for Finance and Governance, director of, 174
  joint degree program (with GSB), director of, 201–202
  Noddings, and, 187

  promotions and tenure, 158, 184
  retirement from, 209
  Smith, and, 184
  Thoresen, and, 158
  Tyack, and, 144–145, 154, 156–157, 191
Stanford University Press, 206
Stanton, Elizabeth Cady
  antislavery conference and, 8
  Declaration of Sentiments and, 7–8, 15
  impact of, 6–8, 10, 13–16, 117, 146, 202, 219
  Mott and, 8
Staten Island, 45, 161, 198
Stimpson, Catharine, 173
Strassmann, Diana, 191–192, 209
Stringer, Eileen, 38–39
Strober, Ari, 204, 211
Strober, Elizabeth
  birth of, 18, 98–99
  canceled bat mitzvah of, 166–167
  childhood of, 4, 18, 20, 99, 101, 112–114, 119, 121, 152, 168
  Hebrew names of, 99
  Jay and, 180–181
  marriage of, 199
  as mother, 204
  parents' divorce and, 164
  Stanford dorm room for, 175
  Ted and, 167–168
Strober, Jared, 204, 211
Strober, Jason
  bar mitzvah of, 160
  birth of, 18, 93
  bris of, 93
  childhood of, 4–5, 18–19, 112–113, 119, 152, 168
  as father, 199, 204–205
  Hebrew names of, 93
  Jay and, 181
  marriage of, 197, 203
  parents' divorce and, 164
  Ted and, 167–168, 177
Strober, Joanna Aptekar, 197, 199, 203–205
Strober, Linda, 197

Strober, Samuel
  arguments with, 18–20, 163–164,
    166, 169–170
  as assistant professor, 96
  current relationship with, 197,
    215–216
  divorce of, 166
  early relationship with, 61–64, 67–
    68, 71–72
  encouragement from, 65–66, 89, 91,
    113, 115–116, 127, 213
  engagement to, 71–72
  as father, 87, 152
  first Rosh Hashanah with, 72–73
  Gowans and, 76
  grant proposals and, 134–135,
    152
  Harvard and, 63
  home division of labor and, 18–20,
    85, 116, 119, 158–159
  immunology research of, 72, 76–77
  internship of, 86, 88, 92
  Lamaze classes and, 92
  marital problems with,139, 152,
    154–155, 163–164, 166, 169
  medical residency at Stanford, 3, 5
  medical school and, 63, 76,
  Mill and, 65
  mother of, 80–81, 88, 95
  Navy service of, 92
  new wife of, 197
  NIH work of, 86, 92, 94, 100
  Vietnam War and, 86
  wedding with, 76–77
  Windsor Hotel union and, 63
Strober, Sarah, 199, 204–205, 206,
  211–212
Strober-Cohen, Leo, 204, 211
Strober Report (Stanford University),
  187
Student Nonviolent Coordinating
  Committee (SNCC), 108
Students for a Democratic Society
  (SDS), 108
Suffrage, 6, 41
Sussman, Theresa, 60–61
Sutch, Richard, 12

Synagogues, 31–32, 44–45, 59, 72–73,
  210–211
Syracuse University, 50

Tallis, 31
Tallit, 183
Tante Annie, 28–32, 40, 45, 56, 73,
  99, 115, 168, 194, 198
Tarfon, Rabbi, 219
Teaching ratings, 133–134
Ted, 167–169, 172, 175, 176–177,
  180, 222
Tefillin, 25–26
Ten Commandments, 211
Thanksgiving, 55, 63, 68, 98–99, 169,
  197, 216
Thesis writing, 74–78, 81, 85–87, 89–
  90, 93, 95–97, 100, 115, 119, 188
Thoresen, Carl, 158
Through the Looking-Glass (Carroll),
  83
Tillich, Paul, 73
Title VII, 108
Tokyo University (Todai), 188
Torah, 25–26, 28, 34–35, 114, 160,
  211–212
Trinity College Dublin, 6, 76
Tufts University, 6, 17, 67, 71–75, 81
Tulane University, 154–155
Tyack, Dave, 144–145, 154, 156–157,
  191

Ulman, Lloyd, 21–22, 101–102, 109,
  115, 120, 206–207
Unemployment, 13–14, 21, 51, 68–70,
  73, 82–83
Union for Radical Political Economics
  (URPE), 116, 118
United Auto Workers (UAW), 120
University of Amsterdam, 192
University of California at Berkeley,
  214
  antiwar demonstrations and, 3, 108
  assistant professorship offer and,
    120
  Break and, 3–5, 7, 10, 12–13, 21, 35,
    103, 113, 115, 120, 125

University of California at Berkeley
(cont.)
discrimination complaints filed
against, 17–18
emerging female faculty member at,
115–120
free-speech movement and, 108
Gordon, Margaret, and, 10–13, 116
Institute for Industrial Relations and,
21
intellectual sophistication of students
at, 13
Kerr, Clark, and, 11
nepotism rules of, 11
Ulman and, 21–22, 101–102, 109,
115, 120, 206–207
University of California at Davis, 191
University of California at Los Ange-
les, 218
University of Chicago Press, 173, 192
University of Maryland, 13, 89–92,
98, 100, 102, 112, 116
University of Michigan, 17, 204
University of Minnesota, 17
University of Southern California, 174
University of Washington, 183
U.S. Department of Defense, 89–90
U.S. Department of Labor, 9, 16–17,
120
U.S. Steel, 7

V'ahavta, 26

Valuing unpaid labor, 193–197
human capital theory and, 195–196
market replacement method and,
195
opportunity cost method of valuing
contribution to marriage and, 195
partnership theory and, 195–196
Van Horne, Jim, 155
Vassar College, 49–51
Vietnam War, 3, 13, 86, 90, 101

Walden Pond, 72
Wallace, Phyllis, 118
Wall Street Journal, 218

Washington Post, 48
Weinberg, Chuck, 133
Wellesley College, 49, 87, 116, 137,
173–174
Wendt, Gary, 193–197
Wendt, Lorna, 193–197
"What Economic Equality for Women
Requires" session, 116
"What's a Nice Girl Like You Doing
in a Place Like This?" (slide show),
123–124
Winchester-Thurston School, 176
Windsor Hotel, 60–61, 63, 139
Witches, 108
Wolf, Margery, 176
*Women at Cornell: The Myth of Equal
Education* (Conable), 56
Women in Management (WIM), 210
Women's Bureau, 16
Women's Center, 129
Women's Equity Action League, 9,
17–18, 120, 214
Women's movement, 15, 41, 107, 173,
213–214
*Women's Place: Options and Limits in
Professional Careers* (Epstein), 135
Women's Self-Government Association
(WSGA), 56–57
Woodrow Wilson Fellowship, 64–65,
68–70, 71, 73, 82, 87
Work and Family class, 201–204
World War II, 30, 69, 132, 170
Written exams, 37, 87

Yale University, 49, 116, 138, 165
Yalom, Marilyn, 147
Yarmulke, 31
Yeager, Ken, 189
YHVH, 160
Yiddish, 26, 29, 32, 59
Yizkor, 161
Yom Kippur, 33, 59, 114, 127, 161,
168, 169
Young, Lili, 123
Young, Rosemary, 141

Zappert, Laraine, 147